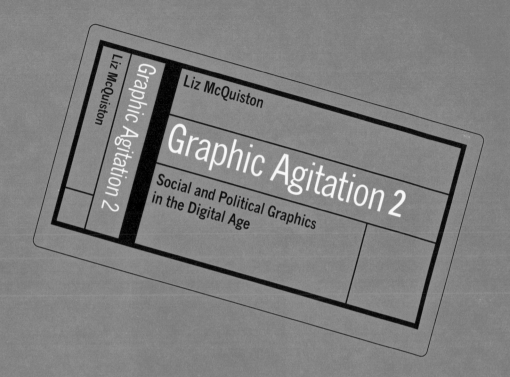

Liz McQuiston

Graphic Agitation 2

Social and Political Graphics
in the Digital Age

For George, Victor and Jeremy

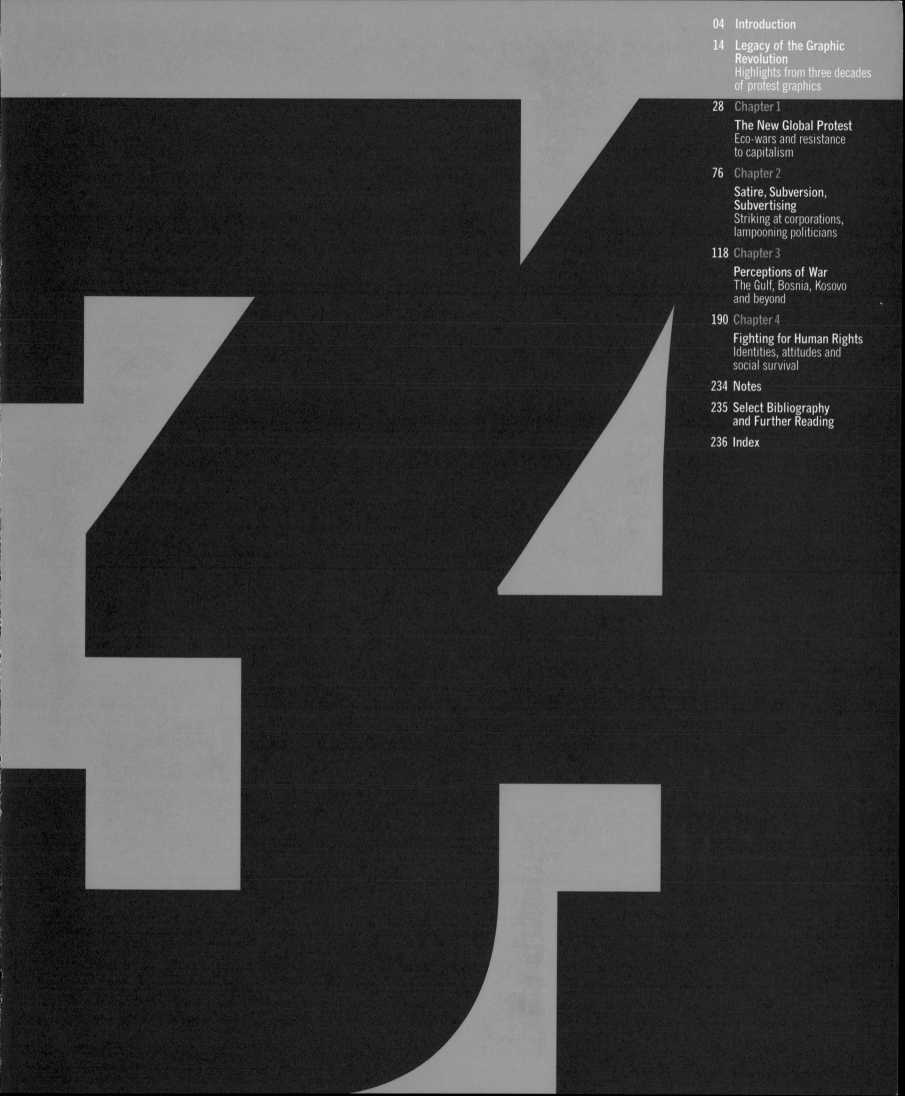

04 Introduction

14 Legacy of the Graphic
Revolution
Highlights from three decades
of protest graphics

28 Chapter 1
The New Global Protest
Eco-wars and resistance
to capitalism

76 Chapter 2
Satire, Subversion,
Subvertising
Striking at corporations,
lampooning politicians

118 Chapter 3
Perceptions of War
The Gulf, Bosnia, Kosovo
and beyond

190 Chapter 4
Fighting for Human Rights
Identities, attitudes and
social survival

234 Notes

235 Select Bibliography
and Further Reading

236 Index

The 1990s marked the beginning of a new political era. The polarities of the Cold War, represented by the contrasting economic and ideological models of capitalism in the United States and communism in the USSR, had disappeared. Where two massive superpowers had been engaged in an arms race and other obsessive attempts to hold each other in check, now there was only one. The old scenario was replaced by a new mass of imbalances: one unchecked major power with its unshakable economic/belief system (capitalism); a dissipating Soviet empire; a shaky ↗

'new world order' of shifting national boundaries; unstable economies; uncapped hatreds. Notions of global annihilation gave way to smaller-scale episodes of shocking savagery, as in the Balkan wars, while old wounds such as the Palestinian–Israeli conflict flared into major new crises. Terrorism – often low-tech and homegrown – became an overriding, end-of-century fear.

Hopes for the peace-making power of global alliances such as the United Nations (UN) and North Atlantic Treaty Organization (NATO) floundered; grumblings against agencies such as the International Monetary Fund (IMF) intensified. A backlash grew in the West against the rising power of multinationals whose influence seemed to challenge governments. Branding and marketing ruled, but came under increasing attack by those who felt that they threatened to undermine or control the basic needs, education, aspirations and lifestyles of current generations. Amid growing concern for environmental devastation, big business and

Graphic 'signs of the times' express the contemporary political atmosphere: the futility of war and fragility of peace; the failures of international bodies and institutions such as the UN; and the ever-present threat of terrorism.

1 'Victory', poster by Fang Chen offering a variety of readings that range from defiance and war to fragility and hope. China 1998.

2 'Bali 12/10/02', postcard produced in October 2003 by Boomerang Media. It memorializes the tragic night, one year earlier, when 202 people died as a result of a terrorist bomb blast in a nightclub on Bali. The card was distributed in youth venues. UK 2003.

3 'Bomb', a subversion of the classic Pan Am logo turns it into a grim remark, suggesting the ever-present danger of terrorism both in the air and in the street. Created by David Fryer for American Retro. UK 1995.

4 A graphic comment by Bruno Souêtre on the slowness and deliberations of the UN during the war in Bosnia. It won first prize in the student poster category of the Festival d'Affiches de Chaumont. France 1994.

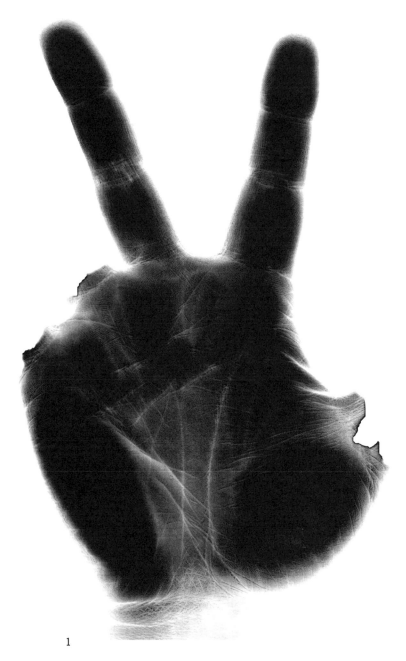

1

2

3

4

With the passing of time and political change, brand logos and symbols take over the world. Evidence of the modern-day marketing and branding of arms, history, dictators, drinks and culture.

1 The old (communist) party is out, and global brands are in. 'McLenin's', front and back of T-shirt. Russia 1993.

2 Portrait of the Iraqi leader Saddam Hussein on a wrist watch in Baghdad. Iraq 1985. Photograph by Steve McCurry, Magnum Photos.

3 'Everything Must Go Bang', front cover of the *Independent on Sunday*'s *Sunday Review* magazine, 22 April 2001, featuring an article on a major international arms fair in Abu Dhabi and the sales hype to be found there. Photograph by Kamran Jebrelli.

4 Front cover of *Time* magazine, USA, 15 May 1950, showing an early depiction of global branding and its cultural impact. Illustration by Boris Artzybasheff.

capitalism were branded as environmental terrorists. A number of political upheavals set populations in movement – seeking political asylum, refuge from conflict or simply a better life. Thus the 1990s saw the start of a new unstable world; it also marked the beginning of a new era of political protest.

Previous decades had already established a global protest culture. In the 1960s and 1970s, the revolutionary concept of 'the personal is political' defined personal concerns and ordinary, everyday actions as part of a broader political context. This led to an even broader shift towards 'global action' in the 1980s, aided by new communications media that brought global concerns within almost everyone's reach. Not only were people more informed of struggles around the world, but they were able to participate in global aid efforts and solidarity movements. Anti-nuclear activities extended from protest camps in the UK to demonstrations in the

South Pacific. AIDS awareness was expressed through poster campaigns and competitions across continents. All became part of the growing trend towards 'personal politics' in the early 1990s – in short, a personal concern for world problems, and an active interest in issues that have an impact on the individual, society and the planet as a whole. Protest and personal expression, particularly in graphic or visual form, continued to be a vibrant aspect of the new personal politics and its global perspective.

Although photographs of the collapsing Berlin Wall (1989) were read as symbolic of the end of the Cold War, it was the 1991 Gulf War – with its televised maps and videogame shoot-outs – that visually signalled the West's embarkation into confusing, new, uncharted territory. The familiarity of Cold War stereotypes vanished, bringing an altered world view, heightened environmental fears and rising grassroots activism, all energized

and brought to our fingertips by developments in digital technology.

Over the following decade the nature and manner of protest changed. The environmental movement grew in strength and joined forces with social justice movements. Violent undercurrents fed into the animal rights movement leading to extreme actions; disparate anti-corporate feelings coalesced into the roots of an anti-globalization movement. A new spirit of activism emerged, driven by individual initiative and a do-it-yourself culture. These changes were accompanied by the emergence and widespread adoption of new technologies – faxes, mobile phones, the internet and the World Wide Web. The image of new technology, used in wartime to dazzle and show videogame-style superiority, was transformed when grassroots activists grabbed control of the internet and made it into the 'power to the people' tool of the 1990s.

1

2

3

4

The internet revolutionized the organization, accessibility and information dissemination of protest movements, giving birth to the global protest network. Whereas in the 1980s global solidarity had still been a long-distance affair, the internet of the 1990s suddenly made possible spontaneous one-to-one communication around the world. A truly 'active' network of emails, lists and chatrooms, coupled with other 'instant' globe-shrinking media, was created. The developing technologies also smashed remaining barriers between professional and amateur modes of production and publishing. Soon nearly anyone could originate a written or visual document or video and self-publish or post it on the web.

Such possibilities greatly expanded the diversity of protest methods. Activism could now take the virtual forms of online 'zines', dedicated websites, text messaging, viruses, spoof websites and hacking; these were

teamed up with more tangible forms of direct action such as street demonstrations, carnivals, tree-sitting, tunnelling and 'guerrilla gardening'. Activists continued to make use of familiar graphic formats such as posters, journals, comics, T-shirts and badges. Far from wiping out conventional forms of protest, the emerging technologies complemented and enhanced them.

Graphic Agitation 2 explores the impact of digital technology on graphic protest over the years since the 1991 Gulf War – or in this context, the so-called 'Digital Age'. This includes the agitational use of new technologies and how they are teamed up with 'old' technologies or formats. A fascinating hallmark of our times is the way that a whole invisible layer of people can be networked dynamically and engaged in political activities in cyberspace, at the same time as working conventionally on the ground: designing posters in studios, plastering signs

up in the street or banging drums outside animal testing labs. The range is vitally important – sometimes banging drums is the most efficient medium for a particular culture or purpose. Not all new technologies can reach everyone or appeal to everyone. Protest groups are often quick to condemn the élitism of new technology, while applauding the power of human contact and shouts rising up from the streets.

This complex scenario – involving high-tech, low-tech and no tech – is viewed and illustrated via a diverse range of modern protest imagery. Satirical jabs at politicians and governments – so long an important graphic mainstay – continue to be popular, with the seamless qualities of digital image manipulation achieving increasingly eerie effects (such as British politician William Hague with Margaret Thatcher's hair on page 105). Crudely scrawled graffiti and cut-and-paste billboard alterations have given way to

Designers and other creatives make provocative use of graphic design as a tool for political expression – and find their voice by criticizing, philosophizing and subvertising.

5 Cards (for distributing by hand) by Sandy K. Germany 2002.

6 Subvertising of a major brand featured on the Adbusters website, 2001.

7 Poster (also used as a postcard) for a designers' exhibition in Holland, by Alejandro Magallanes. Mexico 1999.

5

6

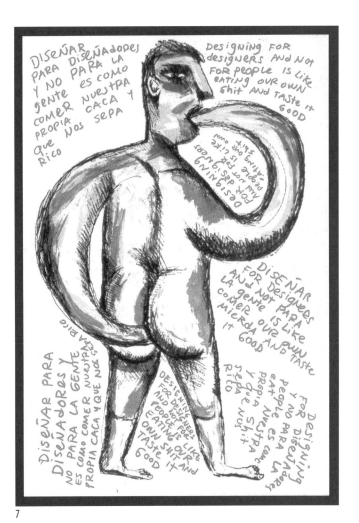

7

The demand for human rights appears in traditional in-your-face graphic form as well as through more subtle agitational techniques involving new technology.

1 Detail from Cathy Davies's website 'NeedCom: Market Research for Panhandlers', a market research-style survey that elicits attitudes to poverty and begging. USA 1999.

2 'Moody Women: More Bitch than Beauty', front cover of magazine focusing on issues for young feminists, designed by Margarita Sada. Mexico 2001.

3 'Women with Rebellious Dignity', sticker/stamp designed by Margarita Sada as part of the series 'Zapata Vive'. Mexico 2001.

'subvertising' – the altering or spoofing of corporate advertisements to communicate alternative messages, an occupation that benefits from sophisticated graphics software. New uses of the net for protest have in themselves generated a whole world of imagery through websites as well as pamphlets and accompanying paraphernalia. An example here is the dynamic online networking and coordination of anti-globalization activism through groups such as People's Global Action and Reclaim the Streets. Alternative media outlets such as online newsletters have built up around such global campaigning ('Have you read your weekly *SchNews*?'), while real-life on-the-ground actions, such as roadbuilding protests, have yielded radical video documentation and illustrated journals. The handbook *Road Raging: Top Tips for Wrecking Roadbuilding* (Road Alert, 1997) is a staunchly thorough account of how to stage an environmental protest campaign, filled with photos, diagrams and instructions. There is advice on everything – from how to survive an eviction attempt by security guards in a hydraulic cherrypicker, to what diseases or infections you might suffer from in a protest camp.

Another part of this new techno-display is the way that designers themselves have made use of the web's international reach. The Zimbabwean general elections of June 2000, for instance, generated internal protest in the form of web-based commentaries and discussions, along with the daily posting of electronic protest posters by graphic designer Chaz Maviyane-Davies, and an agitprop website that cried out for support from designers around the world. At the same time in another context, US artist Cathy Davies was using interactivity, satire and the tools of market research to explore social (and personal) attitudes to poverty in her website 'NeedCom: Market Research for Panhandlers', launched in late 1999.

The technology itself imposes visual qualities. Trio design group, operating in Sarajevo during the Bosnian war (1992–5), produced low-tech postcards imbued with silent trauma. They carry the blurred statement '… printed in war circumstances. No paper, no inks, no electricity, no water. Just good will.' The mottled quality of the printed ink, and its unstable tendency to transfer itself to anything that gets near, speaks volumes about 'carrying on' in the middle of chaos.

Although this book calls upon historical context, it is not a history book. It is a sourcebook of graphics, and its arguments are design and media led. Its interest lies in modern tools of protest and their use: the way that people use graphic imagery (and supporting media) to communicate their concerns, and the defining role technology plays in this.

It presents a snapshot of relatively recent activism, of movements and of graphic developments. It does not attempt to cover a broad span of politics, choosing instead to focus on particular areas of activity and lines of enquiry. It does not attempt to embrace the world. Because the book pursues specific interests, it remains unavoidably biased towards countries of the West.

Graphic Agitation 2 occupies a distinct timeframe. It follows on from its predecessor, *Graphic Agitation* (1993), which covered 30 years of political graphics reaching from the 1960s to the brink of the 1990s. This publication starts a fresh political era – moving from 1990 (with the impending collapse of the Soviet Empire and start of the 1991 Gulf War) to encompass the 11 September attacks on the United States and subsequent war in Afghanistan. But it draws a line in early 2003, when the global War on Terrorism turned its sights on Iraq. A number of additional images are included to suggest the variety of graphics – protest and otherwise – that accompanied the conflict that followed as well as other events later in that year. However, the vortex of personalities, events, issues, slogans and images surrounding the 2003 War in Iraq really mark the beginning of yet another political era – and perhaps eventually another book.

Although *Graphic Agitation 2* is divided into four apparently distinct main chapters, it quickly becomes obvious that issues overlap and some projects belong under more than one heading. The anti-corporate design projects generated by *Adbusters* magazine in Chapter 2, for example, could happily sit within the anti-globalization projects in Chapter 1. The real point is that many of today's global or protest movements interweave or combine interests and concerns, and it is not useful to view them – or their visual material – in isolation.

Large social or historical themes, with their relevant protests and movements, shape the chapters. Chapter 1 is about the wide-ranging anti-globalization movement of the 1990s and beyond, which encompasses the ideals and actions inherent in a new generation's attempt to question the way we live and think, while also trying to halt damage to the planet. The activism featured ranges from roadbuilding protests in the UK throughout the 1990s and the stand made by the Zapatistas in Mexico in 1994 to current graphic design statements on anti-corporate themes from international designers. The internet and other developing technologies play distinct roles, yielding an organized global protest movement, a revolution in media activism and reporting, and a vastly expanded do-it-yourself visual culture.

Satirical attacks on the power and control of multinationals and brands, and of politicians, leaders and governments (also subject to branding and image-building) comprise the social critique in Chapter 2.

1

lunátika
más cabrona que BONITA

2

The tragedy of 9/11 brought harrowing images to mainstream media and evoked images of compassion from designers around the world.

1,2 The day after: on 12 September 2001 images of terror filled the pages of newspapers, including one of the UK's leading national newspapers, *The Times*. Front page photograph (1) of the World Trade Center twin towers right before their collapse, by Spencer Platt, Getty Images. Inside page photographs (2) showing the first and then the second plane, moments before impact, by Sky News.

3 'September 11, 2001', electronic poster by Cedomir Kostovic, Bosnian designer now working in the United States. USA 2001.

The creativity of anti-corporate tactics ranges from the artistry of subvertising to the graphic support systems of the high-profile McLibel Trial, involving the fast food giant McDonald's. In the political arena, satire takes the form of brash lampooning of misbehaving politicians and electoral systems in the West, as well as sour comments from post-communist societies having trouble getting used to that irresistible Western brand, democracy, which rarely seems to live up to its glowing advertisements.

Our modern experience of war is the subject of Chapter 3, in particular the 'distancing' produced by mainstream media and technology. It focuses on attempts by revolutionary outlets to 'close the distance' and offer another view of reality on the ground. The radical role that graphics can play in war is shown with examples from a number of conflicts from the 1990s – from posters and websites that call for opposition to tyrants, to comics used for communicating personal stories of courage or alternative views of events to a wider world.

The ongoing products of wars, economic inequalities and failed social systems have continued to offer graphic design one of its most powerful and traditional roles as a tool for raising social awareness and prompting social change. The issues at stake include racism, poverty, prejudice, homelessness, child abuse, HIV/AIDS, extremism, drug abuse, asylum-seekers and refugees. Chapter 4 features graphic projects and campaigns from the 1990s and later that have used both traditional methods and new technology to address such areas of social survival.

As an aid to orientation, the four main chapters are preceded by an introductory, historical section which provides a brief overview of the legacy of protest graphics of the 1960s, 1970s and 1980s. The graphics from this era are still the source of much

inspiration, as well as demonstrating recurring themes – such as the importance of the underground press – and even personalities such as consumer rights activist Ralph Nader, and groups, including ACT UP (AIDS Coalition to Unleash Power).

As well as the central theme of the impact of digital technology on the nature and manner of protest today, various sub-themes emerge through the book. Contention between the mainstream media (national newspapers, television and so on) and the alternative or underground press – and their contrasting versions of events – not only becomes relevant during major crises such as war but permeates everyday events and reporting. A prime example of this has been the media's stereotyping of protesters as crime-driven thugs, from the roadbuilding protesters of the early 1990s to the anti-globalization protesters of the turn of the century. This kind of colouring, along with skewed versions of many events, gave rise to media activism and new forms of information dissemination over the internet. Running parallel to this is the importance of constantly seeking alternative viewpoints and of keeping alive channels for personal expression.

The combination of violence and children provides a disturbing visual sub-theme: a grim product of many realities of the 1990s, as in all decades. Children are not only depicted as victims of war but as child soldiers taking up arms and posing with chilling gravity (see pages 17 and 119). From other angles, children suffer as victims of domestic abuse; students wield guns at school; other students express concern about their role as potential targets (see page 210).

Marketing and branding appear throughout. War is marketed everywhere – in videogames, in arms trade fairs, in fashion. Revolution is marketed in the sharp advertising campaigns of the student protest movement

Otpor! Irritation with global marketing and cultural takeover finds its voice in McLenin's T-shirts (see page 6) and in various designs in Chapter 2. The tools of branding (logos, symbols, advertisements) and their appropriation or subversion are now an important part of our visual language. If someone hangs a big, plastic, red-headed clown in the middle of a town in Montana (see page 78), we know it is not because they want to vandalize a circus. The subvertising of branding and corporate symbols is now common currency.

But if some people in wealthy, developed countries are protesting in the streets against the power of multinationals and global economy institutions, other people around the world are going to war or sinking into poverty over such issues. The design work shown here by politicized groups, such as El Fantasma de Heredia (The Ghost of Heredia) of Argentina and La Corriente Eléctrica

THE TIMES

When war came to America

Times reporter James Bone was looking up at the World Trade Centre minutes before the twin towers fell from the sky

(Electric Current) of Mexico, makes the conflicts of globalization seem closer and more real. The power of graphic design to cross borders and join cultures in solidarity has never been more pertinent.

The destruction of one symbol of global capitalism came in unexpected and tragic form in 2001 with the events surrounding 9/11, when two jets hijacked by al-Qaida terrorists plunged into the twin towers of the World Trade Center in New York City; a third came down in the fields of Pennsylvania; and yet another crashed into a wing of the Pentagon in Washington, DC. A shocking and sad tapestry of images has since entered our visual culture: footage of the event itself, constantly re-run; stills of the point of impact; photos and descriptions of 'missing persons' stuck to cars, shop doorways and every available surface immediately after the event; flower and picture memorials pinned to the fences at Ground Zero; grey clouds of dust;

firemen; funerals. The event has bequeathed an unforgettable and sinister graphic symbol. The image of a plane or other object headed for a tower – whether the plane represents Zanu PF (see page 12) or another entity – will forever symbolize wilful destruction or tragedy. The occurrence of these events during the writing of this book has had an impact on all the material contained within it. It has not just brought us new imagery; it has altered our reading of the old.

Thus in the jittery post-9/11 climate, when expectations of war appear from ever-new directions, designer Luba Lukova's peace poster on page 13 stands as an example of how images can take on new meaning. In less disturbed times, it might be read as a wish for all things military to be overtaken by one overwhelming movement for peace. Now, however, it can conjure up more fearful ideas – the notion that peace is a facade made up of war-like demons that can erupt out of the

shadows at any time. Its meaning can be hopeful or worrying depending on the viewer's level of paranoia. But it also represents the immense power that a single graphic image can still convey in this age of high-tech digitized information overload, when too much often says too little.

The dozen years spanning 1990 to 2002 covered by this book brought a dramatic shift in world politics and power, glimpses of a future environmental Armageddon and little in the way of peace. Developments in new technologies, however, opened up alternative possibilities for protest and political expression and, coupled with conventional graphic methods, sparked off waves of activism among an ever-widening range of people. For the first time, we can see the vast potential for new resistance and new directions – environmental and political – as the electronic networks of protest movements continue to circle the globe.

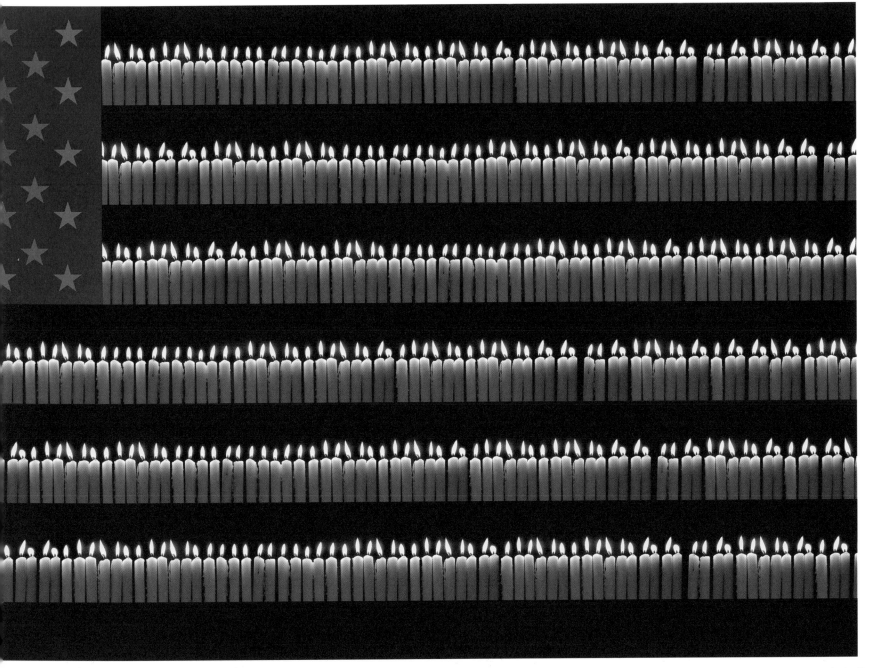

In the post-9/11 climate, a new graphic symbol of destruction – a plane flying into a tower, see page 10 – entered our visual vocabulary, as well as calls not to retaliate.

1 'Televise an Alternative to Retaliation', poster by art activist collaborative THINK AGAIN (D Attyah and S A Bachman), which states its message against a background motif resembling the logos of various US television networks. USA 2001.

2 'State Terrorism': a jet plane labelled with the name and insignia of Zanu-PF (President Robert Mugabe's ruling political party) heads towards the conical tower at Great Zimbabwe, an important national symbol. It is a warning of Zimbabwe's probable destruction in the hands of Mugabe. Designed by Chaz Maviyane-Davies. USA 2002.

3 An image first commissioned as an editorial illustration by the *New York Times* during the conflict in Yugoslavia; it was then taken up and used as a poster by an anti-war organization in New York City. By Bulgarian-born designer Luba Lukova. USA 2001.

1

2

peace

Legacy of the Graphic Revolution
Highlights from three decades
of protest graphics

The social, political and cultural revolutions of the 1960s brought upheaval on an international scale. Mao Tse-tung's Cultural Revolution mobilized the proletariat in the People's Republic of China (at its height from 1966 to 1968, and continuing until his death in 1976). African colonies from the European empires struggled for their independence. The nationwide strikes staged by workers and students in France brought terror to the Gaullist government and riots to the streets of Paris in May 1968. Youth movements launched against authority and 'the ↗

establishment' (or the old social order) spread from the United States to Britain and Europe. Civil rights and black power, feminism, the peace movement and the ecology movement all converged and the spirit of change swept round the world. The aftershocks of this explosion continued to resonate throughout the 1970s and beyond.

The 1960s' spirit of change was expressed through varied aspects of creative culture: through the communicative power of rock music accompanied by a haze of sex and drugs; through new forms of dress and living (especially nomadic and hippie lifestyles); and artistically through popular art and graphics – the visual tools for voicing the ideas and grievances of a new generation. They wanted to discard the values and ambitions of the previous generation, stage a revolution, protest against the Vietnam War and create a new, changed world. Posters became one of the most important renderings of popular dissent and 'liberation' in the 1960s and 1970s, and were produced by professional

The social revolutions of the 1960s and 1970s brought 'power to the people' in the form of the peace movement, black power, sexual liberation and feminism, all expressed through posters and other popular graphic formats.

1 Poster created for the UK peace movement by F H K Henrion. UK 1963.

2 'Critical Mass 74', poster by Arnold Saks for consumer rights activist Ralph Nader's movement against nuclear power. USA 1974.

3 The mark of the US black power group known as the Black Panther Party for Self-Defense, founded in 1966 by Bobby Seale and Huey Newton.

WEST MIDLANDS CND Dr JOHNSON HOUSE 40, BULL ST BIRMINGHAM B4 021 236 8915

1

A nuclear catastrophe is too big a price for our electric bill.

Ralph Nader calls a national meeting of citizens to stop the development of nuclear power until it can be proven safe.

Critical Mass74

A national gathering of the citizens movement to stop nuclear power.
November 15-17 Statler Hilton Hotel Washington, D.C. Phone 20

2

3

In addition to the graphics generated worldwide by liberation movements of the period, US involvement in the Vietnam War (1961–73) prompted intense internal protest and a prolific poster movement. It expressed outrage on many different fronts, including accusations of US imperialism and displays of outright carnage. Children take their traditional role as victim but also appear as soldiers – a horror rarely depicted before that time.

1 A variation on the symbol of the Women's Liberation Movement. 1970s.

2 Poster promoting contraception and a pioneering example of shock advertising, by ad agency Cramer Saatchi for the Health Education Council. UK 1969.

3 'Women's Liberation IS the Revolution!', poster by Pen Dalton. UK 1975.

4 'Protest', poster protesting against beauty contests and women's objectification by See Red Women's Poster Collective. UK mid-1970s.

designers with access to sophisticated reproduction methods as well as amateurs and activists using low cost, homegrown techniques such as silkscreen, or cheap offset-litho printing. Alternative, radical newspapers, magazines and comics – the 'underground' press – spread new ideas and new debates far and wide, while also offering a format for the comments and playfulness of cartoonists and artists in many different countries. This extraordinary period yielded, for example, underground posters and comics produced by artists Victor Moscoso, Wes Wilson, Rick Griffin and Robert Crumb in the United States; magazines such as *Oz* and *International Times* (IT) in the UK; and posters and other press-work by the Student Strike Workshop in the United States, the Poster Collective in the UK, Klaus Staeck in West Germany and the Earthworks Poster Collective in Australia.

These graphic tools shouted out the concerns of the time with a new, free creativity and boldness that influenced the professional studio graphics and advertising of the period, and that echoed around the world from the United States and Europe to Australia. Posters, magazines and other radical graphics were mailed, stuffed in suitcases, handed from friend to friend and sent around the world. One of the outstanding creative characteristics of the period was that a poster printed in an artist's garage by low-tech means could, with a little help from the artist's friends, have an international reach. You could walk into a kitchen in Middle America in the 1970s, for instance, and see a cheaply produced poster by the London-based See Red Women's Poster Collective stuck to the wall. This widespread dissemination was an interesting precursor of the digital age.

War and peace protests

The loudest shout came from protesters against the Vietnam War, a conflict that the United States entered in 1961. Although the conflict provoked music, art, rallies, writings, slogans and graphic comments around the world as the decade progressed, it was protest from within America itself that generated the most intense outpouring of posters, creating a visual lexicon for protest that has been influential ever since. These posters used symbols and clichés such as Uncle Sam; advertisements – often given an ironic twist; dramatic or traumatic news footage; and line sketches and cartoons, snapping with venom and spontaneity. The approaches and methods of treatment were varied, as were the emotions embedded within them, which ranged from stark cynicism to violent anger. The posters also delivered shocking imagery of massacres and of children at war, shown

3

1

Would you be more careful if it was you that got pregnant?

Anyone married or single can get advice on contraception from the Family Planning Association. Margaret Pyke House, 27-35 Mortimer Street, London W1 N 8BQ. Tel. 01-636 9135.

The Health Education Council

2

4

not only as helpless victims but as soldier-fighters. All were a visual aspect of a movement of protest and public anger within America that was instrumental in forcing withdrawal from Vietnam in 1973.
The posters of that era and movement remain an important graphic reference point today.

The creative fires continued to burn brightly throughout the 1970s, working for the causes of feminism and other human rights issues. As the world moved into economic recession in the late 1970s, the UK's alternative presses – including individual artists, printshops, community art groups, and poster and postcard presses – placed their support and energy behind the libertarian movements while also addressing issues of domestic and international politics. Over the following decade, presses such as Leeds Postcards, South Atlantic Souvenirs, Cath Tate Postcards and See Red Women's

Poster Collective would provide a 'graphic voice' for feminism, the burgeoning peace movement, gay and lesbian rights, the UK miners' strike of 1984–5, immigrant communities, environmental issues and solidarity movements (such as the anti-apartheid movement or calls to stop US intervention in Central America), while never missing an opportunity to rail against politicians, the police or the government.[1] As well as covering the disputes of the day, these workshops and presses provided both solidarity and an endless stream of imagery, news and announcements that preceded the networking and activism taking place on the internet in the 1990s.

Also in the late 1970s, the youth-orientated anti-establishment ravings of UK Punk provided a crucial new visual language of social critique – with Jamie Reid's rendition of the Queen with a safety pin through her

nose one of its most famous graphic icons. Punk's emphasis on urban creativity, streetstyle fashion, irreverent do-it-yourself cut-and-paste graphics and the self-publishing of street magazines or fanzines led to the 1980s preoccupation with lifestyles and the use of youth-related formats such as pop music and rock concerts, fashion and style magazines – to redefine politics (environmental and peace issues, and so on) in their own terms.

At the start of the 1980s, Western politics swung towards the right – with Margaret Thatcher elected in 1979, Ronald Reagan in 1980 and George Bush in 1988 – sparking off a chain reaction of events and resulting protest. NATO's move towards nuclear rearmament in the early 1980s brought explosive energy to the international peace movement, resulting in protests such as the Women's Peace Camp at Greenham Common

5 'Vietnamization – Turns Children into Soldiers', anti-Vietnam War poster produced by Clergy and Laymen Concerned About Vietnam, New York. USA 1970. Photograph by Philip Jones Griffiths.

6 'Eat', one of a series of self-published Vietnam War protest posters by artist and illustrator Tomi Ungerer. USA 1967.

7 'Q. And Babies? A. And Babies.', poster by the New York militant Art Workers' Coalition poster committee: Frazer Dougherty, Jon Hendricks and Irving Petlin, with a photograph by R L Haeberle. Produced in outrage at the disclosure of events known as the 'My Lai massacre' of 1968 when many Vietnamese civilians were killed by US soldiers. USA 1970.

8 'I Want Out', poster sponsored by the Committee to Help Unsell the War, a group comprising over 30 advertising agencies. USA 1971.

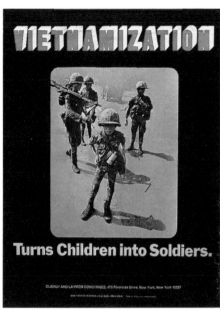

The earth or ecology movement took hold in the early 1970s, promoted by planet-loving, wildlife-friendly imagery. Later in the decade, Punk injected a new, rough energy into graphics and the visual environment. By the 1980s, eco-graphics had taken on a gritty, disturbing presence.

1 An iconic Punk image from the late 1970s: the record sleeve of the Sex Pistols single *God Save the Queen*, designed by Jamie Reid. UK 1977.

2 Anti-whaling illustration by Randolph Holme, contributor to the underground paper, *Georgia Straight*, which reported early Greenpeace actions. USA 1975.

and constant blasts from the alternative press, as well as catapulting the Greens into mainstream politics. The international environmental pressure group Greenpeace, founded in 1971, became a household name in the 1980s with its courageous direct actions. The caring notion of animal welfare became 'animal rights' – an attitude that promoted the same rights for animals as humans, and underpinned a movement of great force and occasional violence. With the disturbing human and environmental threat presented by the world's worst-ever nuclear accident at Chernobyl in 1986, the scene was set for a new breed of emotive, powerful graphics devoted to environmental issues. The 1970s 'Save our planet' graphic ethos of bright suns, smiling animals and cheerful flowers was now overtaken by surreal, often scary, imagery: of fur coats that bled (as in the Lynx anti-fur campaign, see page 57);

radioactive cows; sea animals covered in oily pollutants; children wearing gas masks; and a globe on fire or rotting.

A new era of political and graphic expression
In the midst of this explosive atmosphere, Irish pop musician Bob Geldof masterminded two landmark projects in aid of Ethiopian famine relief. The first was the Band Aid pop single released in November 1984, followed by the global rock concert Live Aid on 13 July 1985, outrageously ambitious in scope (broadcasting to 152 countries by satellite link-up), and in its aim to unite the world in a common cause of goodwill through rock music. Generating unprecedented amounts of famine relief for Africa, Live Aid proved to be a watershed. It changed Western attitudes to charity and ignited a desire in a new generation to act and be involved. It reinforced disillusionment with governments and

politicians, while promoting a positive belief in grassroots activism and 'people power'.

A new era of 'personal politics' opened up, and in the charitable One World atmosphere that followed social and political issues found their way onto a much broader range of public formats. Issues of humanitarian aid, animal rights, environmental protection, anti-drug campaigns and safe sex were all thrown at a receptive public by means of billboard and bus advertising, fashions, street posters and magazines, records and videos, awareness concerts, style magazines, fanzines and cartoons – creating a mood of social awareness that would carry through to the 1990s.

Graphic novels and comic art also climbed out of their prescribed 'box' at this time through Art Spiegelman's graphic novel *Maus*, published in the United States and the UK in 1986–7 (originally existing in an earlier serialized form in Spiegelman's own *Raw*

1

2

magazine, a publication carrying avant-garde comics). *Maus II* followed in 1992.[2] At first glance, the *Maus* epic appears to be a straightforward attempt by Spiegelman to tell his father's experience of the Nazi Holocaust (depicting Jews as mice and Nazis as cats). But in fact it develops a subtext that expresses the pain of a son's difficult relationship with his father, while also forcing the reader to contemplate the complexities of what it is to be 'a survivor'. The comics format allows for leaps through time and views from dramatic angles; the substitution of animals for humans allows horrific scenarios to be told. But the multi-layered narrative conveys the unpredictable emotional forces at work, where a petty exchange of anger over a brand of cereal in the present can produce a flashback to an incident at Auschwitz in the past.

When Spiegelman received a Pulitzer prize for literature in 1992, he was the first comics artist/writer ever to do so, and the *Maus* epic paved the way for other comics to explore new modes of storytelling or documentation. Such explorations include later examples of 'comics journalism' such as Joe Kubert's *Fax from Sarajevo: A Story of Survival* (1996) and Joe Sacco's *Safe Area Gorazde: The War in Eastern Bosnia 1992–95* (2000), shown on pages 152–3. In both projects, the flexibility of the comics format is again used to tackle complex subjects such as the confusion and devastation of war and to convey a range of emotions, from quiet alienation to blood-soaked brutality.

Meanwhile, the fine art tradition of Polish poster design (at its most explosive in the 1950s and 1960s) and the spirit of 'May 68' politics lived on throughout the 1970s and particularly the 1980s in the poster work of Grapus. A highly influential French design collective, Grapus comprised Pierre Bernard, Gerard Paris-Clavel, Jean-Paul Bachollet, Alex Jordan and others. Concentrating on political, social and cultural causes – from the French Communist Party (PCF) to experimental theatre groups – Grapus produced some of the most delightful poster work of this period in a style characterized by a hyperactive scrawl, splashes of bright colour and a general air of playfulness. Hugely inspiring to design students around the globe, its members eventually disbanded in 1991. Splitting into three independent design groups, they continue to demonstrate in their separate ways the inherent vitality of traditional graphic activities such as poster-making.

Graphics and AIDS activism

Another important battleground opened up in the mid-1980s that was crucial to the development of personal politics, and the use of art and design for that political expression.

3,4 'All of Nature Supports the Greens', two posters by Gunter Rambow publicizing Die Grünen, the Green political party founded in West Germany in 1979, which quickly gained power and influence. They also mark the emergence of graphic warnings about the environment through the use of surreal and doom-laden imagery. West Germany c. 1983.

Overleaf 'IQ: Radioactive Contamination of the Environment', poster against radioactive pollution following the nuclear accident in 1986 at Chernobyl in the Soviet Union. Designed by Uwe Loesch. Look closely: the cow is chewing on a radiation symbol instead of a piece of clover. West Germany 1986.

DIE GRÜNEN

Alle Gründe sprechen für Grün

3

DIE GRÜNEN

Alle Gründe sprechen für Grün

4

Youth politics and the peace movement escalated in the 1980s, supplemented by anti-NATO attitudes. Graphics continued to be influenced by the vitality of Punk's do-it-yourself culture and by fine art. It also appeared in a bold, authoritative form when addressing the US AIDS crisis.

1 Poster by the French design collective Grapus (dissolved in 1991) publicizing an exhibition of their work at the Musée de l'Affiche in Paris. France 1982.

2,3 Front covers of *Maus I* and *II*, a two-volumed graphic novel by Art Spiegelman telling the complex story of his father's experience of the Nazi Holocaust, with animals representing humans. Published by Penguin/Pantheon Books. USA 1986 and 1992.

4 'The Sixth March to Torrejón [site of US military base] – We're Continuing the March. NATO, No! Bases, out!', poster produced by the Anti-NATO Commission in Spain. The bride is Spanish president Felipe Gonzalez; the groom is US president Ronald Reagan. In a referendum at that time, the Spanish people voted against entering NATO. Gonzalez created a scandal by making a deal with Reagan, and the country joined, resulting in continuous protests against NATO. Spain 1982.

It involved the anger and protests generated, particularly in the United States, at conservative governments attempting to ignore the growing AIDS crisis. The AIDS activist group known as ACT UP (AIDS Coalition to Unleash Power) was founded in New York City in 1987 to combat US government inaction. It attacked such issues as lack of government funding for research, poor access to treatment and care, inaccuracies in reporting the AIDS crisis and the lack of safe-sex education. Although the epidemic was reported to have started in 1981, US President Ronald Reagan did not utter the word 'AIDS' publicly until 1987. By that time, ACT UP's factsheets were reporting 19,000 deaths.

Visual propaganda was central to ACT UP's operations from the start and it employed a highly distinctive design strategy. Its logo – a pink triangle with the slogan 'Silence=Death' – was actually designed by a group of six gay men known as the Silence=Death Project in 1986, who then gave it to the newly formed ACT UP to use on its demonstrations. The logo in itself was a symbol of strength and historical defiance. A pink triangle (pointing down) was originally the label that homosexuals were forced to wear in Nazi concentration camps. Its use and inversion (pointing up) by ACT UP was an act of defiance, proclaiming that past injustice must not be repeated in the present. The equation 'Silence=Death' was a resounding call to action. The treatment of the entire logo (the pink triangle, the white sanserif type, the black background) lent an authority and sturdiness that allowed various chapters in ACT UP's network to exercise full creative licence with its use and application.

A stark, powerful look became an important facet of all ACT UP's visual propaganda. The group believed that it needed to borrow the sophisticated visual 'power-language' of corporates and advertising in order to fight 'enemies' such as government departments, drugs companies, insurance companies and financial institutions effectively. Its propaganda graphics were used for group identity and strength in demonstrations, highlighting issues, targeting officials and conveying educational information in order to debunk misinformation and myths. They helped to keep the AIDS crisis a live and visible issue and were a crucial element in fundraising activity, particularly T-shirts and badges.[3]

In 1988 members of the ACT UP visual propaganda team established themselves as an autonomous collective entitled Gran Fury, committed to 'exploiting the power of art to end the AIDS crisis' while continuing to produce guerrilla graphics for ACT UP.

1

2

3

4

Gran Fury produced some of the most confrontational and memorable awareness posters of that time. It excelled at targeting different audiences in need of prevention, education and awareness such as women. It also pursued controversial issues, creating a billboard installation called 'The Pope and the Penis' for the Venice Biennale of 1991 which criticized the Catholic Church's position on AIDS. Attempts by Italian customs and Biennale officials to suppress it inevitably aroused much greater media interest and exposure, and allowed it to be exhibited and the issues it raised to be discussed widely.[4]

By the early 1990s, ACT UP had become a global grassroots movement determined to combat a global epidemic, with 180 chapters spread over two dozen countries, held together by the strength of its graphic identity and committed to 'making an impact on national governments and the way they approach AIDS issues'. The book, *AIDS Demo Graphics*, by Douglas Crimp with Adam Rolston (Bay Press, Seattle 1990) chronicles the early days of ACT UP and the central role that graphics played in its demonstrations (roughly 1987–90). The series of events described in the book provide modern-day evidence of the power that graphics can exercise in life-and-death struggles – an inspiration to activists and designers everywhere. And of course, this particular struggle is not over – despite the passage of time and the lack of media attention. ACT UP is still fighting to end the AIDS crisis around the world. Its call to act and demonstrate, along with postings of the latest issues and actions, continues on its highly informative website.[5]

The Iron Curtain falls

While the onslaught of AIDS was becoming ever more visible in the United States (and would eventually develop into a global health crisis), the seeds were being sown for the slow unravelling of the Eastern bloc and the end of the Cold War vision of the world, as well as its stabilities. This showed itself artistically and graphically, as heavily censored cultures began to emerge from behind the Iron Curtain. In the USSR, Mikhail Gorbachev introduced the policies of *glasnost* (openness) and *perestroika* (restructuring) in the mid-1980s, an attempt to breathe life into an economy that was fast becoming out of step with the modern world. The Soviet poster, which had been locked in the role of the 'official art' of Soviet propaganda since Stalin's early days, was one of the first art forms to speak to the West. The Russian 'posters of *perestroika*', as they were called, reflected the political changes taking place and carried social criticism of leaders, of the past and of policies, as well as the views of their creators. Although

5 'Silence=Death' emblem and poster which formed the visual identity of the New York based organization ACT UP (AIDS Coalition to Unleash Power). Designed by members of the Silence=Death Project. USA 1986.

6 Front cover of the book *AIDS Demo Graphics* by Douglas Crimp with Adam Rolston, published by Bay Press. Designed by Carin Berger. Cover photograph by Loring McAlpin from video tape by Catherine Saalfield. USA 1990.

7 'Kissing Doesn't Kill', bus ad by the AIDS activist art collective Gran Fury, which ran in San Francisco and New York. USA 1989.

5

6

7

rarely published in the USSR itself, they were welcomed by the West, where they were exhibited widely, as a new opportunity to discover a culture that had remained hidden for so long.

But Gorbachev's reform policies failed to deliver fast results, simply adding to the discontent and political crises already brewing in countries under communist rule. By 1991 he had been deposed and succeeded by Boris Yeltsin, and by 1992 the USSR had ceased to exist. The visual hallmarks of that immense period of change were ongoing images of statues of Lenin being pulled down, the irreverent use of the old symbols of state socialism (such as the hammer and sickle) on everything from fashions to games, and the arrival of the McDonald's Golden Arches in Moscow in 1990.

At the same time, the grim vision of a regime opposed to the new spirit of change surfaced in May 1989 in Tiananmen Square in Beijing, China. A series of pro-democracy demonstrations was held by students, workers and intellectuals demanding a greater hand in government and an end to corruption. It was a highly visual display that caught the attention of the world, with banners, paintings, a 'Goddess of Democracy' statue and a festive atmosphere. There was live television coverage, while fax and telex machines shot news and messages around the world, generating immense global solidarity and producing iconic images of

bravery carried by the media (most famously the column of tanks stopped in its tracks by one lone protester, see page 25). The party suddenly stopped and the world watched appalled as the protesters were massacred by their own army on 4 June. But their courage and spirit lived on, and ignited popular revolutions across Europe.

The year 1989 proved to be a watershed for Central and Eastern Europe. Long after the workers' strikes in a Gdansk shipyard in 1980 led by electrician Lech Walesa, head of Poland's free trade union, Solidarity, the slow struggle for free elections in Poland finally achieved its goal in 1989. The world-renowned Solidarity logo was very much in evidence, and on voting night a Solidarity poster was to be found hanging on polling booths throughout Poland. It showed Gary Cooper striding down the street, making his way to a confrontation in the classic American western *High Noon* (1952) – a sign that Poland was about to have its own confrontation with fate in the election.

The Communist Party also met its own High Noon on a broader scale – it soon lost its grip in the Eastern bloc and gave way to popular calls for democracy. The Iron Curtain, for so long a symbol of the Cold War, began to crumble. Throughout 1989 a wave of popular revolutions swept through Central and Eastern Europe, including Poland, Hungary, East Germany, Bulgaria, Czechoslovakia (the bloodless 'Velvet Revolution') and Romania (a particularly

bloody uprising, which ended with the execution of the despot Nicolae Ceausescu and his wife).

Spontaneous graphics played an important role in these events, as a tool for revolution and social change produced by amateurs and professionals alike. Posters, flags, handbills and handheld signs accompanied many of the demonstrations. They brought words of anger, cries of police brutality, news of strikes and demonstrations, symbols to rally round, slogans and calls to action. They were carried around and pasted on everything from people and monuments to moving vehicles. As fast as they were torn down by state police and militias, they were replaced with fresh comments and pictures. While signs and posters provided a constant, mobile and fast-moving news stream of daily events, other forms of mass media such as television were still struggling against political repression.[6] (Romania was an exception: when the revolt finally happened in December 1989, rebels headed straight for the state broadcasting centre, took it over and used it to broadcast news of the revolution to the Romanian people, with fighting still taking place in the street outside.)

Amid this atmosphere of growing dissent artists also produced posters critical of the Communist Party and its officials (although they still had to express their anger using symbols or metaphors); or reminders of the past or past injustices (for example, the

1

posters of Czechoslovakia's Velvet Revolution and their reference to the Soviet invasion of Prague in 1968); or posters showing uncertainty over the future. Posters were produced for political parties, international competitions, protest groups or simply for themselves. Poster artists also travelled to help revolutions in other countries, offering solidarity and visual support, and helping to document events – another example of pre-digital artistic networking.

On 11 November 1989, in a historic moment of joy and freedom, the Berlin Wall – symbol of the ideological division between East and West – was breached and pulled down by the crowds it had managed to divide for so long. And in the following year, in the

shadow of the excitement and clatter caused by the pro-democracy sweep, the apparatchik Slobodan Milosevic slipped into his pseudo-democratic seat as president of Serbia.

The stage was set for new crises, new wars, new world events and new protests. For three decades, graphics – in its traditional two-dimensional printed poster, postcard, magazine and comic forms – had been pasted on walls, paraded down streets or distributed by protesting crowds, from the anti-establishment movements of the 1960s to the Vietnam protests of the 1970s and the pro-democracy revolutions of the late 1980s. It had provided a voice for libertarian movements and for unrepresented

groups such as immigrants or strikers. It had not only mirrored the crises and revolutions of the time, but had often acted as a tool for social and political change. In performing these many roles, the use of slogans, bold typography, graphic symbolism and often crude or experimental print techniques had passed from decade to decade. The range of formats and media used became more imaginative and varied as the decades rolled on. With the advent of the 1990s, all these roles and qualities – some traditional, some still developing – would be put to use in a new political era, and enhanced by the creative and global networking possibilities of the emerging digital technologies.

2 'Solidarity with Chinese Students', Czech poster inspired by the pro-democracy protests staged in Tiananmen Square. Czechoslovakia 1989.

3 On 5 June 1989, the day after the Tiananmen Square massacre, student Wang Weilin stood in front of a column of 20 tanks leaving the square and, shouting defiantly, stopped them – giving television cameras the enduring symbol of the pro-democracy spirit. By the end of the month, newspapers were reporting worldwide that the authorities had executed him.

4 Front page of the UK newspaper *Today*, 5 June 1989. The previous day China's hard-line regime had ordered its troops to open fire on the Tiananmen protesters. The massacre left over 2,000 dead.

5 Election poster by Tomasz Sarnecki for Poland's Solidarity party. The image of resolute sheriff Gary Cooper, taken from the classic American western, *High Noon* (1952), represents Solidarity's own resolute march to the ballot for a showdown with the communists on 4 June 1989.

Overleaf 'The fall of the Berlin Wall' (11 November 1989), photograph by Jan Sibik, Germany. To many, the breaching and subsequent tearing down of the wall marked the end of the Cold War and the ideological divisions between East and West.

2

3

4

W SAMO POŁUDNIE
4 CZERWCA 1989

5

The nature of activism and graphic protest has been revolutionized since the early 1990s. A global resistance movement, incorporating anti-globalization and environmentalism, has engaged with the networking, information accessing and distribution possibilities of digital technology. It has created a new episode in direct action culture (sometimes called the New Activism), with do-it-yourself methods as wide ranging as tree-sitting and consumer militancy, and with a burgeoning visual culture that encompasses professional design projects as ↗

well as street graffiti. It defies age, it defies class, it defies social or economic groupings. Nothing has been quite the same since this energetic mood of resistance took hold.

The most prevalent call for change in recent years has come from the anti-globalization movement. Although experts may define and over-define globalization, it remains to many people a confusing and intimidating term. A quick working definition is therefore helpful. Globalization can be summarized as the process whereby a growing number of countries of the world have become part of a global economy involving 'free trade', which is run and regulated by international agencies such as the International Monetary Fund (IMF), the World Trade Organization (WTO) and the World Bank. The diverse groups encompassed by the anti-globalization movement feel deeply about the inadequacies and failures of this process – and where it may lead the world in future. Anti-globalization is used here to describe an umbrella

A new and urgent form of environmentalism appeared in the 1990s, bringing with it brash and unusual messages, protest methods and imagery.

1 'Human Being – Contradiction', poster by Makoto Saito for IUCN, the World Conservation Union. Japan 1993.

2 Photograph by Andrew Testa of an anti-road protester. UK mid-1990s.

1

2

The international anti-globalization movement was launched in solidarity with the Zapatista rebellion in the Chiapas region of Mexico. It later found an important voice in the publication, *No Logo*.

1 'Zapaptota', a project conducted in early April 2001 by La Corriente Eléctrica (Electric Current), and a group of 200 people. They commemorated the anniversary of Emiliano Zapata's death in April 1919 by painting this super-sized portrait on the tiles of the Zócalo – the main square of Mexico City. Photograph by Ernesto Lehn. Mexico 2001.

movement of discontent, with many related but divergent parts and a plethora of concerns. It has no leaders, only numerous spokespeople – activists, writers, campaigners – who have popularized the movement. It also has no manifestos, although it acquired an important text in Naomi Klein's best-selling book, *No Logo* (2000), a thorough study of the economics and marketing that gave rise to the movement. Anti-globalization is in essence about people power vs. corporate power. It is not the surfacing of a 'new issue', but has grown out of concerns over the years for the imbalance of wealth that marks the North from the South, the First World from the Third – an imbalance that places much of the world's land and wealth in the hands of the very few.

The movement has anti-corporatism and anti-capitalism at its core, and thus a deep suspicion of the power that multinational corporations wield over world economies and people's lives – particularly the power exercised by highly visible brand names such as McDonald's and Nike. It berates the debt-handling activities of Western governments and institutions, like the IMF, for stifling the progress and livelihood of the developing world. It rejects the realities of the 'free trade' model that have ensured that poorer nations of the developing world have become even poorer and that fosters the exploitation of working people in sweatshops around the world. It demands a search for alternatives. It is a movement of many separate but interlocking concerns and of many voices.

The inspirational Zapatistas

A key ignition point for the anti-globalization movement was the rebellion staged in Mexico by the Zapatistas, a collectively based group taking their name from the legendary hero Emiliano Zapata, who fought for land reform or *'tierra y libertad'* ('land and liberty') in the early part of the twentieth century. On the day that the North American Free Trade Agreement (NAFTA) between Mexico, Canada and the United States came into being – 1 January 1994 – the Zapatista army (the EZLN) declared war against the Mexican government. They occupied a cluster of towns in the poverty-stricken Chiapas region (in the southern-most part of Mexico) in defence of land rights, resources and the rights of the indigenous people. Rich in resources the region was ripe for development by multinationals, who were encouraged and welcomed by a Mexican government eager to pull the country into the First World and its lucrative deals.

Captured local radio stations were used to announce the declaration of war and broadcast further developments. But the

2 Emblems for the Mexican agitational groups La Corriente Eléctrica and Fuera de Registro. Both have been involved in projects calling for peace in Chiapas. Mexico 1990s.

3 Front cover of Naomi Klein's book *No Logo*, published by Flamingo/HarperCollins in 2000 and tagged by the mainstream media as the bible of the anti-globalization movement. Designed by Bruce Mau.

internet proved to be the most important mouthpiece for the Zapatistas and played a major role in ongoing events. The news of the uprising, the Zapatistas' actions, their organization of self-governed, democratically run 'autonomous municipalities', and their struggles with government forces over the following years were transmitted in the form of messages carried by hand (often through lines of military encirclement) to 'solidarity networks' of people connected to the internet. The messages were then sent round the world electronically to make front page news, creating an international outcry in their defence. It brought a stream of journalists, activists and human rights monitors to the conflict zone, and generated solidarity movements and anti-NAFTA protest demonstrations around the world.

By 1998 this protest had grown into a global coalition of resistance to the symbols of global capitalism, such as the G7 and G8 summits. The new technology distributed Zapatista ideas and words, as well as their challenge to people everywhere to seek practical alternatives.

The Zapatistas continued to be inspirational: full of poetic statements and collective/democratic ideals, and spreading the age-old cry of the dispossessed, *'Ya Basta!'* ('Enough is Enough!') around the world. They created a potent and romantic image of ski-masked guerrilla fighters descending from the mountains and the jungle to stage the uprising ('the ones without faces, the ones without voices').[1] As well as projecting a memorable image the masks ensured that voices and words would be seen as coming from the collective voice, rather than the personality of the individual; they also served to protect the wearers from the cold of the Chiapas highlands. Individuals inevitably did stand out, such as the articulate and well-known spokesperson Subcomandante Marcos, who received a great deal of attention from the mainstream media in their attempt to assign leadership to someone. However, the mask became the distinctive visual identifier of the Zapatistas, and was on its way to becoming the hallmark of the international protester.

Even before the armed uprising, the indigenous women of Chiapas were questioning the inequalities they suffered, which were grounded in centuries of tradition and religion. They made their bid for revolution, demanding changes in the home and in public life to give them equal rights, and a greater role in community meetings and decision-making. They participated at the forefront of the armed resistance – approximately one-third of the Zapatista combatants were women, providing yet another fiery masked image of radicalism (see page 9).

Solidarity with the Zapatistas and calls for peace in the Chiapas region were expressed throughout Mexico itself, and particularly by a younger generation of creative people. This included La Corriente Eléctrica (Electric Current), a mixed group of agitators in Mexico City known for their large-scale social and political projects. One of their most ambitious ideas took place in April 2001 to commemorate the death of rebel icon Emiliano Zapata in April 1919. They organized around 200 people – young people, old people, artists, collectives and Zapatistas – to paint his portrait on the tiles of the city's main square, producing a literally massive tribute to the spirit of Zapata and the indigenous peoples' struggle. The finished piece was 50 x 70 metres (165 x 230 feet).

In the year of the Zapatista uprising, as its influence was spreading around the globe, the Conservative government in Britain passed the Criminal Justice and Public Order Act of 1994 (popularly known as the Criminal Justice Act or CJA). A controversial act that tightened definitions of public order and increased the powers of the police, it was obvious in its targeting of rave parties (what

it called 'unlicensed assemblies') and rave culture. The Criminal Justice Act also had wide-ranging implications for other groups. Participants of various forms of peaceful protest, such as road protesters or hunt saboteurs, were slotted under the new offence of 'aggravated trespass'. Other groups fitting the terms of 'unlawful trespass' – such as squatters, New Age travellers and gipsies – could now be committing the new offence of 'unauthorized camping in vehicles'. Hence a new generation of young British activists, inspired by the fight for rights taking place in Chiapas, saw the new Criminal Justice Act as an attack on their rights and particularly their right to protest. The result was to bring together many single-issue protests into solidarity protests over the Criminal Justice Act, creating a growing hot spot of action that would converge with the forces of anti-globalization (see page 36).[2]

UK roadbuilding protests
Another movement that would join forces with anti-globalization was environmentalism, bringing with it militant, uncompromising methods of direct action that had been practised for decades by the radical, environmental movement Earth First! in the United States. A loose network operating in defence of wilderness and wildlife since 1979, Earth First!ers were renowned for their imaginative approach to non-violent civil disobedience. Their tactics included street dances, guerrilla theatre, tree-sitting, banner-hanging, occupation of premises and road blockades. They were also associated with the introduction of methods such as 'monkeywrenching' – eco-tage or environmental sabotage – including the sabotage or disabling of industrial equipment, cutting through fences, cutting down billboards and other acts aimed at inanimate objects.

Inspired by Earth First!'s strategies and direct actions against roadbuilding, and disillusioned with pressure groups and party politics which offered only legal challenges and lobbying, roadbuilding protests in the UK in the early 1990s took a dramatic new turn. The protest against the extension of the M3 motorway over Twyford Down in Hampshire in 1992 involved massive resistance from a wide range of people including on-site protesters, known as the Dongas Tribe (young people, many of them New Age travellers), UK members of Earth First!, Twyford Down Road Alert! and other activists, as well as trenchant Conservative voters and local Greenham Common activists (see page 38). Although the road was completed in 1994, mass anti-road protest grew.

The renowned 'No M11 Link' campaign of north London began when, in September 1993, contractors' bulldozers moved in to begin clearing trees for a new commuter link road into London. The campaign involved a squat in a roofless house and months of obstruction of the tree-clearing process, conducted by protesters living in treehouses or self-made shelters. Protesters finally squatted a row of houses in Claremont Road, which became the focal point of the campaign (until their eviction in November 1994).

1

They were joined by protesters from the July 1994 national demonstration against the Criminal Justice Bill, later to become an Act of Parliament.

By this time, evidence of the protests had spread throughout the graphic environment. Reports appeared on television, in newspapers and in magazines carrying battle-like, high-contrast imagery that pitted the man-made vs. the organic; bulldozers vs. trees; police vs. protesters; destruction vs. creativity and life. Calls to action, news-bites and slogans emanated from alternative journals or newsletters, graffiti was daubed on walls and hoardings, and stickers were plastered on anything – one spotted in the interior of a commuter train said simply, 'M11 Shove It', with a phone number.

Direct action anti-road protests burgeoned around the country. Campaigners lived in trees in the Cuerden Valley, site of an intended M65–M61 link road in Lancashire. In 1995, Stanworth Valley, also related to the M65, hosted an elaborate treehouse community called the Cosmic Tree Village with over 30 treehouses and four kilometres (2½ miles) of aerial walkways.[3]

The campaign against the Newbury bypass in 1995–6, one of the largest protests, saw many arrests. It also propelled tunneller and cult personality Swampy to celebrity as the mainstream media searched for human interest stories, initiating a pattern of biased or trivializing portrayals of protesters while ignoring the real reasons behind the protest. Other protesters who were arrested and evicted Swampy-style with accompanying bruising and broken limbs received little or no media coverage. Their anger would fuel the cause of media activism as the decade moved on.

The roadbuilding protests of this period rarely (if ever) stopped the building of roads – they merely postponed them, although sometimes for substantial amounts of time. But they made real the notion that a relatively small number of people with determination and daring could seriously stand up to big business interests as well as memorably

challenge authority in general. This growing culture of resistance would add its strength to the mass anti-globalization protests at the end of the decade.

Media activism

Many varieties of media activism grew out of the protests described so far. The Brighton-based group Justice? came together in 1994 in opposition to the Criminal Justice Act. They squatted a derelict courthouse and turned it into a thriving community and organizational centre for their campaigns and demonstrations. They were moved on, but quickly settled in new premises and continued to throw free parties alongside running a telephone helpline and publishing pamphlets. They also produced a directory of the national campaign against the CJA (called *The Book*) and carried on producing the free weekly newsletter *SchNews*.

Written by activists with a wicked sense of humour, *SchNews* delivers an alternative view of the stories of the day – local, national and international – as well as 'the inside story from the direct action frontline'. Events, parties, demonstrations and other actions are all to be found there, along with the 'crap arrest of the week'. *SchNews* has since expanded into a highly popular website, an online version of the newsletter, and several compilation annuals. *SchNews* provides living evidence of the massive direct action movement originally generated in opposition to the Criminal Justice Act. The weekly newsletter continues to be essential reading for anyone not wishing to define their world via mainstream media – or simply wanting to know what's going on underground. As their header says, 'Wake Up! Wake Up!'.

Out of the roadbuilding protests rose other media activists – video activists, internet hackers, radio pirates, digital photographers and text reporters. A collective called Undercurrents was formed in 1993 by four people: Paul O'Connor and Zoe Broughton (veterans of the M11 road protest) and two producers. Born out of a dissatisfaction with mainstream media that, in its words,

'trivialized', misrepresented or ignored the protest movement, it decided to 'demystify activism', while also maintaining its taste for provoking authority. Developments in technology were on its side: lightweight, easy-to-use camcorders had become available for popular use.

Undercurrents produced alternative news videos labelled 'the news you don't see on the news', taught camcorder skills to fellow activists and made camcorders and video activism a feature of protests in Europe, Australia and the United States. It became a global collective, with as many as 800 people contributing news stories.

By 1999, the original coalition of four had moved on. However the Undercurrents Foundation has continued to provide video-activist training, which some mainstream reporters have been known to attend, while managing its substantial archive of 1990s British protests and a website that acts as a central information point for how to engage with and train in video activism. Undercurrents was also instrumental in setting up the Indymedia network in 1999 which, using the internet and an open access website, allowed Independent Media Centers (IMCs) to be set up at protests to report news throughout the day.[4]

Undercurrents and other media activists set up real alternatives to the six transnational media corporations that have dominated world news distribution over the past decade. And that has not always been a safe position to occupy. Many still shudder to recall the reports that emerged from the G8 Summit in Genoa (July 2001) with regard to the violent attack by Italian paramilitary police on the volunteer-run Independent Media Center set up there.

The rise of such media alternatives was, and still is, all part of the on-going anger felt by activists, across many campaigns and causes, about the way that activism and protest is reported by corporate news agencies. The media's need for provocative headlines leads them to focus on the lifestyles (even the hairdos) of protesters. Protests tend to be depicted as battles between thugs,

2 Front cover of the *SchNews Annual*, a collection of the free, weekly information sheet (Issues 101–150, December 1996–January 1998) that provides 'the news the mainstream media ignores' as well as information on parties, protests and grassroots organizations. Published by the Brighton group Justice?. UK 1998.

3 Web page from eco-action.org. Children's character Miffy appropriated for a bit of monkeywrenching on the Ecological Direct Action website, providing contact with branches of Earth First! and information on protest camps, tree-sits and so on. 2002.

4 Page from the Virus Foundry catalogue, displaying the anti-corporate typeface known as 'Bastard'. Designed by Jonathan Barnbrook. UK 1997.

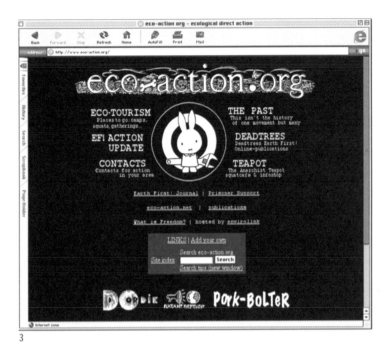

Key symbolic elements of the new global protest: new methods of direct action; the iconic symbol of the protester's mask or bandana; a new brazen attitude to hurling verbal abuse at corporations; and a focus on the workings of the global economy.

1 Photograph by Steve Johnson of protesters occupying trees at the 'No M11 Link' road protest. From the journal *East Ender*. UK 1994.

troublemakers or anarchists and the police, and scaremongering about the violent nature of protesters far outweighs the coverage of issues or events.

Digital agitation

Video activism is only one of many ways in which the agitational role of digital technology has had a profound impact on graphic protest since the early 1990s.

'Cyberactivism' in itself surfaced quite early in website development. Greenpeace had a website before most leading corporates and pioneered its use to help its audience follow campaigns and actions, thereby subverting the control of the newspapers. This proved to be highly effective during the 1995 Brent Spar incident. When the Shell oil company decided to dump their disused North Sea oil platform Brent Spar at sea, Greenpeace occupied the platform – even as it was being towed to its

burial site. This occupation mustered European public opinion and forced Shell to dismantle and dispose of the platform by other means. The protest campaign was viewed as an important strike against governments and industries taking the kind of irresponsible attitude that this dumping of waste in international waters represented. But Greenpeace had also undermined Shell through the campaigning power of its website. Anyone, anywhere in the world could follow the Greenpeace campaign on the web and lend their support. Most corporates still had no website at that time, and could not challenge web protest campaigns by posting their own version of events. Today corporate websites subject to protests and hacking can recover with great speed, although spoof websites remain an irritation.

Since the Brent Spar episode the internet has made possible the online networking,

organization, coordination and information dissemination of protest movements and activities through groups such as People's Global Action, Reclaim the Streets and People & Planet (the student environmental network). Most direct action groups or campaign organizations now have their own websites – examples include People for the Ethical Treatment of Animals (PETA) (see page 58) and the AIDS activist group ACT UP in New York (see pages 22–3). Mass demonstrations and protests usually acquire their own specific website where participants can find information. Add to this online newsletters such as *SchNews*, online petitions, mailing lists, discussion groups and chatrooms. Spoof websites are regularly set up to denigrate or rattle politicians, corporations and other groups, usually by posing as official websites using a disguised web address, or by following the company

or brand name with 'sucks', 'kills' or 'stinks'. So annoyed have some US companies been in the past that, unable to wait to do battle with the American Civil Liberties Union or Ralph Nader's Consumer Project on Technology (both of which come to the aid of such sites), they have instead resorted to buying up potentially rude sites or domain names using their brand name.

All of this online activity carries graphic impact and has introduced a whole new world of imagery in the form of website design, subvertising, games, photogalleries and video archives of protest imagery, comics and cartoons, illustrations and animated graphics. Visitors to the website of Free Range Graphics, a design group based in Washington, DC, can view animated Flash-movies on particular political topics. At the end of each movie, the viewer can link up (at the push of a button) with a campaign that allows them to take

immediate action by, for example, signing a petition or sending a letter of protest.

One of the essential aspects of this dynamic cyberactivist scenario is its direct connection with tangible actions taking place on the ground: street demonstrations, carnivals, street parties, tree-sitting, tunnelling, guerrilla gardening, marching, boycotting, and so on. More often than not it teams up with conventional graphic forms of protest and agitation: posters, signs and banners that go up in the street; mailings of announcements, pamphlets, stickers and other ephemera; and more robust printed publications such as *Adbusters* and *Car Busters* magazines. Protest actions and campaigns in themselves have given rise to illustrated journals such as Kate Evans's book, *Copse* (see page 39), which offers an inside view of tree protests and protesters, as well as the issues that underlie the protests.

New technology has not made conventional forms of protest (or graphics) obsolete, but has formed a partnership with them.

The alternative press goes to great pains to point to the élitist connotations of the new technology, pointing out that most people in the world have never even made a phone call. When the British mainstream media repeatedly reported that the London 'J18' (18 June 1999) demonstrations against capitalism had been organized clandestinely on the internet, the organizers responded in the alternative press, saying that in addition to email and website use they had also sent out letters in several languages, printed leaflets in runs of 30,000 or more, and attended meetings and conferences. They also stated that although the media may feel free to ignore such old-fashioned methods of organizing, 'any movement serious about confronting inequalities of power and creating

2 Front cover of *Adbusters* magazine, No 31, August/ September 2000, showing a painting by Evie Katevatis entitled *Unidentified (Activist, Seattle)*. Canada 2000.

3 Lollipop from the StopEsso campaign, a high-profile boycott of Esso/Exxon products prompted by their stance on global warming. Designed by Paul Hamilton of One Another. UK 2001.

4 Stickers by El Fantasma de Heredia design group (Anabella Salem and Gabriel Mateu), Argentina 1993. An introduction to Argentina as 'the culture of the big drum' — and a vision of happier times. By the end of the century, Argentina's thriving economy would crash.

3

2

4

The visual displays and graphic ephemera surrounding mass protests against capitalism at the turn of the century were colourful, energetic and (at times) full of humour.

1 Spoof newspapers produced by the direct action movement Reclaim the Streets (20,000 printed of each): *Maybe*, 1 May 2000 (*Metro*); the *Spun*, November 2001 (the *Sun*); *Evading Standards*, 18 June 1999 (*Evening Standard*); and *Financial Crimes*, September 2000 (*Financial Times*). UK 1999–2001.

free and ecological communities can ill afford to do so'. They underlined the need for a radical grassroots movement to benefit from human togetherness and the excitement and rawness of the 'shout in the street'. Hence the ongoing line, 'the revolution will not be televised', and it's highly unlikely that it will be emailed either.[5]

Meltdown at the turn of the century

A succession of events, under the banner of anti-globalization protests, showed that protesters were not simply content to tune in to the web, they were also keen to show up on the doorstep and pursue the symbols of global capitalism – the IMF, the World Bank, the WTO, the G8 and the world leaders – to wherever necessary. After the clarion call of the Mexican Zapatistas in 1994, the first meeting of the global campaign, People's Global Action, was held in Geneva in 1998. Following on from that, 18 June 1999 became J18, the International Carnival Against Capitalism. Protesters then stalked the world summits and forums wherever they went: these included 30 November 1999 or N30 in Seattle, a watershed protest against the WTO that caused the shutdown of the World Economic Summit; May Day 2000 in London; and summits in Prague (September 2000), Nice (December 2000) and Davos (January 2001). Quebec City prepared itself mightily for protests during its hosting of the Summit of the Americas and negotiation of the Free Trade Area of the Americas in April 2001. It became known not only for the numbers of protesters attending (between 40,000 and 80,000)[6] but also for the amount of tear gas used on them.

By May Day 2001, London's anticipation of rioting by protesters was high and heavy-handed countermeasures were put in place. On the day, protesters were trapped within a circle of police in central London's Oxford Circus and held for seven or eight hours. On 14 June 2001, the EU–US Summit in Gothenburg brought a visit by George W Bush and failure to ratify the Kyoto Treaty. And in July 2001, the protests at the G8 Summit in Genoa brought not only violence but death, as one of the protesters was shot dead by paramilitary police.

All of these events consolidated the iconic graphic image of the anti-globalization protester and the romanticized wearing of 'the mask' (see page 32) – often a bandana or scarf, which paid homage to the Zapatistas, but mainly served to hide identity or protect against pepper gas. All of the protests carried their own iconic photo-images – the police with batons guarding Nike Town in Seattle (see page 44); the kicking-in of McDonald's on May Day 2000 in London (see page 47). All generated protest paraphernalia – flyers, newspapers, banners, signs, costumes and large street puppets (see page 54). All sparked off websites with information, list discussions and so on, some of them still in operation.

As protests raged over global and corporate summits and conferences, designers and campaigners found expressive

ways of denouncing the widening gap between rich and poor nations and the failure of the G8 nations and global agencies, and of highlighting environmental and other concerns. Opinions tended to be more extreme than in previous decades, and graphic statements more coarse and upfront.

To take animal rights as an example: although there had been much international activity surrounding this cause for some time, it was the UK and the United States that led the way with aggressive animal rights campaigns in the 1990s. The Stop Huntingdon Animal Cruelty campaign (SHAC) in the UK regularly intimidated workers at Huntingdon Life Sciences (a laboratory involved in animal experimentation) by standing outside the offices shouting abuse, banging on drums and wielding large posters depicting animals as torture victims. Some animal rights groups used extreme measures to threaten shareholders, including holding vigil in front of their homes while dressed in animal costumes, sending hate mail and making death threats. (Such anger harked back to a landmark image that appeared in a national newspaper and kick-started the UK campaign as early as 1975: the smoking dogs photograph [see page 56], showing beagles in a lab being forced to smoke cigarettes.)

Anti-fur campaigning took forward the graphic legacy of the UK's renowned Lynx anti-fur campaign of the 1980s with banned posters by the group Respect for Animals. British fashion designer Stella McCartney – daughter of Linda McCartney, outspoken vegetarian and supporter of Lynx – not only spoke out against fur but also refused to use leather in her collections or sit on leather

seats. Campaigns by the large US animal rights organization PETA (People for the Ethical Treatment of Animals) included catwalk attacks and online protests such as voguesucks.com.

The anti-GM (genetically modified) food campaign turned tough with a scary symbol, the biohazard sign (see page 61), and protesters in even more scary (protective) gear destroying GM crops by hand. Greenpeace produced an anti-GM food campaign with posters, shop boycotts and, on their website, an online game that allowed players to trash GM crops à la Lord Melchett (see page 61). The new crowd arrived: GenetiX Snowball, a non-violent direct action campaign against the release of GM plants in the UK, was set up by five women in 1998; they took a crack at media stereotypes of protesters by projecting themselves as solid, ordinary people of varying ages. GenetiX Snowball's main interface with the public has been a highly informative website, giving fully documented written and photographic accounts of their protests and their substantial experience of lengthy court actions.[7]

Many graphic designers over the decade practised their own particular version of activism by making comments via the tools of their trade. The varied selection of their work included here demonstrates the extent to which anti-globalization and environmental issues have become intertwined. Graphic comments are shown from designers ranging from Jonathan Barnbrook, whose statements on US cultural imperialism are sometimes portrayed in the form of typefaces, and Yossi Lemel, whose bold and sophisticated photographic posters emanate from the volatile

1

ongoing situation in Israel, to designer/ activists in Mexico City (including Leonel Sagahón, Alejandro Magallanes and Margarita Sada) who produce massively powerful posters as individuals but also band together in collectives such as La Corriente Eléctrica (Electric Current) and Fuera de Registro (Off the Register). As collectives they produce large-scale socially orientated projects involving many people and complex projects such as photographing defaced election posters all over the city in order to expose and document the distrust and anger people feel towards their politicians. The politicized design group El Fantasma de Heredia (the Ghost of Heredia), run by Anabella Salem and Gabriel Mateu, offers up a portrait of Argentina as a society traumatized by past military government, generations of 'disappeared', and in December 2001, the implosion of their bankrupt economy. But it is also a portrait of resilience and courage, for a national revolt took place on 19 and 20 December 2001, as people in Buenos Aires took to the streets and stormed the seat of government, forcing the resignation of the president and starting a new political era. Argentina may be a living, breathing example of IMF and global economy devastation, but as its people force social and economic change through grassroots self-management movements – such as the creation of local assemblies, which handle neighbourhood needs ranging from food to unemployment – it may also provide the first surviving challenge to the global economy.

The events of 9/11 sent shockwaves through the anti-globalization movement, particularly in the United States where protest and anti-corporate dissent were increasingly viewed as 'anti-American'. With the passage of time, however, the movement has entered a new phase. Activity has continued worldwide on many fronts – for example, anti-globalization protesters joined 10,000 people marching from the township of Alexandra to the UN Earth Summit held in Johannesburg in South Africa at the end of August 2002. With the ongoing War on Terrorism, a great deal of its energy has gone into anti-war activities, a logical development for a movement that has viewed recent conflicts, such as the one in Afghanistan, as being driven largely by corporate and economic interests, including oil reserves.

All these protests and movements, from anti-roadbuilding to anti-globalization, constitute a new oppositional force for change, charged electronically by digital technology. This global resistance movement has created a new and memorable direct action culture. It has visually defined the 1990s with new images and icons – of mass demonstrations and fighting in the streets, of new heroes in the form of people living in trees, of science fiction-style creatures wielding scythes and trashing crops. Most importantly, it has generated global conversations via new technology such as the internet, bringing issues, debates and alternative viewpoints to all – an essential development for a world that is now attempting to question its directions and consider its actions.

2,3 Street flyer (front and back) by the London Mayday Collective, announcing planned May Day festivities. UK 2000.

4,5 Crowds, flags, bandanas and an example of protest art commenting on US militarism, at the mass protest against capitalism and the FTAA in Quebec City, Canada 2001. Photographs by Brian Holmes of Ne Pas Plier.

2

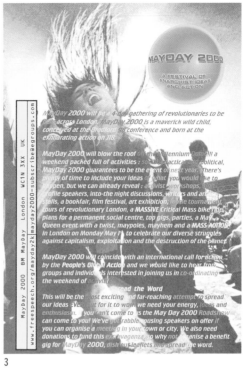

3

4

5

1 'Vote Swampy!', joke badge illustration celebrating the eco-activist and tunneller known as Swampy, famed for his protests at the Newbury bypass site. It emerged around the time he was evicted (with others) from a later protest to stop the building of a second runway at Manchester Airport which would destroy over 40 hectares (100 acres) of farmland and mature woodland. Published in *The Face* magazine, No 12, January 1998. UK.

2 Logo for The Alliance Against an M11 Link Motorway, a national alliance of campaigning groups, local associations and individuals, responsible for peaceful mass protest against the proposed motorway. UK 1994.

3,4 Front cover and spread from *Road Raging: Top Tips for Wrecking Roadbuilding* by Road Alert! UK 1997.

5 Greenpeace's gift to the anti-road protest in Cuerden Valley near Preston — two flowered JCB diggers (painted by graphic artist Tod Hanson) to keep the security men at bay and slow down progress. UK 1994.

6 Photograph by Tod Hanson of the Greenpeace diggers, nicknamed Flora and Daisy. UK 1994.

Anti-road protests: the UK

Driven by environmental concerns, a desire to challenge authority and disillusionment with party politics, the British roadbuilding protests of the early 1990s brought a surge of do-it-yourself culture and direct action that embraced people of all backgrounds, ages and experiences and generated a visual culture all its own. Protest tactics to delay construction ranged from tree-sitting to tunnelling and environmental art. Certain protests became legendary.

The protest against the extension of the M3 motorway over Twyford Down (1992–3) was renowned for the variety of its participants — from young New Age travellers to comfortable Conservatives. It was also marked by the violence that was to plague many of the protests thereafter.

With protesters squatting on land that was about to be dug up, security guards were hired to ensure that contractors could carry on their work. On 'Yellow Wednesday' (9 December 1992) yellow-jacketed private security guards — not required to wear ID numbers on their jackets as police do — used what has by many accounts been described as shocking violence, and evicted protesters from the site. Protests carried on in one form or another, usually causing delay to construction. This included one of the largest actions in May 1993, when 300 police reinforcements in riot gear took all night to remove over 200 people occupying a temporary bridge that had been constructed for the use of bulldozers. The road was eventually completed, but anti-road protests were on the rise.

The north London campaign against the building of the M11 Link Road (1994) drew attention through colourful protest tactics such as the erection and habitation of a treehouse in a now-famous chestnut tree — followed, eventually, by eviction using a cherrypicker (high-hoist hydraulic platform) in full media glare. In January 1994 a number of Edwardian houses due for demolition to make way for the road, declared themselves an independent country — the Independent Free Area of Wanstonia. Their occupiers were eventually evicted. A bender site of protesters (living in benders, or self-made shelters) was declared Leytonstonia — and trashed. Attention then focused mainly on Claremont Road, a row of squatted houses that became a public art installation — the whole street was transformed into a living room with furniture, sculptures, murals and so on — until the inevitable eviction.

Other anti-road protests included Cuerden Valley (aka Cuerdenia, 1994) in Lancashire, site of another motorway extension, where protesters lived in trees. They received a surprise delivery in July 1994 when

1

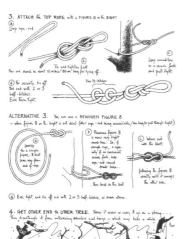

2

3

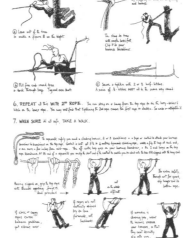

4

5

6

two multicoloured JCBs (road diggers) arrived, painted with rainbows and doves—courtesy of Greenpeace—and began digging up the current construction work, as security men tried to stop them.

At around the same time came the passing of the controversial Criminal Justice and Public Order Act of 1994, which targeted rave culture and criminalized forms of peaceful protest, such as road protests and unauthorized camping in vehicles by travellers and gipsies. This galvanized protesters from different causes into a consolidated direct action movement pitted against the Act.

One of the most famous anti-road protests was still to come: the campaign against the

Newbury bypass (1995–6) in which contention between protesters and mainstream media ran high. The elevation of the tunneller Swampy to cuddly, celebrity status brought worries to protesters about the media's ability to create entertainment-led stereotypes, while trivializing the environmental issues. Or in another mood, the media was equally capable of stereotyping all protesters as thugs.

Out of this clash of intention grew wide-ranging art and media activism, including photographers who began to document the protest movement from within—not only to show protest in a different light but also to catch evidence of the brutality inflicted on protesters.

As well as the traditional flyers, newsletters and pamphlets that had normally accompanied UK demonstrations, heavy documentation in the form of illustrated journals began to appear. *Road Raging: Top Tips for Wrecking Roadbuilding* (1997) stands as the ultimate resource manual, with contents ranging from how to build a camp to how to deal with evictions and legal issues. Highly organized and detailed, it provides invaluable information on how to construct and weather an environmental protest campaign while at the same time shedding light on the issues and difficulties to be faced. Kate Evans's book *Copse: The Cartoon Book of Tree Protesting* (1998) is more of an illustrated

rendition of what makes protesters tick. It is a diary-like journal of events, actions, personalities and feelings that shows protesters as people (warts and all), at the same time offering a compelling, historical chronicle of the anti-road actions themselves. Both publications offer insights into and graphic expression of one of the most important environmental movements of our time.

7 Photograph by Nick Cobbing of a 'Mass Trespass' against the Criminal Justice Act on Twyford Down in Hampshire, also the scene of heavy anti-road protest. UK 1994.

8 Front cover of Kate Evans's illustrated book *Copse: The Cartoon Book of Tree Protesting*, published by Orange Dog Productions. UK 1998.

9 Front cover of the second issue of *East Ender*, the journal for The Alliance Against an M11 Link Motorway. UK 1994. In the background are houses on Claremont Road — focal point of the 'No M11 Link' road protest. Tweedledum is the then Home Secretary Michael Howard (responsible for the Criminal Justice Act), and Tweedledumber is Prime Minister John Major.

7

8

9

1 *SchNews Survival Handbook,* annual compilation of the weekly information sheet (Issues 151–200, January 1998–February 1999) including survival guides on activities such as DIY Tunnelling, Subvertising or How to Set Up a Co-op. Published by Justice?. UK 1999.

2 Front cover of Undercurrents alternative news video compilation No 8. UK 1997.

3 Home page from the SchNews website. UK 2003.

4 Home page from the Undercurrents website. UK 2002.

Media activism: videos, the alternative press and Indymedia

Anger at the way in which the mainstream news media reported the early roadbuilding protests gave rise to the UK video-activist collective known as Undercurrents. Founded in 1993, Undercurrents provided an alternative news service. It created highly informative news videos that were shot by campaigners with domestic camcorders and covered the main campaigns around the UK at that time.

Undercurrents not only attempted to provide an alternative view of protests taking place and the people involved but also challenged the mainstream media notion of 'news', the priorities given to certain topics and the unsettling omission of others. Most disturbingly of all, its videos captured an atmosphere of heavy intimidation aimed at protesters and camcorder operators. They also showed, in the case of the roadbuilding protests, examples of outright violence (visited upon protesters by security guards and others) that have never appeared on our television screens.

Undercurrents also provided workshops and training in camcorder skills for activists, creating a vast network of video-activists and helping to establish the camcorder as an essential protest tool around the world. It also helped establish the now-renowned Indymedia network.

The first Independent Media Center was set up to cover the Seattle anti-globalization protests in 1999, providing on-the-spot grassroots coverage – reports, photos, audio and video footage – through an open access website, as well as a printed publication called *The Blind Spot*, handed out to protesters in the street. There is now a network of over 50 Independent Media Centers around the world (known as Indymedia), each operating autonomously but dedicated to non-corporate, grassroots reporting and open exchange of and access to information. The organization Indymedia.org coordinates international independent media projects through its website. It has no actual address or office, it only exists in cyberspace. Local IMCs, however, have been known to meet face-to-face.

The concept of open publishing is the key to the globally accessible Indymedia.org website. Anyone can post an article on the site and receive instant feedback. The internet does not reach everyone, however, and IMCs are aware that they must branch out into other formats and media. Some IMCs publish offline printed newsletters and newspapers, and in some countries, set up radio and television initiatives.

The Indymedia.org web page is the window to the new world of independent media, aspiring to involve everyone, everywhere in an openly fluid information

1

3

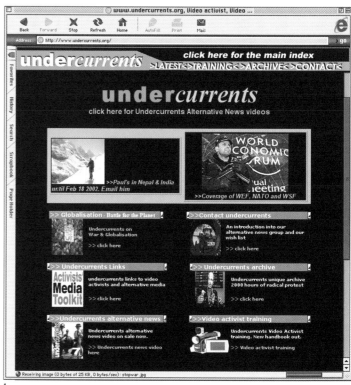

2

4

exchange, all in the hope of shaping a better and more just society.

Meanwhile, the long-established tradition of an alternative press with an international reach has carried on through publications such as *Fifth Estate* (in the United States) and *YearZero* (in the UK). Even more of this activity can be found on the internet. The online newsletter *SchNews* (founded in 1994) provides sharp but acerbic weekly news reports — and remains available in hard copy form for those not online. Its popular website, heavy with postings of protests and festivals is blatant evidence that anti-capitalist and eco-protests are not part of a clandestine network —

as sometimes intimated by mainstream news — but are hanging right out there for anyone who is interested to see and to follow. *SchNews* is only one of the many press alternatives that are now vocal in cyberspace as well as in the streets.

5 Front cover of the radical Detroit-based publication *Fifth Estate* (Spring 2000 issue), published since 1965. Cover illustration by Maurice Spira. USA 2000.

6 Front page of *The Indypendent*, the offline newspaper of the New York IMC (Independent Media Center), January 2002.

7 Front cover of the subversive magazine *YearZero*, Issue 3, carrying the unforgettable byline 'Live on your feet not on your knees'. UK 2000.

Overleaf Media activists aimed to tell an alternative story about protests and their violence. Photograph by Michael Donoghue showing the removal of a protester by the police. UK 2002.

5

6

7

1 One of the iconic images to emerge from the mass protest against the World Trade Organization which became known as the 'Battle of Seattle' in November 1999: US riot police stand guard at the entrance to Nike Town. Photograph by Andy Clark.

2,3 'Squaring up to the Square Mile', the information booklet and accompanying map (available by post) which laid the foundation for the J18 protest held on 18 June 1999 in London's financial district. Written by the Oxford-based research group Corporate Watch and London Reclaim the Streets – a popular movement using direct action to liberate city streets and public spaces.

Mass protest against capitalism: London and Seattle 1999

A number of protests against capitalism and globalization took place in different countries around the turn of the century. They have become legendary, galvanizing pockets of discontent into a global movement which now operates through networks such as Indymedia (see page 40), as well as many other websites and organizations around the world. The volume and the force of the discontent was their overriding and most shocking feature: right there, on hard pavement, dancing in the street or running from tear gas. They changed any mainstream media notions of straggly little street protests as has-been events – and showed the full power of current,

new generation collective action, as well as the frightening, destructive forces that take charge when it all goes wrong. The images and memories that emanated from those events will be with us for a long time.

Festive, open-air protest came to London's Square Mile – the financial district – with 'J18' (18 June 1999) otherwise known as the 'Stop the City' protest, part of the global 'Carnival Against Capital'. More than 10,000 protesters piled into the Square Mile for the festivities, which later erupted into riots sweeping across the city: two million pounds' worth of damage, 46 people in hospital. Although the press muttered about clandestine plots and subversion over the internet, the day's guide and map were available to anyone willing to lick a stamp and send for them by

post. At the same time, the Carnival Against Capital – International Day of Action took the form of protests, street parties, festivals and other actions and events in 27 countries around the world, with photos and reports placed on websites. From thereon, most of the mass protests had their own website for information and organization.

November 1999 brought the 'Battle of Seattle', known for the range of groups linked arm-in-arm in solidarity, including trade unionists, students, environmental campaigners, feminists and other activists. This massive protest against the IMF and the WTO, involving an estimated 50,000 to 100,000 protesters from all over the world, resulted in the shutdown of the World Economic Summit that was being held there.

Riots broke out, large quantities of tear gas and pepper spray were used against protesters, a state of civil emergency was declared and a curfew imposed. The sinister photo below of riot police in body armour guarding Nike Town appeared in newspapers around the world. The episode was to be repeated soon after when in April 2000 clashes between protesters and police shut down Washington, DC, for six hours and disrupted a meeting of the IMF's financial committee.

1

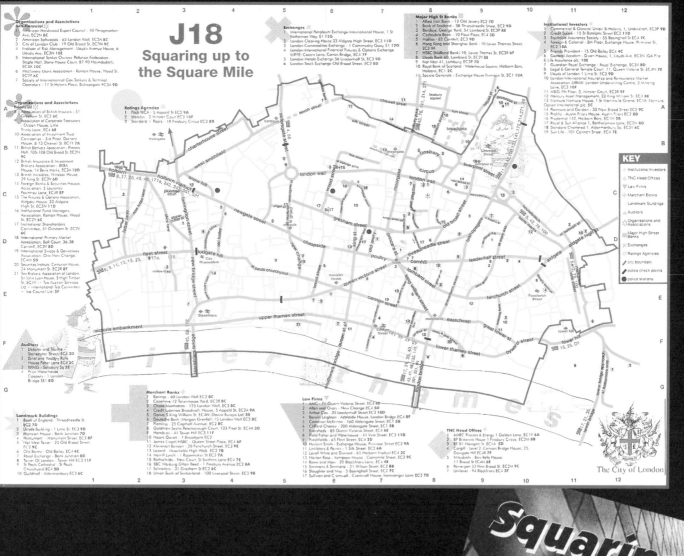

1 May Day 2000 in London. Photograph of a May Day fairy dusting off a policeman's riot shield in Trafalgar Square. Photograph by Adrian Dennis, AFP.

2,3,4 Photographs by Michael Donoghue of May Day 2000 in London: guerrilla gardening — turf begins to invade tarmac; a banner in a crowd of clicking cameras; and dealing a blow to the multinationals with violence against a McDonald's restaurant.

Mass protest against capitalism: London 2000

May Day 2000 in London brought a four-day series of anti-capitalist events. On May Day itself, an estimated 4,000 people gathered around Parliament Square and nearby Trafalgar Square. (Some 5,500 police officers were also present at the event.) It started peacefully enough: a May Day fairy appeared in Trafalgar Square and demonstrators engaged in guerrilla gardening with the symbolic digging up of Parliament Square — a gesture towards reclaiming public spaces and greenery from cars and congestion.

But as the day wore on, violence broke out — including the smashing up of a McDonald's restaurant — and fighting between police and protesters carried on into the evening. The following day, newspapers were full of photographs of violent clashes, the defaced Cenotaph (war memorial) and the vandalized statue of Winston Churchill, painted with the word 'murderer' and sporting a Mohican haircut modelled out of grass turf. Much of the mainstream media declared the protesters to be anarchists or thugs, and the scene was set for heavy security measures on every protest to come.

1

2

3

1,2,3 Swiss artist Johannes Gees's protest contribution to the World Economic Forum in January 2001 in Davos – an interactive installation involving a laser projector beaming messages, submitted by visitors to Gees's website, onto the mountainside overlooking Davos and within view of the delegates.

Mass protest against capitalism: Prague and Nice 2000 and Davos 2001

September 2000 found around 5,000 protesters rioting during the World Economic Summit in Prague attended by representatives of the IMF and World Bank; and violent protest accompanied by clouds of tear gas greeted European leaders on their way to the conference centre for the European Union Summit in Nice in December 2000.

Switzerland launched one of the country's biggest security operations ever in January 2001 in an attempt to keep protesters away from the business and political leaders attending the World Economic Forum in the mountain resort of Davos. Water cannon, tear gas and rubber pellets were used on protesters to quell demonstrations. Swiss artist Johannes Gees found an imaginative way to bypass the chaos and get at the participants of the congress. He aimed a 15 metre (50 foot) high laser beam at a slope above the resort and beamed messages to the delegates from people who logged on to the 'Hello Mr President' website. Although the site was only online for 24 hours, he was able to project one-third of the 7,200 messages that rolled in from 81 countries.

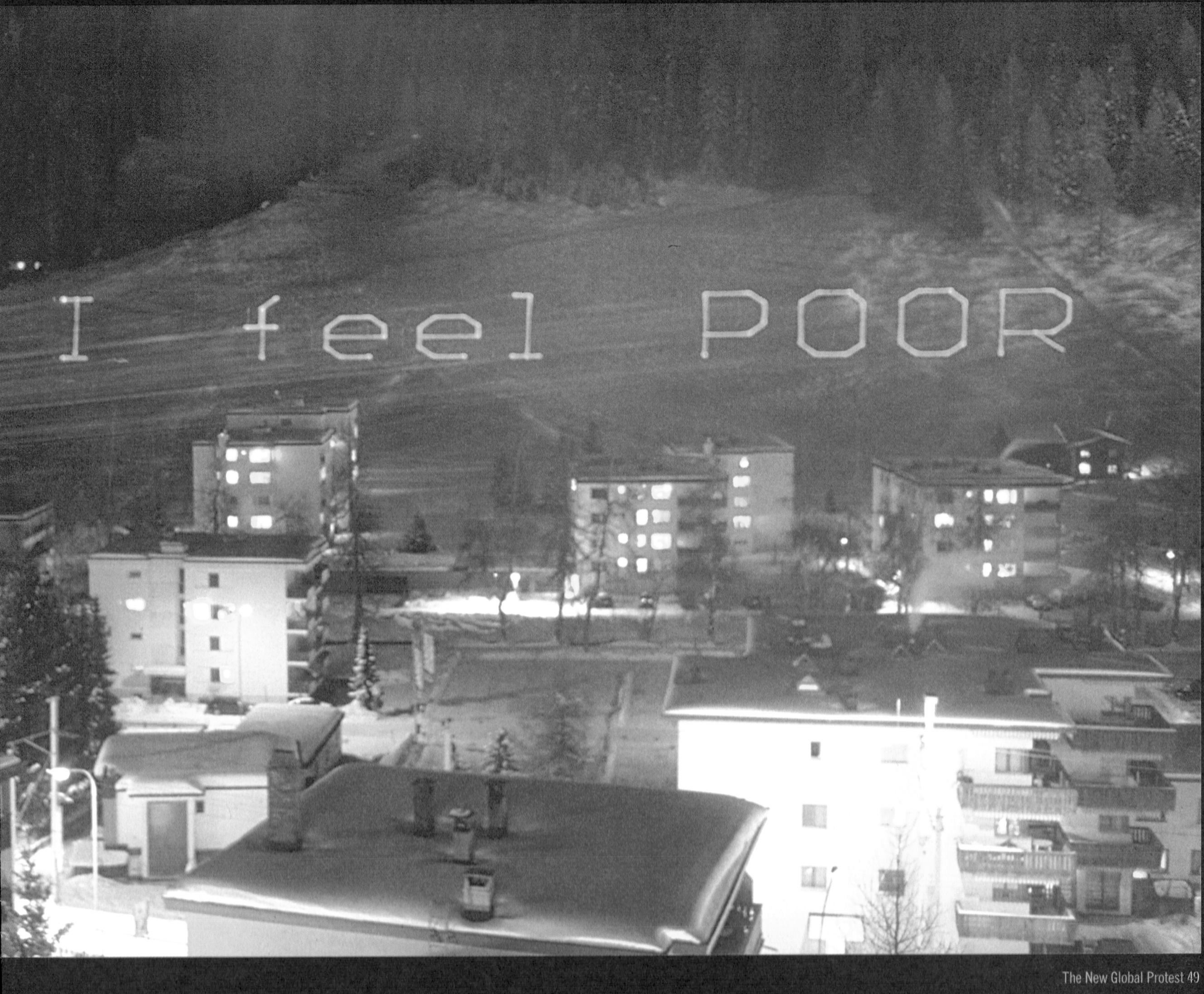
I feel POOR

1 Protest in the form of street theatre during the demonstrations against the FTAA in Quebec City, April 2001. Photograph by Caleb Huntington.

2 Front and back cover of a CD compilation aiming to generate funds to aid activists and organizations, and promote awareness of the harmful impact of globalization, by GASCD: Governments Accountable to Society and Citizens = Democracy. Canada 2001.

Mass protest against capitalism: Quebec City and London 2001

By April 2001 it was obvious that wherever summits and economic forums met, anti-globalization protests would follow. The Canadian authorities therefore set up a 3 metre (10 foot) high steel and concrete fence closing off the centre of Quebec City, the location for the three-day Summit of the Americas. This closed meeting resulted in the creation of the Free Trade Area of the Americas (FTAA), a free trade zone comprising 34 nations. The city councils of Saint-Foy and Quebec City passed bylaws (which they later dropped) prohibiting the wearing of masks or scarves covering part or all of the face by protesters or activists.

The Carnival Against Capitalism protest against the FTAA in Quebec City attracted demonstrators from around the world. With carnival events from many different groups, it became a protest event of great theatre and intensity – but subsequent reports were shocking. After three days of protest, during which the steel fence came down, 400 people were arrested, 120 were hurt and human rights groups condemned police for their heavy use of plastic bullets and tear gas (allegedly without provocation) on people staging peaceful protests.

Spurred on by the city bylaws relating to masks, Lydia Sharman and her students from the Design Art Department of Concordia University joined together with the French design group Ne Pas Plier (Do Not Bend) and other European activists to create a carnival event called 'The Gift of Masks'. They designed a bandana mask with, on one side, a mouth smiling and laughing, and on the other, a gagged mouth behind the fence. Four thousand of these masks, laboriously silkscreened by hand, were distributed for free early on at the protest site, along with stickers and posters. The group then had the experience of seeing their masks dispersed throughout the crowds, appearing again and again in different circumstances throughout the days of protest. This served to generate strong feelings of connection. Sharman says, 'Masks, even fabric ones, offer some protection against tear gas and pepper spray, and a degree of anonymity and solidarity'.

Fear of protest – whipped up to hysteria levels by government and media – hit its zenith in London on May Day 2001, when much of central London was boarded up in anticipation of anti-capitalist protests. 6,000 police lined the streets (with half as many reserves) in an unprecedented show of force. Despite the 'Monopoly' game theme and the jolly printed graphics that accompanied it all (an essential complement, it seems, to any organizing taking place over the internet), the Critical Mass bike ride which took place early in the

1

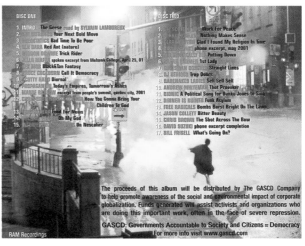

2

day was the only truly visible event. Most of the protesters heading for the main event in central London were herded into Oxford Circus, a central junction of streets, where they were kept penned in by police for seven to eight hours. Complaints about this treatment filled the newspapers for days, coming from journalists and ordinary bystanders caught up in the mess as well as anti-capitalist protesters and activists.

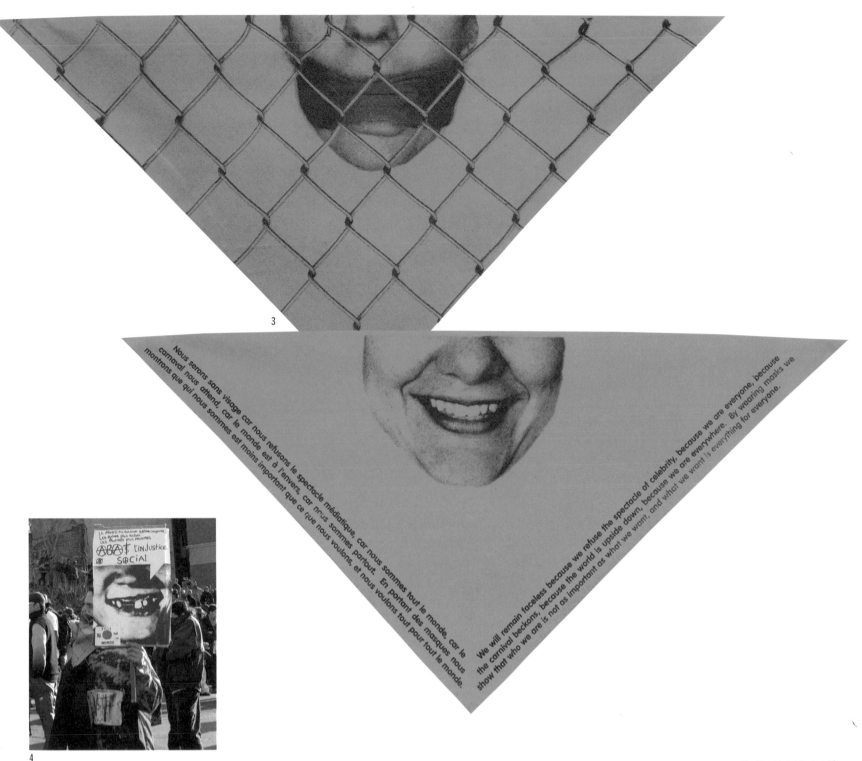

Nous serons sans visage car nous refusons le spectacle médiatique, car nous sommes tout le monde, car le carnaval nous attend, car le monde est à l'envers, car nous sommes partout. En portant des masques nous montrons que qui nous sommes est moins important que ce que nous voulons, et nous voulons tout pour tout le monde.

We will remain faceless because we refuse the spectacle of celebrity, because we are everyone, because the carnival beckons, because the world is upside down, because we are everywhere. By wearing masks we show that who we are is not as important as what we want, and what we want is everything for everyone.

3

4

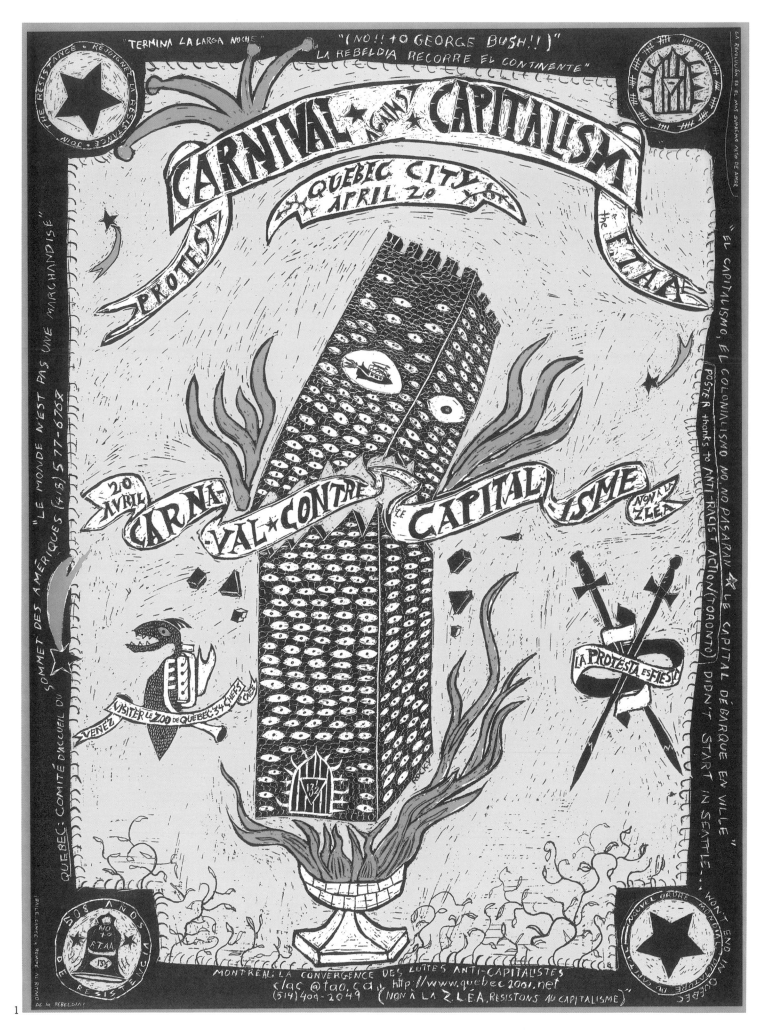

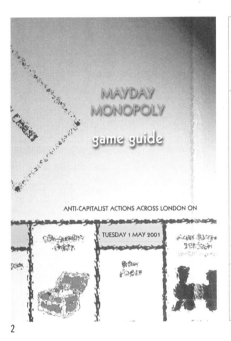

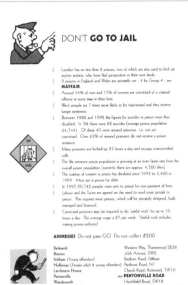

1 'Carnival Against Capitalism: Protest the FTAA, Quebec City, April 20', poster by the artist Rocky. Produced by Anti-Racist Action (Toronto) in March 2001 in preparation for the demonstrations in Quebec City against the FTAA and the Summit of the Americas.

2 Cover and page from *Mayday Monopoly Game Guide*, an information and survival guide to anti-capitalist actions in London . on May Day 2001. Published by the London Mayday Collective.

3,4 Flyers and stickers announcing May Day events in London, 2001. Published by the London Mayday Collective.

2

3

4

1,2 Demonstrators use street puppets and 'mass mooning' in protests against US President George W Bush's visit to Gothenburg, Sweden, for the EU–US Summit in June 2001. Photograph (1) by Jockel Finck and photograph (2) by Wolfaram Steinberg, both Associated Press.

3 Front page of the French newspaper *Libération*, 22 July 2001, showing the tragic death of protester Carlo Giuliani during anti-globalization protests at the G8 Summit in Genoa. Photograph by Dylan Martinez, Reuters.

Mass protest against capitalism: Gothenburg and Genoa 2001

The EU–US Summit in Gothenburg, Sweden, in June 2001 was visited by George W Bush, who was dubbed the 'Toxic Texan' and met by elaborate street puppets and protests against his refusal to sign the Kyoto Treaty (see page 62) and his plans for the 'Star Wars' missile defence shield. As the EU Summit then convened, 25,000 people came out to protest, confrontations ensued and three people were shot and wounded by police. It was a vision of things to come.

In July 2001, three days during the G8 Summit turned Genoa, Italy, into a battlefield, with reports of brutality by paramilitary police against the volunteer-run Independent Media Center, and the fatal shooting of protester Carlo Giuliani.

From then on, international summits and meetings were doomed to insulate themselves from protesters and the public they claimed to serve, located in distant or isolated places—the WTO meeting in November 2001 was planned for Dohar in Qatar, a Gulf state. But world events took over with the tragedy of 9/11, and anti-capitalist protest was forced to start a new and different chapter in its history. Protest activities around issues of environmental and social justice would certainly continue. But a great (if not greater) deal of energy would also be channelled into protests against upcoming conflicts, promoted by many—including governments—under headings such as War on Terrorism, but suspected by some to be driven by corporate interests.

1

2

Les juges sur la piste du patrimoine de Chirac page 11

Libération

Mort au G8

Les affrontements entre les militants antimondialisation et la police ont tourné au drame vendredi à Gênes, avec la mort d'un manifestant. Le sommet des pays les plus riches continue. Page 2

Le jeune manifestant tué n'était pas encore identifié vendredi soir.

M 0135 - 721 - 7,00 F - 1,07 €

www.liberation.com

1,07 euro
France métropolitaine

Antilles,Réunion-Guyane 10 F, Allemagne 3,30 DM, Autriche 30 Sch, Belgique 48 F, Cameroun 1000 CFA, Canada $2,95, Côte d'Ivoire 1000 CFA, Danemark 15Kr, Egypte 7,50 L, Espagne 270 Ptas, Finlande 13 Mkf, Gabon 1000 CFA, Grande-Bretagne 1,20 L, Grèce 550 Dr, Irlande 1,50 L, Israël 11 Nis, Italie 3200 L, Liban 2500 LBB, Luxembourg 48 F,Maroc 12 Dh, Norvège 18 Kr, Pays Bas 3,75 Fl, Portugal Cont. 320 Esc, Sénégal 1000 CFA, Suède 20 Kr, Suisse 2,40 F, Tunisie 1,20 Din, USA $ 3 (N.Y. $ 2,50)

PREMIERE EDITION NUMERO 6277

1 The controversial 'smoking beagles' photograph published in the UK in 1975.

2 Cartoon taken from the website of the Animal Liberation Front (ALF), which comprises activists who engage (anonymously) in direct action against animal abuse, often through the damage and destruction of property. 2002.

3 Animal rights protester dressed as a beagle pickets the house of an 'anonymous' investor in Huntingdon Life Sciences, pressuring him to sell his shares. UK 2000. Photograph by Geoff Robinson.

Animal rights: anger and extreme protests

Animal welfare became a mainstream issue in the UK with the publication in 1975 of an article and photograph in the *Sunday People* tabloid newspaper exposing the use of beagle dogs — forced to smoke 36 cigarettes a day — to test a 'safe' cigarette in a British laboratory. Over the following decade, new underground militant animal rights groups felt driven to free animals from labs or send letterbombs to scientists or politicians associated with such practices.

Hence animal rights protest groups of the 1990s could draw on a wealth of emotional associations from the past.

The Stop Huntingdon Animal Cruelty campaign (SHAC) has run a long protest against Huntingdon Life Sciences, a laboratory which conducts experiments on animals in order to test the safety of new drugs. They have intimidated workers by standing outside the offices shouting and banging on drums. Their protests are usually accompanied by large posters showing animals as victims of torture.

Far more extreme measures have been taken by unnamed, underground animal rights groups. (Despite their underground nature some of them have websites, with accompanying cyber-graphics.) Computerized investor lists have been accessed and both corporate and individual shareholders targeted, receiving hate mail, bomb warnings, attacks and death threats. Individuals have even found protesters in animal costumes holding vigil in front of their homes.

In the end, the tactics worked — investors were scared off and the Huntingdon Life Sciences' share price collapsed in 2000. Although Huntingdon Life Sciences was rescued by a US backer, the protest campaign carries on as a reminder of the deeply emotional debate surrounding animal rights in the UK. The UK fox hunting debate arouses similar emotions, and became a political issue under the Labour government, when a vote was taken to ban it.

3

1

The world is not dying, it is being killed, and those who are killing it have names and addresses.

ALF

2

Anti-fur protests: the Lynx legacy

The Lynx anti-fur campaign in the UK produced some of the most dynamic pieces of graphic activism of the 1980s. This included the landmark 'Dumb Animals' campaign created by Yellowhammer ad agency, which comprised a billboard and cinema ad showing a fashion model dragging a bloody fur coat behind her. Still hailed as a graphic icon, the Dumb Animals campaign was followed by other equally startling Lynx campaigns, as well as photographs by Linda McCartney and slogan T-shirts designed by Katharine Hamnett that snapped 'Yuk! Your disgusting fur coat'. Lynx's aggressive visual campaigns

played a heavy role in damaging the fur industry: shops were boycotted, fur sales plummeted. Perhaps more significantly, their efforts attached a stigma to the wearing of fur that still causes debate on the issue even today.

When Lynx was transformed into the organization Respect for Animals in the 1990s — devoted to campaigning against the international fur trade — it carried on its tradition of producing highly controversial graphic images. Its poster 'One Fur Hat. Two Spoilt Bitches', shown here, featured a model bedecked with a real, dead, skinned fox (a roadkill victim) to startling effect. Its 1996 poster 'Do You Have the Face to Wear Fur' — depicting a skinned fox head on top of a fur coat — was eventually banned by the

Advertising Standards Authority. Respect for Animals also engaged the support (and merchandise designs) of fashion designer Stella McCartney, renowned for her pro-animal rights views, and fashion photographer Mary McCartney — both daughters of Linda McCartney.

1 'Two Spoilt Bitches', poster by ad agency Palmer Hargreaves for Respect for Animals. UK 1990s. Photograph by Bob Carlos Clarke.

2 Groundbreaking billboard and poster for Lynx anti-fur campaign by Yellowhammer ad agency. Art direction by Jeremy Pemberton, photograph by David Bailey. UK 1985.

3 'Hands up if you wear fur', poster created for Respect for Animals. Conceived by Jeremy Pemberton of IMP London, photograph by Mary McCartney. UK 1999. The poster was translated and launched in France, Spain and Italy in 2000.

1

2

3

1 Highly successful poster campaign by PETA featuring celebrities and supermodels, including Naomi Campbell. USA 1995.

2 Detail from one of PETA's spoof websites, voguesucks.com. It targets the editor of a leading fashion magazine for running fur spreads in her magazine, writing pro-fur editorials, refusing ads from animal protection groups and other 'furry' offences. USA 2001.

3 PETA activists storm the catwalk during the annual Victoria's Secret fashion show in New York City, protesting against Brazilian supermodel Gisele after she agreed to model fur for leading US fur company Blackglama. USA 2002. Photograph by Mike Segar, Reuters.

Anti-fur protests: the style tactics of PETA

Alongside Respect for Animals, the animal rights group PETA has also employed Stella McCartney to help their campaigning. McCartney introduces a fur farming exposé – a film shot on a fur farm in the United States showing foxes being electrocuted for their pelts and enough appalling cage conditions to sicken any viewer. PETA was launched in 1980 and is a large, international non-profit-making organization based in the United States. Over the years, it has used a wide range of media and high-profile campaigns to 'educate policy-makers and the public about animal abuse'. It also became known in the 1990s for bringing a sense of style and cool to animal advocacy, causing the well-known UK magazine *Time Out* to declare PETA responsible for making animal rights the number one 'hip' cause.

PETA managed to recruit a stream of models and celebrities, including Christy Turlington and Kim Basinger, to pose for its 'I'd Rather Go Naked Than Wear Fur' campaign. More recently, its humorously biting websites, bearing names such as voguesucks.com or meatstinks. com, have targeted magazines, companies and even personalities which it felt promoted the use of fashion fur or lifestyles supporting the abuse of animals. It has produced two animal rights albums, held 'Rock Against Fur' benefit concerts and engaged film-makers such as Martin Scorsese to pledge to keep fur off movie sets. Lastly, no Fashion Week is safe: PETA's catwalk protests have put fur-toting designers and fur-wearing models in their place.

1

2

3

Sophie Ellis-Bextor by Mary McCartney Donald

4 Anti-fur campaign by PETA showing British pop singer Sophie Ellis Bextor holding up the carcass of a skinned fox. USA 2002. Photograph by Mary McCartney.

Here's the rest of your fur coat.
www.furisdead.com

Anti-GM campaigning: trashing crops and other tactics

The controversy surrounding genetically modified (GM) food and crops reached fever pitch in the UK during 1999–2000. Campaigning groups launched armies of activists dressed in protective white suits and masks to descend on farms, ripping up GM crops and destroying test sites. They were usually accompanied by flags, banners, bags and other gear carrying the biohazard symbol, all functional but adding to the science fiction-like appearance of a decontamination job. The armies could be quite large. The 'Stop the Crop National Rally' and GM test site visit in July 1999 involved coachloads of activists – around 700 in all, from 'ordinary' people to anarchists – who donned white suits and masks, and smashed their way through 10 hectares (25 acres) of farmland in Watlington in Oxfordshire, destroying a farm scale test site.

One of the most famous actions involved the arrest of Greenpeace UK's Executive Director Lord Peter Melchett and 27 Greenpeace activists, all caught in the act of pulling up a Norfolk farmer's field trial of GM maize in July 1999. The 'Greenpeace 28' went on trial, pleading not guilty to theft and causing criminal damage – and were acquitted by a sympathetic jury, a clear signal of public concern. Greenpeace lapped up the publicity, even sporting a little computer game on their website entitled 'Cropraider', offering players the chance to guide a Pac-Man-like creature named MunchIt (a pun on Melchett) through a maze, while avoiding GM monsters, eating organic food and getting the chance to trash GM crops. Moreover, the combined efforts of different activist groups were by now achieving results. Not long after the Greenpeace trial, *Do or Die* – a journal involving people from the Earth First! UK network and other environmental movements –

reported that by July 1999 more than a third of all test sites had been trashed.

With consumer activism on the rise, Greenpeace targeted supermarkets, restaurants, schools and other public food outlets with colourful print materials for their True Food campaign, which opposed the use of GM ingredients, at the same time as promoting organic food.

At about the same time, the name GenetiX Snowball began to appear in the press. It ran a non-violent, anti-GM direct action campaign which declared 'active resistance to the new gene technology' by encouraging people to remove GM plants from the ground and then accept the consequences of their actions. Their use of non-violent resistance was intended to challenge opponents with their vulnerability – and their name was borrowed from the 'snowball' effect of gathering support used in the 1980s peace movement.

GenetiX Snowball also gained column inches and photo opportunities by breaking the media stereotype of protesters as young lunatics. The 'GenetiX Five' who launched the group were all women, a mixture of ages, fairly reserved and civilized, and prone to describe themselves as 'ordinary people'. Nevertheless, all had been arrested and roughed up at various points along the way, and were viewed as eco-terrorists and hooligans by biotech companies, supermarket bosses and food giants. Documentation of their activities and actions exists on their website: a photo and information archive of their substantial contribution to the anti-GM crop movement.

Anti-GM campaigning continues. In the UK its main focus is environmental; on the world stage it also battles with issues such as corporate power versus the devastation of local communities, and the question of agricultural control.

Opposite Photograph by Julia Guest showing protesters destroying a field of genetically modified oilseed rape. The flag emblem is the international biohazard symbol. UK 1999.

1 Logo from the Greenpeace True Food campaign, working to oppose the introduction of GM foods and increase the availability of organic food. UK 1999.

2 Demonstration against GM crops staged outside a courthouse, allegedly by members of GenetiX Snowball. UK 1999. Photograph by Garry Weaser.

3 The international biohazard symbol.

3

1

2

Environmental concerns and eco-crimes: globalization versus the environment

Graphic statements or protests relating to the environment over the past decade or so are very different in both content and attitude from many of the campaigns of earlier years. They are grittier and less endearing or 'fluffy', and they often harbour the dark subtext that corporate interests are somehow at the bottom of it all. Cyberactivism has also come into play, through the hard-driving, campaigning websites of groups such as Greenpeace and the student environmental network, People & Planet, as well as the graphically playful websites and printed magazines belonging to forums for direct action such as Car Busters and Adbusters.

In the examples shown here and overleaf, symbols of business, indulgent lifestyles and overdevelopment or corporate interests are never far away. Certain targets stand out. When George W Bush made one of his rare trips to Europe in June 2001, protesters showed up in force and not without reason. Early in his presidency, environmentalists reeled in shock at his agreement to introduce exploratory drilling in the Arctic National Wildlife Refuge in order to ensure future US energy supplies.

The high-powered StopEsso campaign – a global boycott of Esso/Exxon products due to the corporation's stance on global warming – has spent most of its existence spreading the word that ExxonMobil gave more money towards the Bush election campaign than any other oil company. Once elected, President Bush pulled the United States out of the Kyoto Protocol, an international agreement to reduce the emissions that cause global warming. The United States has refused to ratify it ever since. Bush has featured large in StopEsso's campaign imagery, alongside calls of 'Don't put a tiger in your tank'.

Petrol-guzzling, status-seeking, street-choking cars are subjects of satire on the cover of the Czech magazine, *Car Busters*. Deforestation is condemned in a poster by Argentinian design studio El Fantasma de Heredia; air pollution provokes angry comment in a poster by Mexican designer Alejandro Magallanes. US-based artist Luba Lukova's 'Eco Crime' poster series shows environmental destruction by humans as one of a number of crimes against humanity. All the usual suspects are delivered here with sarcasm or sinister undertones, although World Car Free Days manages to raise a smile of hope and a promise of global resistance.

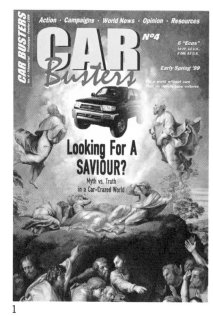

1

2

3

4

DON'T BUY E$$0

THEY DON'T GIVE A DAMN ABOUT **GLOBAL WARMING**

Boycott E$$0

No.1 global warming villain

www.stopesso.com

5

6

5 'Don't Buy Esso', front of leaflet by Paul Hamilton of One Another showing the Esso tiger (mascot) holding a match to the world. UK 2002.

6 'Boycott Esso', poster by David Gentleman for the StopEsso campaign. UK 2001. The poster was not used after 9/11 due to its visual association with the burning towers.

7 'George W Bush Memorial Park', a comment on connections between the US President and environmental disasters. Illustration by Knickerbocker, copy by Jesse Gordon. USA 2001.

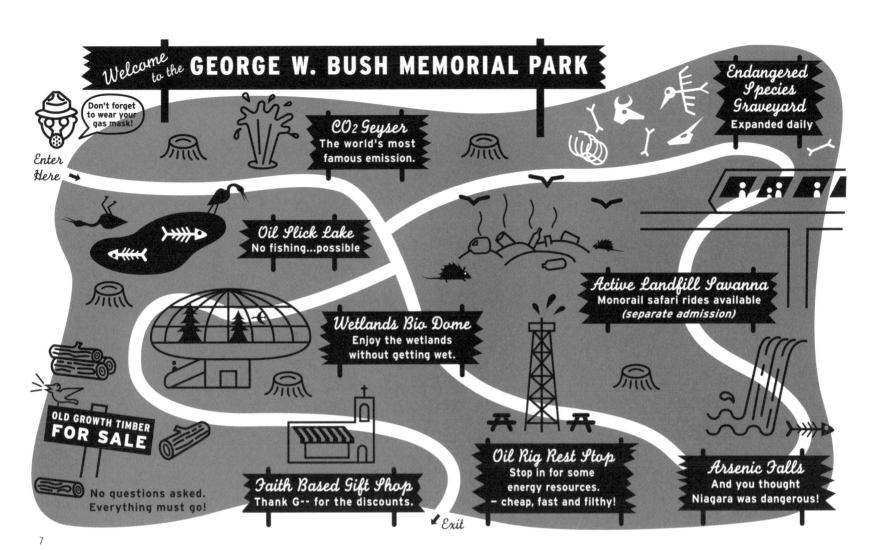

Welcome to the **GEORGE W. BUSH MEMORIAL PARK**

Endangered Species Graveyard
Expanded daily

Don't forget to wear your gas mask!

Enter Here →

CO$_2$ Geyser
The world's most famous emission.

Oil Slick Lake
No fishing...possible

Active Landfill Savanna
Monorail safari rides available
(separate admission)

Wetlands Bio Dome
Enjoy the wetlands without getting wet.

OLD GROWTH TIMBER FOR SALE

No questions asked. Everything must go!

Faith Based Gift Shop
Thank G-- for the discounts.

↙ *Exit*

Oil Rig Rest Stop
Stop in for some energy resources. – cheap, fast and filthy!

Arsenic Falls
And you thought Niagara was dangerous!

7

1

2

1 Front cover and spreads from the *Water for Human Kind* catalogue, designed by Thierry Sarfis. France 2000.

2–5 Four of the images selected for the web-based 'Water for Human Kind' image bank, a project created in 2000 by French designer Thierry Sarfis. A total of 750 projects were received from 42 countries.
(2) Masutera Aoba, Japan.
(3) El Fantasma de Heredia, Argentina. It says: 'Clean Water Now!'
(4) Liu Xingrui, China.
(5) Marion Le Masurier, France.

Environmental concerns and eco-crimes: water markets, water wars

'Water for Human Kind' was the theme of a project conceived by French designer Thierry Sarfis in 2000. A call for images was made to graphic designers, associations and colleges around the world. Out of the substantial amount of work received, a database of images was constructed on the web as a resource for future campaigns. A panel of judges chose award-winning pieces and a printed catalogue was designed by Sarfis. But this was no soft exercise – the issue of drinkable water for everyone is fiercely political, and the bank of images (which can be found on the web at www.eauhumanite.com) shows an interesting if worrying barrage of ideas from many angles. Sanitation, privatization, population increase, dwindling supplies, pollution, economic development – they're all in there, imaginatively expressed, and sounding alarms about issues that are often ignored and lack of change. The same messages continued to be put across at the World Summit on Sustainable Development in Johannesburg in August–September 2002, many of them a grim portent of things to come.

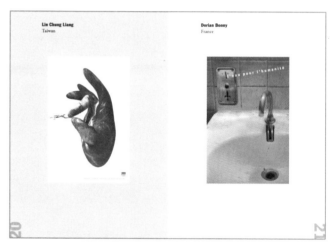

1

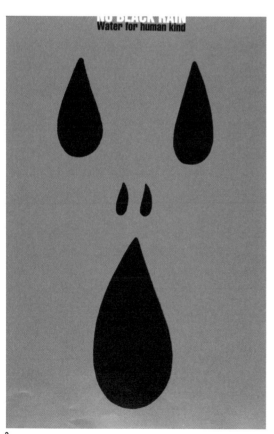

2

3

4

L'eau pour l'humanité

1 'Just Say No', poster by James Victore protesting against cultural takeover by corporations. USA 1998.

2 'Sudan, Struggle Against Poverty', poster by Luba Lukova decrying the shameful global imbalance of those who go hungry and those who are too well fed. USA 1999.

3,4 'Supersize', two images created by Plazm for a special issue of the Japanese magazine IDEA that focused on American design. Both comment that the USA's most deadly export is its fast food. (Creative direction by Joshua Berger, Niko Courtelis, Pete McCracken, Enrique Mosqueda; art direction by Enrique Mosqueda; photography by Dan Forbes.) USA 2000.

5 Page from the Virus Foundry catalogue displaying Nixonscript, 'a font for telling lies with', designed by Jonathan Barnbrook. UK 1997.

6 'Stop American Cultural Imperialism', poster by Jonathan Barnbrook. UK 2000.

The anti-globalization debate: international graphic comments

While mass protests, do-it-yourself culture and other aspects of popular activism rose up from the streets, graphic designers in studios around the world also lent their voices and skills to the anti-globalization debate.

US cultural imperialism and political deceit were addressed by British designer Jonathan Barnbrook in the form of typefaces and posters; American designer James Victore attacked the sellout of Times Square (and New York City) to corporations in his poster work. Bulgarian-born designer Luba Lukova commented on the global imbalances and injustices of food and nutrition; US design group Plazm graphically described the United State's most deadly gift to the world, exported far and wide, as being fast food.

Israeli designer Yossi Lemel and French designer Pierre Bernard both remarked on the global economy, its hidden alliances and its imbalances in wealth (see overleaf). Meanwhile Argentinian design group El Fantasma de Heredia made a bitter depiction of their country as a 'banana republic' (a derogatory term, usually applied to poor Central American countries, describing a small state dependent on foreign capital through one trade, such as banana growing). Such visual expressions of anger and biting criticism continued to target global injustices in the years surrounding the turn of the century.

1

2

3

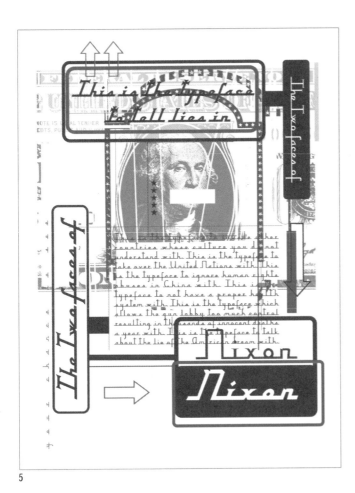

5

6

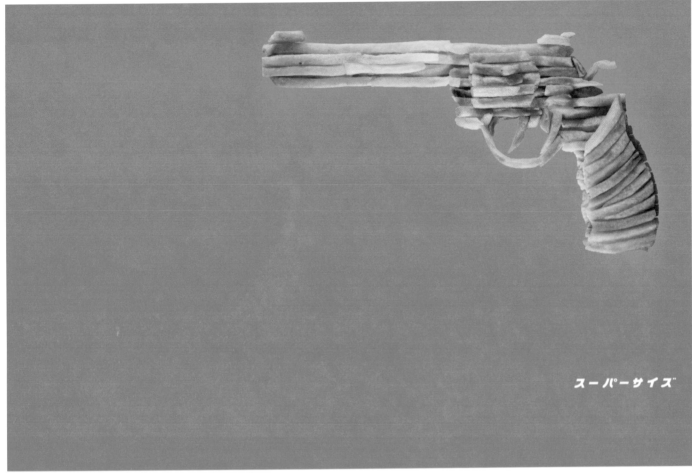

4

1,2,3 'Poverty vs. Prosperity', billboard and posters from a membership campaign for Amnesty International in Tel Aviv. Designed by Yossi Lemel. Israel 1998.

4 'Banana Republic', postcard by El Fantasma de Heredia. Argentina 1997.

5 'Tout va bien! (All's Well That Sells Well)', poster by Pierre Bernard of Atelier de Création Graphique in which the UN logo becomes a tangled mess of economic and trade ties. France 1997.

1

2

3

4

1 Electronic image by Ricardo Peláez showing a masked member of the Zapatista Liberation Army smoking a peace pipe. Mexico 2001.

2 'Zapata Vive' series of stickers organized and produced by Fuera de Registro (Off the Register) and La Corriente Eléctrica (Electric Current) to support the peace process in the Chiapas region. They coordinated the participation of the following designers: Ricardo Lopez Castro, Margarita Sada, Alain Le Quernec (France), El Fantasma de Heredia (Argentina), Andres Ramirez, Ricardo Peláez, Edgard Clement, Heraclito Lopez, Alejandro Magallanes and Leonel Sagahón. Mexico 2001.

The anti-globalization debate: views from Latin America

Powerful anti-corporate comments have emerged from the studios and collectives of Latin America. The combined efforts of the groups Fuera de Registro (Off the Register) and La Corriente Eléctrica (Electric Current) in Mexico City produced the sheet of stickers shown opposite. During a weekend in March 2001 when the commanders of the Zapatista Liberation Army (EZLN) arrived in Mexico City to make demands for the rights of indigenous people – and a stand against corporate power – 75,000 copies were distributed and stuck all around the city. With about 15 artists and designers involved, the stickers were part of a series called 'Zapata Vive', produced to support the peace process in Chiapas. Some of the stickers also make comments against the government and official media viewpoints.

Since their launch in 1993, the design studio El Fantasma de Heredia, directed by Anabella Salem and Gabriel Mateu, has been engaged solely in social, cultural and political projects. The name means 'the ghost of Heredia', the name of the street in Buenos Aires where Salem and Mateu first started to plan their vision of a studio. Much of the studio's work to date has presented the 'face' of Argentina, and although it can be a warm and playful face, El Fantasma de Heredia excels at showing that there can also be pain and struggle behind the laughter. For it is a society which is still recovering from the 'disappearance' of 30,000 people (associated with or part of the Left) during the 1976–83 military dictatorship (see page 116).

By the start of the new century (after years of following the IMF's lead), Argentina's economy was crumbling under the weight of its huge external debt. Its citizens were spiralling into poverty and hunger. Reacting to this climate, El Fantasma de Heredia created an art interaction entitled 'Laugh Upon Request' – beginning with an open exhibition involving photographs, eight large posters, each 1.2 x 2 metres (4 x 6½ feet), and texts intended to motivate exchange and discussion between inhabitants of the San Telmo neighbourhood of Buenos Aires. The use of the symbol of laughter – seen on the faces of 400 people asked to smile for the camera – was intended to help people gain strength from each other and feel better about facing the future. El Fantasma de Heredia also produced an interdistrict guide of the 'organizations of civil society' (OCS), to be given away in the weekly markets in the neighbourhood square. All these were ways of establishing bonds between neighbours and initiating local solutions to daily problems.

Then in December 2001, Argentina's economy plummeted into bankruptcy. On 19 and 20 December there was a national revolt – a people's uprising, now referred to as the 'Argentinazo' – and the president, cabinet and other politicians ran for cover. Some placed the blame for the catastrophe at the door of Argentina's own government; many more placed it at the door of the international lender, the IMF. But despite half the population reportedly existing below the poverty line in March 2002, Argentina's people are fighting back, with the creation of local, neighbourhood-driven 'assemblies' of self-management, providing alternative economic models that may yet challenge the forces of corporate globalization.

1

!YAPA$

22 DE DICIEMBRE DE 1997, ACTEAL, CHIAPAS

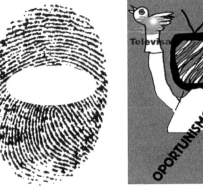

MEXICO

PAZ con JUSTCIA y DIGNIDAD

El EZLN no viene a firmar la paz

El EZLN no viene a apoyar la iniciativa de Vicente Fox. Televisa y TV Azteca son oportunistas al promover ahora un concierto por la paz.

El viaje de los zapatistas desde la selva Lacandona hasta la capital del país, es mucho más que una simple manifestación; vienen a hablar ante los diputados y senadores de la República, para exigirles que los acuerdos de San Andrés, plasmados en la iniciativa de la Cocopa, se conviertan en ley.

El EZLN no viene a "firmar la paz". Es más, la aprobación de esta iniciativa de la Cocopa es tan sólo una de las tres condiciones que el Ejército Zapatista exige para sentarse a negociar una salida pacífica al conflicto. Las otras dos son: la liberación de todos los zapatistas presos en diferentes cárceles y el retiro del ejército de los 5 campamentos que todavía ocupa en los Altos de Chiapas.

La aprobación de la iniciativa de la Cocopa, sobre los derechos y cultura indígena, depende de los diputados y senadores; la liberación de los presos zapatistas corresponde a los gobiernos de los estados donde están recluidos; sólo el retiro del ejército depende del gobierno federal. Mientras no sean satisfechas todas estas demandas, no habrá ni negociación, ni paz.

Vicente Fox ha cambiado radicalmente la estrategia que durante 7 años enfrentó a los mexicanos en una guerra de baja intensidad. Ahora el gobierno ha declarado su deseo de atender las demandas indígenas y así lograr la paz. Pero la forma en que el gobierno y las dos grandes televisoras nacionales manifiestan sus intensiones, encierra el peligro de hacer creer a la sociedad que para lograr la paz, basta con sentarse y firmar. Vicente Fox confunde a la población al insistir en que los zapatistas vienen a firmar la paz y a apoyar su iniciativa (que es de la Cocopa). Por otro lado, y a pesar de que todavía hace poco, Televisa y TVAzteca promovían el repudio al EZLN; con su concierto por la paz y su campaña de firmas, las dos grandes televisoras nacionales, alimentan una presión social sobre el movimiento zapatista, al promover una visión ingenua de la pacificación en Chiapas. Todo esto contribuye a que si el EZLN no "firma la paz" pronto, la población sentirá que los zapatistas son intransigentes, que no quieren negociar y justificarían una salida de fuerza.

No queremos cualquier paz. La paz de verdad y duradera, no puede pasar por encima de las demandas indígenas. Aunque un entendimiento entre el gobierno y el EZLN está más cerca que nunca, el proceso es mucho más complicado de lo que la propaganda oficial ha difundido. Es necesario hacer un contrapeso a la campaña de desinformación y participar en la difusión de información precisa, que permita a la sociedad formarse una opinión realista del estado de la pacificación en Chiapas.

ADIOS A LAS ARMAS

!YAPA$

MIENTEN

JUSTA Y DIGNA
POR UNA PAZ CON ADJETIVOS
JUSTA Y DIGNA

LAS MUJERES CON LA
DIGNIDAD REVELDE

NO QUEREMOS CUALQUIER PAZ
EZLN EN DF MARZO 2001

22 DE DICIEMBRE DE 1997, ACTEAL, CHIAPAS

LA PAZ NO ES UN CONCIERTO POR TV
EZLN EN DF MARZO 2001

ANTES NO, AHORA SÍ, ¿MAÑANA QUÉ?

COMO LO VIÓ EN LA TELE
PAZ
LAVE SU CONCIENCIA

PAZ con JUSTICIA y DIGNIDAD

LIBERTAD A LOS PRESOS POLITICOS

MEXICO

Aprobación de la ley • Libertad de los presos zapatistas • Retiro y cierre de las 7 posiciones militares

1 'One for You, One for Me', one of eight large posters designed by El Fantasma de Heredia as part of their 'Laugh Upon Request' project. The project included an open exhibition for the people of the San Telmo neighbourhood in Buenos Aires. Argentina 2001.

2 'Urbania, Children's Museum', poster by El Fantasma de Heredia. Argentina 1997.

3 'Argentina Hurts', poster created by El Fantasma de Heredia at the time of Argentina's national revolt in December 2001.

engl. one for you, one for me (laughs under order) to smile for the picture!
to look at all of them / to look at each of them. and see. can you see something? / no yes. girl from the neighbourhood
fr. un pour toi, un pour moi (rires sur demande) sourire pour la photo!
regarder tous / regarder à chacun d'eux. et voir. pouvez-vous voir quelque chose? / non oui. fille du quartier

1

Urbania, un museo a escala de los chicos

2

3

ADG | Concurso-Muestra Composición Tema: «La vaca». 1987/2001
Asociación de Diseñadores Gráficos de Buenos Aires.
Diseño: El Fantasma de Heredia / Foto: Andrew Stern

4

4 'Composition Topic, The Cow: "Undernourishment of Our Children"', poster by El Fantasma de Heredia. The first part of the title is a phrase used in children's writing exercises. The poster shows a man using tyres for a *piquete*, a large protest or demonstration where unemployed people use burning tyres to block main highways and camp out on-the-spot with their families. (According to the artists, almost half the country was unemployed at this time.) Argentina c. 2001.

5 Front cover and inside page of a booklet for CEISI, a centre for the study of street children. Designed by El Fantasma de Heredia. Argentina 1999.

5

Resistance to the power of governments or political doctrines has manifested itself historically in familiar forms — whether through actions, as in revolutions, strikes and protests, or through graphic opposition, as in cartoons, caricatures, poster campaigns, graffiti and the underground press. In recent years, however, resistance has grown towards another source of control — that of global corporations or multinationals. This new power is perceived as an invasive force that creeps through societies, cultures and individual lives with stealth. More powerful and potentially ↗

more manipulative even than governments, multinationals control or make an impact on matters as wide ranging as health, food, the environment, energy and economies – and have been doing so for decades. Their scope seems limitless; their damage can be tracked back through many years. Through the instruments of branding and advertising, they play with our desires, values and aspirations. Governments and political parties are now borrowing corporate methods of manipulation and image-building, and the lines are becoming blurred between politics and brands.

Resistance to the power of corporations or multinationals now comes in both traditional forms of protest and in new forms such as subvertising (the subversion of ads and their messages), all of them energized by the global reach of modern communications media. All wield the devastating weapons of humour and satire, expert tools for undermining or disarming power in its many forms and guises.

Subvertising became the activist's tool of sharp critique in the 1990s: the more polished the presentation, the more biting the result.

1 'Impotent Man', anti-smoking campaign produced by the California Department of Health Services in Los Angeles. USA 1999.

2 'Obsession, for Men', the subvertisement of a major fashion brand and its perfume advertisements. Ad parody by Adbusters; photographer Nancy Bleck; model Cayvan Econmi. Canada 1993.

The build-up of brand subversion

The escalating power of corporations since the mid-1980s (if not earlier) is synonymous in many people's minds with the rising power of brands, and particularly the big-name brands which have taken over our shopping malls, our high streets and, many feel, our lives. The long process that saw corporations change from selling products to selling brands is well charted in Naomi Klein's *No Logo*.[1] Although notions of brand awareness date back to the 1950s, a new frenzied era of branding (and branding concepts) began in the late 1980s and early 1990s with companies like Nike, Gap and Starbucks. On one level branding is about the marketing of a lifestyle associated with a certain brand image and identity. On a deeper level, it can mean the brand almost taking on a life of its own, endowed with values and meaning that go far beyond the original branded product itself – and the promotion of these values can be almost religious in its fervour. These are big concepts which, fed over time to a thinking public, will eventually start to appear prescriptive – or controlling. The corporations behind the brands start to look as if they are making huge profits out of telling people how to live their lives.

Add to that the sheer increase over the past decade in the numbers of billboards and shops, and suddenly brands are everywhere: in our faces, on the streets, on TV, in every city and country we visit. Brand ubiquity, together with rumblings about sweatshop manufacturing, Third World exploitation and environmental issues, has put brand identity on trial – at least in the minds of a new generation of activists.

Anti-corporate attitudes – expressed visually – were present throughout the 1990s, certainly in the environmental and anti-tobacco camps. Visual protests emanating from this 'backlash', as Klein calls it, set as their target the visual symbols of corporate brands – slick logos, cuddly mascots (often cartoon characters) and other aspects of brand advertising such as billboard ads.

The US organization Doctors Ought to Care (DOC) was giving the brand icons for Marlboro and Camel cigarettes a good pasting long before it was fashionable (or safe) to do so. Artist Doug Minkler produced confrontational, subverted cartoons of Marlboro Man and Mr Camel for DOC as early as 1990. DOC was founded in 1977 by Dr Alan Blum to challenge the 'promotion of lethal lifestyles in the mass media', particularly the marketing of tobacco and alcohol to adolescents. Its humorous and imaginative campaigns often incorporate the ideas of young people themselves. Originally a group of physicians, DOC grew into an international network of more than 150 groups in 29 countries, including health professionals, teachers, students, and business and community leaders.

DOC has always used counter-advertising to ridicule tobacco and alcohol promotions, sometimes running campaigns in the broadcast and press media, sometimes devising counter-promotions or 'house calls' (personal appearances). In 1993, for example, DOC took exception to a Marlboro campaign called the Marlboro Adventure Team, which was seemingly aimed at young people. Marlboro vans drove across the United States, giving away jackets, watches and hats in return for proof of purchase coupons, and then staged an 11-day rafting, riding, biking and driving event in Colorado and Utah. Infuriated by what it felt was an attempt by Marlboro manufacturer Philip Morris to target young people, DOC formed the Barfboro Barfing Team. (Barfing means vomiting.) The Barfboro Barfing Team toured the West in the official Barfmobile, which was driven by Barfman Erik Vidstrand, accompanied by his faithful companion Barfy the Wonder Dog. In the San Francisco Bay area, California DOC held an event called the Barfboro Barfing Team Challenge, with prizes for the quickest death, slowest death, most dramatic death and a freestyle barfing competition.[2]

From the series, THE SEVEN EARLY SIGNS OF CANCER.
Doctors Ought to Care   5510 Greenbriar, Suite 235   Houston, Texas 77005   713-798-7729

1

2

Barfboro was not far off its objective. Tobacco manufacturer R J Reynolds, the makers of Camel cigarettes, was eventually taken to task by the US Federal Trade Commission for unfair advertising practices – its cartoon character 'smooth' Joe Camel was deemed too appealing to children.[3] By 1998, tobacco advertising had been banned in the United States, and a major US cigarette manufacturer admitted in 1999 that smoking kills. The tobacco industry was forced to make reparation payments by financing anti-tobacco advertising campaigns and turning over their hoardings to state health agencies, while still paying for the sites (until January 2000).[4] An example: the Marlboro Man became the Impotent Man on billboards in Los Angeles in 1999, in a poster that was commissioned by the California Department of Health Services but allegedly financed by tobacco reparation money.

Culture jamming

Another notable organization out to subvert the media, advertising and corporates, and literally reshape culture, is Adbusters (the Adbusters Media Foundation, Vancouver) headed by Kalle Lasn. It describes itself as 'a loose global network of artists, writers, environmentalists, ecological economists, media-literacy teachers, reborn Lefties, eco-feminists, downshifters, high school shit-disturbers, campus rabble-rousers, incorrigibles, malcontents and green entrepreneurs', although the list is fluid and changes periodically. Its magazine *Adbusters* (founded in 1989), subtitled 'the Journal of the Mental Environment', has at its heart the criticism that commercial mass media has been overtaking our lives and our brains – our mental space. Over the years it has become best known for encouraging 'culture jamming' – the subversion of the dominant, corporate-run culture through a variety of creative means in order to initiate a re-thinking of how we all want to live in the twenty-first century.

One of the most popular forms of culture jamming, particularly for visual artists and designers, has been subvertising, the production of corporate ad spoofs. Tactics include simple graffiti on billboards, cut-and-paste to change the message or meaning of an ad, and elaborate photo or film parodies which mimic existing ads as well as criticizing their corporate source (as shown on page 77). Fashion brands such as Calvin Klein and Nike have been traditional targets. Subvertising has grown to become the favourite pastime of many artists and designers around the world, who subvert the messages of all sorts of commercial organizations from fast food chains to computer manufacturers.

Culture jamming – as 'creative resistance' on many fronts – can take many different shapes and forms and keeps evolving as time goes on. With its website and magazine operating as information and inspiration centrepoints, Adbusters encourages culture jamming through competitions, campaigns and other activities, all with an international scope. The best known includes 'First Things First 2000', an updated version of a manifesto originally written in 1964, calling on designers to use their skills to solve today's social and environmental crises, rather than simply serving the cause of consumerism. It acquired thousands of signatures, generated immense debate, was published in magazines internationally and gave birth to conferences and other public events. Adbusters then followed it up with a special 'Re-design' issue of its magazine – guest art-directed by the renowned graphic designer, Jonathan Barnbrook – which called for entries and then printed a survey of design projects that promoted and created new ways of thinking and living.

Always controversial, Adbusters has provided a much-needed wake-up call to the design industry, has been responsible for a proliferation of culture jammers around the

3 'DIKE' T-shirt photographed by Mark Ritson. Subvertisement of the Nike brand identity and a reference to the company's lack of acknowledgement of one enthusiastic Nike consumer group – lesbians. USA 1997.

Satirical subversion of national symbols and icons is used to communicate anger at corporate and political power.

1 'Now Poland', poster by Marcin Wladyka which subverts the national symbol of Poland (a white eagle on a red ground with a gold crown). Poland 1999.

world and has remained a vital creative player in the social meltdown taking place around the turn of the twentieth century. It is still operating as feverishly as ever: a magazine of continual provocation and one of the few websites that actually succeeds in being an active meeting place of many minds and a colossal amount of energy.

A telling, high-profile example of activists vs. corporate might was the McLibel case. London Greenpeace had been encouraging boycotts and distributing 'What's Wrong with McDonald's?' leaflets since 1986. In 1990 McDonald's issued libel writs against five London Greenpeace activists, targeting the contents of the leaflet. Three of the activists apologized; two did not. McDonald's took David Morris and Helen Steel to court for libel, starting the longest running civil libel case in British history. (The case began on 28 June 1994 and ran for 2$^{1}/_{2}$ years, with the verdict finally delivered in June 1997.) The equally long-running McLibel Support Campaign coordinated publicity around the world and raised money for costs through donations and sales of T-shirts and other merchandise. An autonomous group of volunteers from 14 different countries created the McSpotlight website, which acts as a comprehensive library for all things relating to the court case, as well as a centrepoint of worldwide anti-McDonald's activity.[5]

In the end, Morris and Steel were unable to prove all of their claims and were found guilty of libel on a number of counts. However, the case was widely acknowledged as a public relations disaster for McDonald's; it was ruled that 'they "exploit children" with their advertising, produce "misleading"

advertising, are "culpably responsible" for cruelty to animals, are "antipathetic" to unionization and pay their workers low wages.'[6] Attention was thus drawn to areas of activity that McDonald's would have preferred remain unpublicized.

Constant references in the press to this David and Goliath battle helped to rally the public to the activists' cause. Steel, a gardener, and Morris, a postman, handled their own legal defence in court against the corporate giant and its imposing lawyers. For them it was a fight for freedom of speech and against censorship by powerful corporations. The result of the struggle was summed up by a McLibel Support Campaign poster showing the McDonald's mascot Ronald McDonald, terrified and trapped in the heavy beam of the McSpotlight (see page 91).

Both Adbusters and the McLibel Trial are landmark examples of how small groups of people, volunteers or organizations can take on and do battle with corporate might. They also show the crucial role that websites can play. In both cases, the websites have supplied an up-to-date information source and an active forum for debate (through discussion rooms and so on) as well as initiating and organizing many forms of direct action, protest and solidarity on a global scale.

New political brands, West and East
It does not require a giant leap to move from the branding of corporates to the branding of governments, political parties and even individual politicians. But branding provides no protection against the satire and lampooning that is dished out by artists, illustrators, cartoonists, caricaturists and

activists and that can be zapped across the internet.

There has been a lot to target. When the Cold War died and the Soviet Empire fell apart, the 1990s and its New World Order introduced new heights of intrigue and mockery to Western politics. America's politicians provided a wealth of opportunities to satirists in the 1990s. The Clintons created a circus of scandal in the White House – most famously, the Monica Lewinsky affair in 1998–9. Bill Clinton's affair with a young intern brought embarrassment, investigations, an impeachment trial, acquittal by the Senate of charges of perjury (by lying about his involvement) – and finally, forgiveness, after an apology to the public and a trip to church. Indeed, scandal-prone Clinton seemed so adept at landing on his feet that sharp satirists such as the *Spitting Image* team in the UK began to imagine divine interference (see page 82). The jokes and embarrassment made a big impact in all areas of the graphic environment. Images and wisecracks filled national newspapers, magazines and books, and appeared in smaller, personalized graphic forms such as the birthday card shown on page 101, on sale in a smalltown supermarket in West Virginia. To a much larger and even more cynical international press, the Clintons were easy targets and were pilloried mercilessly.

So too was the incoming President George W Bush. His oil connections, his minimal experience of the world outside America – abroad less than six times, and only once to Europe – and his seeming inability to put a decent sentence together were ridiculed throughout the mainstream media on both

Teraz Poland

1

sides of the Atlantic. One of the biggest targets was the 'democratic' process that put him into the White House in 2001: a demonstration of the failure of the electoral system, where the final result depended on the votes from one state, bringing about miscounts, re-counts, mis-readings of the ballot by voters, and discussions over the weight and indentation of the pencil mark used. A final decision was reached only after the US Supreme Court voted by 5 to 4 to prevent a further re-count of contested votes in Florida, thereby giving Bush victory in that key state. This 'victory' provoked a tide of cynicism and jokes, such as satirist Michael Moore's references to Bush as '"President" Bush' or 'the Thief-in-Chief' in his best-selling book, *Stupid White Men*.[7] But underneath the laughter, America faced uncomfortable issues: the need for electoral reform and review of the two-party system, the issue of corporate funding of candidates, and the public's dwindling use of the vote.

But all of this seemed relatively straightforward, if clumsy, compared to the unnatural calm and even more unnatural smiles worn by British politicians in the 1990s, where 'what you see' definitely was not 'what you get'. The imagery on pages 102 to 105 presents a world of things that are not what they seem – of post-Thatcher modernists who might be deep traditionalists; of people versed in double-speak; of supposedly left-wing parties operating on the centre-right. Perhaps this is why the caricatured images that emerge tend to smack of lunacy, showing a host of maniacal smiles.

As a major political force of the 1980s, Margaret Thatcher was highly distinctive in politics, character and appearance, and a gift

for caricature and other forms of visual ridicule. Her hair and her handbag became graphic icons of the period. With her resignation in 1990, John Major brought visual blandness, a love of road-side cafés and ambiguous politics, and satirists went to extremes to try to make him interesting. Tony Blair, however, arrived in 1997 in a flurry of spin doctors, photo-opportunities and designer lifestyles. He re-branded Old Labour as New Labour (moving it from the left to the right) and has spent much of his time since re-branding British politics, complete with slick government websites. By the start of the new century, there was revived potential for British satire and nastiness – not only on the homefront, but in the 'special relationship' between Tony Blair and George W Bush and the resurfacing of old villains such as Saddam Hussein.

But new visions of twenty-first century branded 'democracy' and its fulfilment have left some countries of Europe and beyond (and their graphic artists) unimpressed. Artists who had operated under the totalitarian regimes of the former USSR and other Iron Curtain countries, and were well practised in circumventing government censorship and expressing 'unofficial' ideas or criticism through coded symbols and metaphors, often applied heavy doses of black humour to their work. As circumstances brought release from totalitarian constraints – in the USSR, by *glasnost* and *perestroika*, and in Central and Eastern Europe, by the following pro-democracy revolutions of 1989 – graphic art, and particularly posters, played a dramatic role as carriers of discontent or the voice of 'truth' and opposition.

Once the short-lived euphoria of the 'new dawn' was over, artists such as the late Yuri Bokser of the USSR continued to express their finely honed sense of irony, cynicism and black humour. In the following decade there would be extraordinary political failures or downfalls, including the crumbling of the Soviet Empire itself. With Mikhail Gorbachev deposed, Boris Yeltsin installed in 1991, the new Russia – or Russian Federation – embarked on a decade of economic collapse and social change – bringing with it the continued impoverishment of the Russian people. Corruption and gangsterism ensured that, by 2001, 25 to 40 per cent of the economy still ran on the black market. Alongside a nascent market economy run by young, post-communist entrepreneurs, Russia also acquired one of the highest rates of increase in HIV in the world. Drug abuse had reached epidemic proportions and was blamed for the rapid spread of HIV. The social stigma attached to AIDS was high; the availability of Western-style drugs treatment was low; the interest of Russian leaders or officials was virtually non-existent.

In other post-communist countries the 1990s would bring more fallen heroes, such as Czech President Václav Havel (marked by public disillusionment due to perceived scandals in his private life); terrors on the horizon, such as Serbia's export of war and decline into isolation (see pages 110–13); disappointment and dismay over the 'rewards' of the free market, such as unemployment (see visual comments on pages 108–9). Most particularly the open door to the West brought features of Western culture such as the proliferation of brands (like Benetton and

2 'Images of an Ideal Nation', poster by James Victore for an exhibition of social and political work from the nineteenth and twentieth centuries in the United States, held at DePaul University Art Gallery. USA 1998. Historically, a ribbon carrying the words *E Pluribus Unum* (Out of Many, One) has accompanied the American eagle.

3 Poster by Yossi Lemel for Israel's fiftieth anniversary of independence, making a cynical comment through the use of the McDonald's brand symbol. Israel 1998.

4 Front cover of Michael Moore's satirical book *Stupid White Men …and Other Sorry Excuses for the State of the Nation!*, a blistering attack on George W Bush as the man who 'stole' the presidency in the 2000 election. Published by ReganBooks/HarperCollins. USA 2001.

2

3

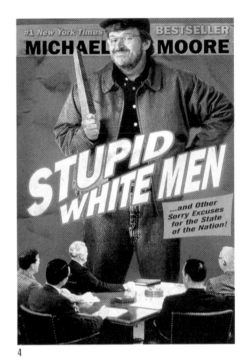

4

Traditional visual satire in the form of caricature and cartoons continues to ridicule world leaders, politicians and their power plays.

1,2 Former Iraqi leader Saddam Hussein and former US President George Bush, Sr (both veterans of the 1991 Gulf War) are caricatured as latex puppets by *Spitting Image*. UK mid-1990s.

3 Bill Clinton makes a deal with God in a scenario created by *Spitting Image*. UK mid-1990s.

4 'Silly Season', cartoon in the *Guardian* newspaper by Martin Rowson, a comment on things to come. UK 2002.

others) and of Western party politics, such as never being able to tell 'the bad guys from the good guys'. Not surprisingly, much of what artists have to say about post-communist or pro-democratic society is laden with sarcasm, obscenities, dog droppings and vomit.

Social comment from Latin America

Another of the world's frontlines for multinational exploitation (as well as International Monetary Fund havoc) lies in Latin America. Although always rich in revolutionary heroes and images, it remains racked by inequalities and social hardship imposed over the years by governments and rulers who are at times catering to the interests of global corporations or their large neighbour to the North. Latin American artists have harsh things to say about politicians and dictators both past and present.

For around 70 years the pseudo-democratic Institutional Revolutionary Party (PRI) was the dominant ruling party of Mexico, scarred in its later years by power and drugs corruption. Calls for a greater democracy began to be heard. The Zapatista uprising that took place in the Chiapas region of Mexico in 1994 (see page 30) – demanding land and rights for indigenous people, and resisting multinational development forced on them by the government – put Mexico at war with itself. The subsequent military and media campaign waged by the government (and its troops) against the Zapatistas brought worldwide concern and solidarity, and calls for peace throughout Mexico. According to Mexican designer Leonel Sagahón, 'Young people knew that it was urgent to do something to stop the armed confrontation and to help the thousands of families that had to run away to the depths of the rainforest without food,

clothes or medicines. But also to stop the dirty war, and preserve the nation from rotting.'[8]

It was in this climate that La Corriente Eléctrica (Electric Current) was formed in 1995 by Sagahón and others as a loose group of graphic agitators, devoted to supporting the peace process for the Chiapas region. They have worked on other projects involving social or political issues under different group names, such as Fuera de Registro (Off the Register) or El Cartel de Medellín (the Medellín Cartel).[9] The people involved (who alter slightly with each group or project), are not all necessarily artists or designers, but they possess shared objectives: to maintain the non-commercial status of the groups and their projects; to challenge the official propaganda pumped out by the commercial media; to promote inclusiveness in project work by encouraging young people and different underground groups to work with them; to help other people through their work; and to urge everyone (including themselves) to take action.

A project conducted by Fuera de Registro, shown on pages 114–15, explores the public's underlying attitude towards politicians, with cynical if not frightening results. The photographs of defaced campaign posters were taken just before an election in Mexico City in June 2000 and appear exactly as they were found. They were published in a book which was then distributed in Mexico City's main square by members of Fuera de Registro and discussed with the public.

Other ongoing Latin American themes for creative comment (see pages 116–17) include the United States' obsessively difficult relationship with Cuba, continuing and unlikely to improve as long as the socialist Fidel Castro remains in power. Despite UN

condemnation, the long-established and strangulating US economic embargo against Cuba still exists, only in newer forms such as the Helms-Burton Bill, signed into law by Bill Clinton in 1996. A shadow is cast over Latin America by memories of past dictators and the 'disappeared'. The Argentinian design group El Fantasma de Heredia (The Ghost of Heredia, Gabriel Mateu and Anabella Salem) offers a graphic reminder that in the period 1976–83, Argentina survived a bloody military dictatorship that resulted in 30,000 people arrested or missing, while most of the military men involved remain free.

However, Steve Caplin's cover illustration for *Guardian Weekend* magazine showing Margaret Thatcher in the uniform of General Augusto Pinochet (see page 117) points at one military man whose past did catch up with him. Following an alleged US-backed military coup in Chile in 1973, the years of General Pinochet's brutal regime brought the torture, murder and 'disappearance' of thousands. He finally lost power in 1990. A frequent visitor to the UK, Pinochet was arrested in 1998 and held in London on charges of genocide, terrorism and torture, throwing a spotlight on his connections with the Thatcher administration over the years. (The former prime minister herself increased the spotlight by protesting strongly at his arrest.)[10] He was never extradited to Spain, where the charges originated, but was instead released on medical grounds and flown back to Chile – despite many cries from protesters. There ended an attempt to punish, or put to rest, a horror which many in Chile (as in Argentina) are forced to keep reliving, while the image serves as a chilling reminder in itself of the many sinister entanglements and 'friendships' that continue to exist in the New World Order.

1

2

3

Striking out against the brands: anti-tobacco protests

Throughout the 1990s, anti-corporate attitudes were directed against the power of the brands and particularly targeted their symbols or logos and their advertising.

Major battles were waged with heavy bouts of direct action, aided by the visual satire of artists and activists. The frontline of health activism was tobacco. Inventive campaigns and graphics against tobacco promotions were produced by the United States-based group Doctors Ought to Care or DOC (see page 78). For example, the founder of DOC, Dr Alan Blum, created the Barfboro theme in the mid-1980s and collaborated with artist Doug Minkler on many of its applications. Their outlandish support graphics and promotions included the Barfboro Barfing Team in 1993, Barf Bags and Doug Minkler's sensational posters. Publicity was also generated by the Barfman, who toured many of the same spots as the Marlboro Adventure Team vans in 1993 while driving the official Barfmobile.

At around the same time, artist Ron English's disturbing billboards attacked the child-appeal of cartoon character 'smooth' Joe Camel, used to sell Camel cigarettes and eventually to fall foul of federal regulations. Later in the decade, as the tobacco industry was forced to pay compensation to health victims and 'reparation payments' by financing anti-tobacco ad campaigns, one of the world's most recognized brand icons, Marlboro Man, was subjected to billboard humiliation and chemotherapy (see pages 86 and 88).

1

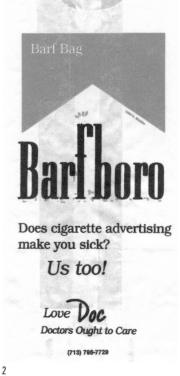

2

3

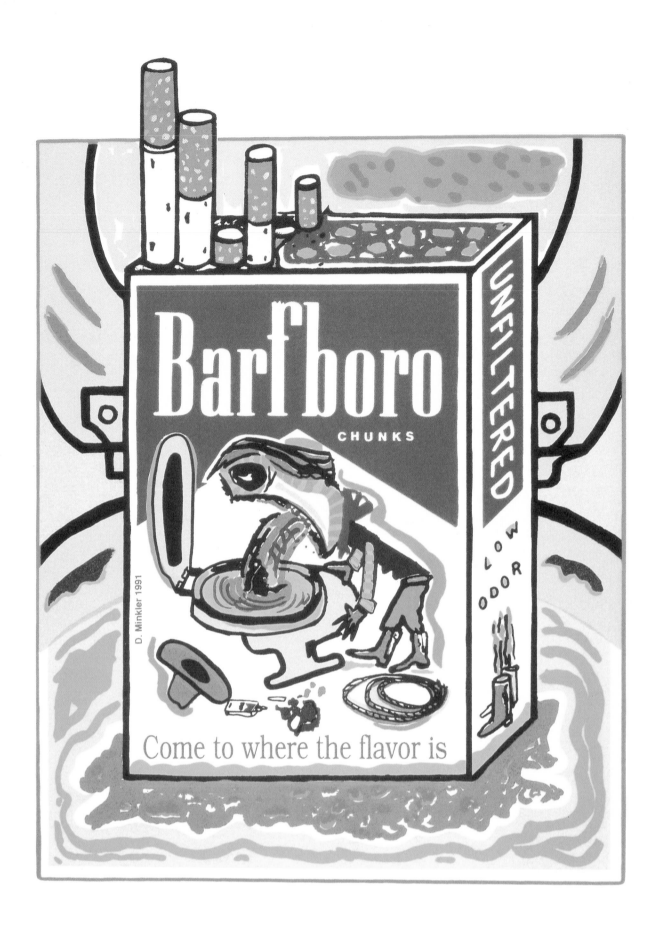

Bob, I've got

1 Billboard and image (previous spread) from an anti-smoking campaign using Marlboro Man ad parodies, created by ad agency Asher and Partners (art director Nancy Steinman, photographer Myron Beck, writer Jeff Bossin) for the California Department of Health Services. USA 2000.

2 Double-page spread showing brand icon 'Joe Camel', created by leading US ad-man Mike Salisbury, and alluding to the controversy surrounding cartoon ads and their appeal to children. From the book *Art Director Confesses: I Sold Sex!, Drugs & Rock'n' Roll* by Mike Salisbury, published by RotoVision, 2000.

3 'The Official Camel Cash Catalog' (Vol IV), a catalogue showing products – from nightshirts to jewellery, and often bearing the brand icon of Joe Camel – that could be obtained with the 'Camel Cash' (C-Notes) that came with cigarette packs. USA 1993.

4,5 Billboard subvertisements by artist Ron English, using the creation of 'Camel Kids' to attack the use of cartoons in cigarette advertising. USA 1991–4.

Getting into Trouble with Animals

Chapter 14

JOE CAMEL

THE GOVERNMENT CENSORS THE WORLD'S MOST RECOGNIZED BRAND IMAGE

2

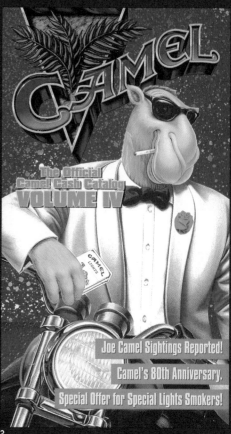

CAMEL

The Official Camel Cash Catalog VOLUME IV

Joe Camel Sightings Reported!

Camel's 80th Anniversary.

Special Offer for Special Lights Smokers!

3

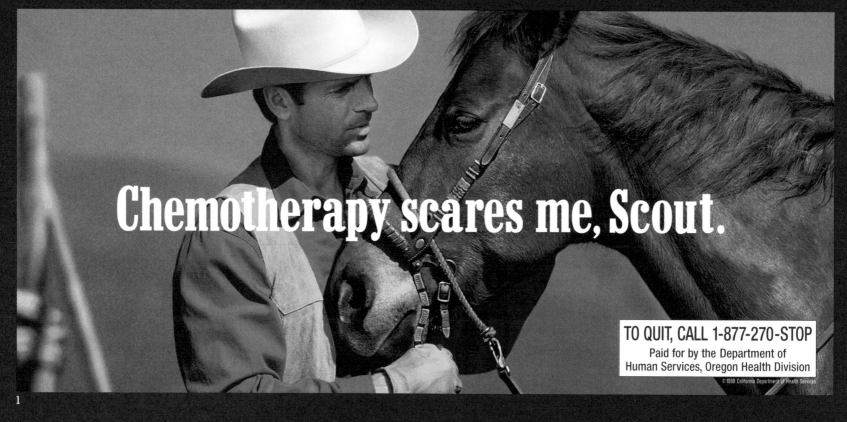

Chemotherapy scares me, Scout.

TO QUIT, CALL 1-877-270-STOP

Paid for by the Department of Human Services, Oregon Health Division

© 1999 California Department of Health Services

1

1 Photograph by Nick Cobbing of 'The McLibel Two' (Helen Steel and David Morris) shown in the mainstream press at the end of the trial. UK 1997.

2 Front of the leaflet, distributed by London Greenpeace (1986–90), that eventually led to the McLibel Trial.

3 T-shirts from the McLibel Support Campaign. UK 2000.

4 Stickers from the McLibel Support Campaign. UK 2000.

5 Poster publicizing the McSpotlight website. Produced by the McLibel Support Campaign. UK 2001.

6,7 Web pages taken from the McSpotlight website, created by the McInformation Network and an important information carrier for the McLibel Support Campaign, 2002.

8 Anti-McDonald's advertisement by PETA. USA 1999.

9 'Do You Want Fries With That?', controversial international poster campaign designed by London-based Lawrence and Beavan for PETA. When the UK media and ad industry refused to carry it, PETA paid for it to tour the UK on a mobile billboard. UK 1999. Photograph by Giuseppe Fassino.

Striking out against the brands: anti-fast food activism

A major battlefield has been declared over the years by campaigns against the fast food corporation, McDonald's. In the McLibel Trial (1994–7), McDonald's took UK activists David Morris and Helen Steel to court over the contents of one of their leaflets – 'What's Wrong with McDonald's?'. The trial itself attracted heavy media focus, and substantial amounts of trial-related and anti-McDonald's material entered popular culture. In addition to news coverage of events surrounding the trial in the mainstream media (cameras are not allowed in UK courtrooms), there were books, CDs and documentary films telling the story of the trial and 'The McLibel Two', and the McLibel Support Campaign churned out T-shirts, stickers and posters to help finance the legal costs.

The crowning feature was the McSpotlight website, created at the time of the trial by the McInformation Network, an international group of volunteers. The website serves as the main database and epicentre of international anti-McDonald's campaigning. Designed with the feel of a highly organized strategic operation, it carries a complete archive of material relating to the trial and is the hub for anti-McDonald's activists, with topical issues and campaigns, opportunities for discussion or debate, dates of protests and appeals to join the fight. There are also ongoing anti-McDonald's protests staged by other groups such as US animal rights organization PETA, originators of some of the most ghoulish anti-McDonald's ads.

1

2

3

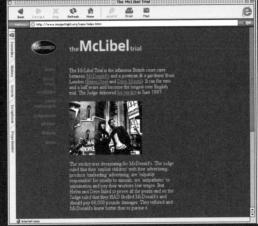
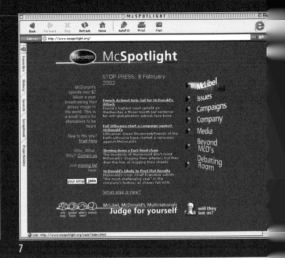

Striking out against the brands: Adbusters

Adbusters Media Foundation in Vancouver is another strategic stop for anti-corporate hell-raisers. Adbusters promotes resistance to corporate and mass media takeover of our culture, and our lives, through its energetic website and even more energetic magazine. To this end it encourages 'culture jamming' (creative resistance) and subvertising, an important tool with which visual artists, designers and activists around the world can revolt against the system creatively and (often) with a sense of humour. Through its many ad alterations and parodies Adbusters have spearheaded a veritable visual revolution.

Adbusters also encourages culture jamming through competitions and campaigns. Buy Nothing Day, for example, is an international 24-hour halt to consumer spending held every November. It inspires spin-off activities around the world, such as the No Shop project shown overleaf, used by the organization Friends of the Earth for its UK launch of No Shop Day in 1997. Designed by thomas.matthews, No Shop was a real shop filled with nothing to buy. It used double-sided banners with 'sales' messages such as 'Prices slashed' backed by 'At what cost?'; its walls were lined with photocopies of product-free shelves; and it contained a till that was empty of cash and a receipt that urged people to 'not shop the planet'.

One of Adbusters' most popular campaigns to date has been the 'First Things First 2000' manifesto, calling on designers to direct the use of their skills towards social needs, not consumer requirements. It is in this arena that its website plays a motivational and inspirational role, encouraging conversations and debate with activists and designers around the world, showcasing ideas and projects, and acting as a high-speed accomplice to the magazine.

1

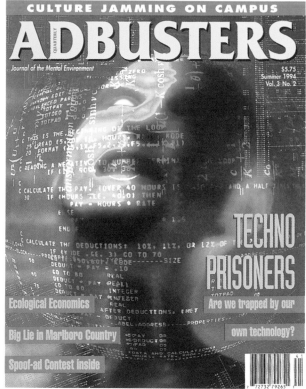

2

ADBUSTERS

No.37

SPECIAL DOUBLE ISSUE.

DESIGN ANARCHY

3

DESIGN EGO

DESIGNERS ARE FALLING OVER EACH OTHER TO KISS CORPORATE ASS

our humanity has become DISLOCATED

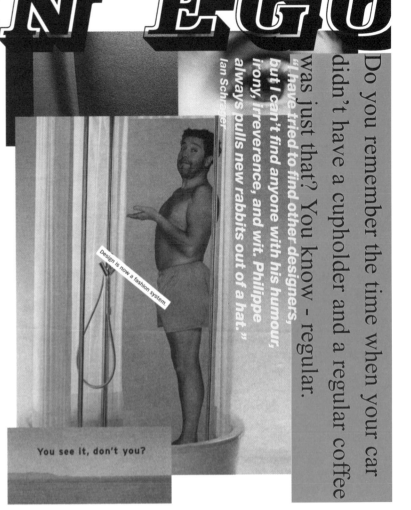

Do you remember the time when your car didn't have a cupholder and a regular coffee was just that? You know - regular. "I have tried to find other designers, but I can't find anyone with his humour, irony, irreverence, and wit. Philippe always pulls new rabbits out of a hat."

Ian Schrager

Design is now a fashion system

You see it, don't you?

4

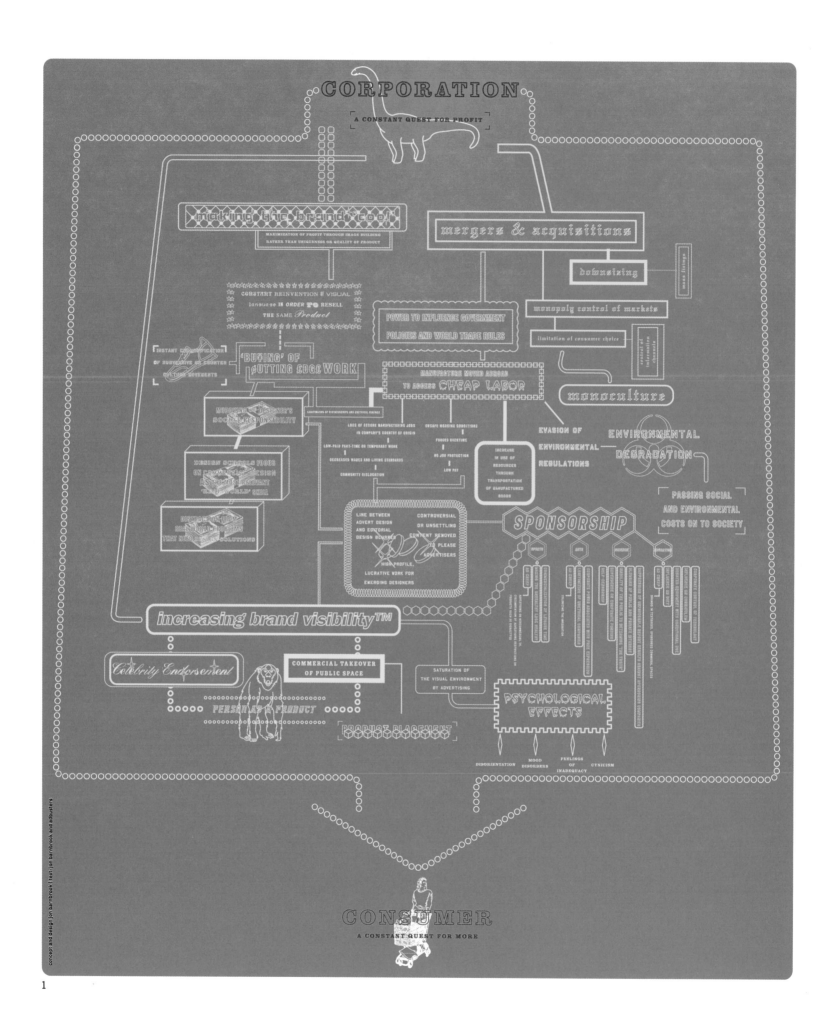

concept and design jon barnbrook | text jon barnbrook and adbusters

1

first things first 2000 **WE**, THE UNDERSIGNED, ARE GRAPHIC DESIGNERS, ART DIRECTORS AND VISUAL COMMUNICATORS who have been raised in a world in which the techniques and apparatus of advertising have persistently been presented to us as the most lucrative, effective and desirable use of our talents. many design teachers and mentors promote this belief, the market rewards it, a tide of books and publications reinforces it. ¶ encouraged in this direction, designers then apply their skill and imagination to sell dog biscuits, designer coffee, diamonds, detergents, hair gel, cigarettes, credit cards, sneakers, butt toners, light beer and heavy-duty recreational vehicles. commercial work has always paid the bills, but many graphic designers have now let it become, in large measure, what graphic designers do. this, in turn, is how the world perceives design. the profession's time and energy is used up manufacturing demand for things that are inessential at best. ¶ many of us have grown increasingly uncomfortable with this view of design. designers who devote their efforts primarily to advertising, marketing and brand development are supporting, and implicitly endorsing, a mental environment so saturated with commercial messages that it is changing the very way citizen-consumers speak, think, feel, respond and interact. to some extent we are all helping draft a reductive and immeasurably harmful code of public discourse. ¶ there are pursuits more worthy of our problem-solving skills. unprecedented environmental, social and cultural crises demand our attention. many cultural interventions, social marketing campaigns, books, magazines, exhibitions, educational tools, television programs, films, charitable causes and other information design projects urgently require our expertise and help. ¶ we propose a reversal of priorities in favor of more useful, lasting and democratic forms of communication – a mindshift away from product marketing and toward the exploration and production of a new kind of meaning. the scope of debate is shrinking, it must expand. ¶ in 1964, 22 visual communicators signed the original call for our skills to be put to worthwhile use. with the explosive growth of global commercial culture, their message has only grown more urgent. today, we renew their manifesto in expectation that no more decades will pass before it is taken to heart.

NEW KIND OF MEANING ¶ in 1964, a small number of british graphic designers lent their names to a quietly radical document. first things first was a rebuke to the design industry as it drifted deeper into commercialism and away from more vital and lasting forms of communication. the manifesto struck with the force of truth and inspired a generation. ¶ in 1999, adbusters' editor kalle lasn and art director chris dixon were visiting new york city and stopped in to meet the legendary designer tibor kalman. tibor was ill with the cancer that would, less than eight months later, claim his life, but his eyes were clear. he thumbed through the latest issue of adbusters, in which we had reprinted the 1964 declaration, then paused and gazed out the window. finally he turned back to kalle and chris and said "you know, we should do this again." ¶ so we did. ¶ we re-drafted the original manifesto, bringing the language up to date and editing a provocative new thrust. ian garland, the driving force behind the 1964 document, visited the adbusters office and gave his nod to the project. with rick poynor and rudy vanderlans, we solicited endorsements from some of the most prominent designers around the world. finally, poynor and max bruinsma inspired us to launch the manifesto simultaneously in the design industry's most influential publications. ¶ first things first 2000 set the design world on fire. it was applauded, criticized, fought over, torn to bits and put back together again. over one thousand designers signed the manifesto at www.adbusters.org now, in the aftermath of the storm, as biodiversity plummets, consumer culture spreads and corporations control an ever-greater share of global information flows, it's time to heed and deliver on the manifesto's most urgent demand: "a mindshift away from product marketing and toward the exploration and production of a new kind of meaning." ¶ the staff and volunteers at adbusters

1,2 Adbusters poster/magazine double-sided insert, designed by Jonathan Barnbrook. Canada 2001. On one side, the 'First Things First 2000' manifesto, including many of the signatures acquired by 2001. On the other, poster diagramming the relationship between corporation and consumer.

3 'No Shop', a project created by thomas.matthews for Friends of the Earth. UK 1997.

4 Poster publicizing international Buy Nothing Day, by Adbusters. Canada 1999.

1 'Same F**king Difference', a bitter comment on the indistinguishable features of the candidates or policies of the two main political parties in the US election, 2000. Created by Frogopolis (Brett Doran and Jan Williamson); production by Elbop at Kind Greetings in Los Angeles. USA 2000.

2 'Don't Vote (And No one Will Hear You)', poster sponsored by the American Institute of Graphic Arts encouraging people to vote in the US 2000 election. Designed by Robynne Raye of Modern Dog Design Co. USA 2000.

3 Bumper sticker from Florida, alluding to its position as the determining state in the US election of 2000, as well as the difficulties in vote-counting that took place there. USA 2002.

4 Cartoon circulating the internet during the US presidential election of 2000, created by Mike Collins. USA 2000.

US politics: presidential elections and personalities

The US presidential election of 2000 underlined many of the United States' then current political difficulties, including the process whereby it elected its president. The two main parties, Democrat and Republican, and their policies seemed to many to be indistinguishable; and the election process itself was an advert for electoral reform.

Visual satire of the time therefore poked wicked fun at the ambiguity of the two main political parties via their mascots – the Republican elephant and the Democrat donkey were either combined or shown doing nasty things to each other. Even a spoof campaign website, shown here, commenting on the widening gap between the rich and poor in the United States was directed at both candidates as if they were one monster.

The American Institute of Graphic Arts encouraged designers to help get the public out to vote; and Adbusters (see page 92) appealed to young voters by pictorializing consumer activist Ralph Nader, the Green candidate for the presidency, as a radical alternative worthy of sporting the symbolic protester's bandana-mask. But Nader's insistence on maintaining an independent stance proved to be too much for the two-party system. In the election itself, a stalemate occurred between the two main parties that left one state (Florida) as the final decision-maker, followed by an episode of vote-counting and re-counting that forced the decision into the lap of the Supreme Court. Visual jokes and cartoons circled the globe on the internet and popped up in popular culture in the following months, and the electoral system's credibility was seriously undermined as George W Bush took over the presidency.

US presidents of the past decade have been a gift to visual satirists. Bill Clinton's presidency (1992–2000) dominated the 1990s with its scandals, including his affair with Monica Lewinsky in 1998–9 and subsequent impeachment trial. But if the visual satire surrounding Clinton smacked of womanizing, dirty jokes and narrow escapes, the satire surrounding the new president 'Dubya' preyed on notions of inexperience and ignorance (of the rest of the world), a peculiar use of the English language (see the map on page 100) and down-home Texas-style family connections. His father George, Sr was a former US president (1988–92) and his younger brother Jeb was Governor of Florida – the determining state – during the presidential election of 2000.

2

3

4

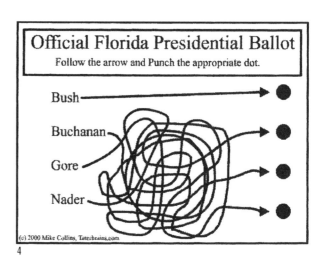

1

5 'Radical Democracy', poster supporting Ralph Nader's campaign for the US presidency, designed by Bill Texas for Adbusters. Canada 2000.

6 Poster from the spoof website 'Billionaires for Bush (or Gore)' and a satirical comment on both the sameness of the candidates (partially reflected in the closeness of the results) and the widening gaps, socially and economically, resulting from current wealth-driven politics. Created by Andrew Boyd. USA 2000.

7,8 Web page and Donkeyphant logo from 'Billionaires for Bush (or Gore)' by Andrew Boyd. USA 2000.

RADICAL DEMOCRACY
www.votenader.com

★ Help launch the Nader TV campaign! Preview the "Tweedles" TV spot at <www.adbusters.org>. Buy a 30-second timeslot on CNN Headline News for $2,000.

★ Copy this poster, or download it at <www.adbusters.org>.

★ On November 7, get your ass out and vote. Bring friends!

5

BUSHGORE

Because inequality isn't growing fast enough.

Paid for by Billionaires for Bush (or Gore). www.billionairesforbushorgore.com

6

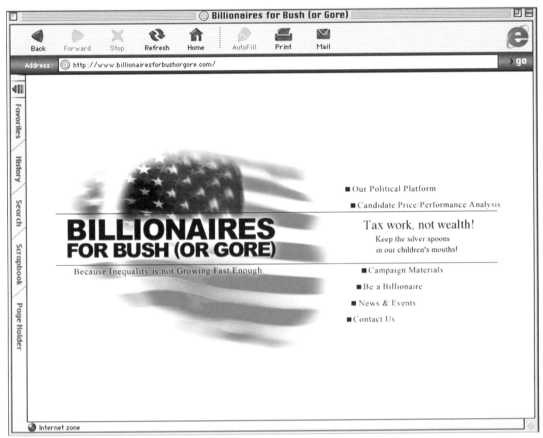

@ Billionaires for Bush (or Gore)

Back   Forward   Stop   Refresh   Home   AutoFill   Print   Mail

Address: @ http://www.billionairesforbushorgore.com/   go

Favorites History Search Scrapbook Page Holder

BILLIONAIRES
FOR BUSH (OR GORE)
Because Inequality is not Growing Fast Enough.

■ Our Political Platform
■ Candidate Price/Performance Analysis

Tax work, not wealth!
Keep the silver spoons in our children's mouths!

■ Campaign Materials
■ Be a Billionaire
■ News & Events
■ Contact Us

Internet zone

7

BILLIONAIRES
FOR BUSH (OR GORE)

8

1 'Impeach Clinton Now!' badge. USA 1998.

2 'Six Degrees of Monica', an absurdist joke on the theory that 'everyone is connected to everyone else through a chain of no more than six people' – applied here to Bill Clinton's favourite intern, Monica Lewinsky. An illustration for the *New York Times*. Writer David Kirby, designer Paul Sahre, art director Nicholas Blechman. USA 1998.

3 Front cover of *Spy* (February 1993 issue), New York's satirical magazine, launched in 1986 by Graydon Carter and closed down due to financial problems in 1994. This photomontaged cover was published just after Hillary Clinton became First Lady, and questions were being raised about her influence in the White House. It was one of their best-selling covers.

1

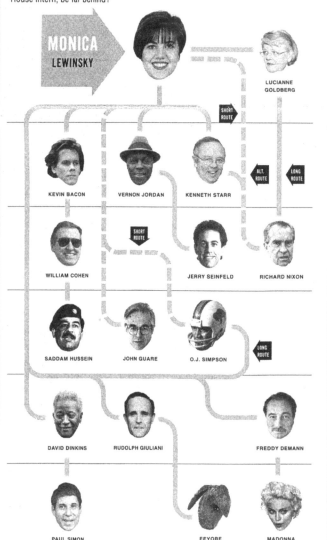

Op-Art

DAVID KIRBY & PAUL SAHRE

SIX *Degrees of Monica*

First came John Guare's play **"SIX DEGREES OF SEPARATION,"** with its theory that everyone is connected to everyone else through a chain of no more than six people. Then some college students with too much free time inexplicably began connecting the dots to the actor Kevin Bacon, and a small industry on the theme of "Six Degrees of Kevin Bacon" was born. Can "that woman," the world's most famous former White House intern, be far behind?

MONICA LEWINSKY

LUCIANNE GOLDBERG

KEVIN BACON · VERNON JORDAN · KENNETH STARR

WILLIAM COHEN · JERRY SEINFELD · RICHARD NIXON

SADDAM HUSSEIN · JOHN GUARE · O.J. SIMPSON

DAVID DINKINS · RUDOLPH GIULIANI · FREDDY DEMANN

PAUL SIMON · EEYORE · MADONNA

MADONNA for years had a manager named FREDDY DEMANN, whose daughter NEYSA DEMANN ERBLAND recently testified to the Whitewater grand jury about conversations she had with her childhood friend MONICA LEWINSKY.

PAUL SIMON created a Broadway catastrophe starring RUBEN BLADES, who is friends with the former New York City Mayor, DAVID DINKINS, who sits on the board of the Cosmetics Center, which is run by a subsidiary of the Revlon Corporation, which put forth and then withdrew a job offer to MONICA LEWINSKY.

O.J. SIMPSON (short route) lives in Brentwood, which is also home to the father of MONICA LEWINSKY.

O.J. SIMPSON (long route) was investigated by MARK FUHRMAN, who wrote a book that was handled by LUCIANNE GOLDBERG, who persuaded LINDA TRIPP to record conversations with MONICA LEWINSKY.

EEYORE will remain in New York thanks to RUDOLPH GIULIANI, who is a big fan of PLACIDO DOMINGO, whose sex life was the subject of a book by the self-described "glamorous Beverly Hills writer" MARCIA LEWIS, who gave birth to MONICA LEWINSKY.

JASON ALEXANDER plays a neurotic, self-obsessed New Yorker on a show starring JERRY SEINFELD, who appears in commercials for American Express, on whose board sits VERNON JORDAN, who arranged job interviews at the company's New York offices for MONICA LEWINSKY.

RICHARD NIXON (short route) tried to cover up a break-in at Democratic headquarters in the Watergate complex, which is home to MONICA LEWINSKY.

RICHARD NIXON (long route), in the 1972 election, trounced GEORGE McGOVERN, who flew around with Nixon-spy-masquerading-as-a-reporter LUCIANNE GOLDBERG, who (you know the rest) MONICA LEWINSKY.

RICHARD NIXON (alternate long route) was almost impeached by a Congressional committee that included Senator HOWARD BAKER, who is now part of the tobacco lobby, which is represented by a law firm that includes KENNETH STARR, who is making life very difficult for MONICA LEWINSKY.

SADDAM HUSSEIN may be about to be bombed by American warplanes in an attack directed by Secretary of Defense WILLIAM COHEN, whose top military spokesman is KENNETH BACON, who is in no way related to KEVIN BACON but who once hired a White House aide named MONICA LEWINSKY.

JOHN GUARE, whose play introduced this whole concept, once stayed overnight at the White House, which may or may not remain on the resume of MONICA LEWINSKY.

My mother, BARBARA KIRBY, once ate lunch in a Los Angeles restaurant that is said to be a favorite of NANCY REAGAN, who lives in Bel Air just down the way from ELIZABETH TAYLOR, who was dear friends with NATALIE WOOD, whose daughter graduated from Beverly Hills High School, which also matriculated MONICA LEWINSKY.

2

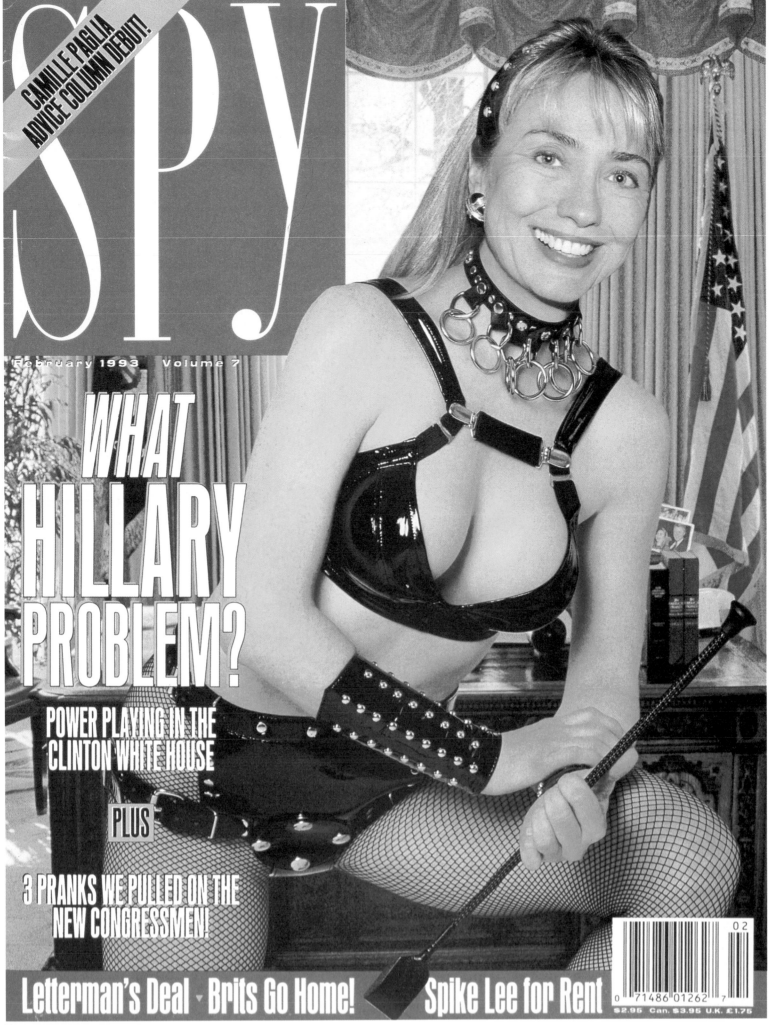

SPY

February 1993   Volume 7

WHAT HILLARY PROBLEM?

POWER PLAYING IN THE CLINTON WHITE HOUSE

PLUS

3 PRANKS WE PULLED ON THE NEW CONGRESSMEN!

Letterman's Deal · Brits Go Home!   Spike Lee for Rent

$2.95 Can. $3.95 U.K. £1.75

0 71486 01262 7

02

1 Post-US election cartoon by
Charles Nevin and Jim Robins,
which appeared in the *Independent*
newspaper. UK 2000.

2 Birthday card showing Bill and Hillary Clinton waving. Inside it says, 'See … there are scarier things than growing older. Happy Birthday.' Bought in a supermarket in West Virginia. USA 1998.

3 Front cover of *The Bill Clinton Joke Book* by Mitchell Symons, a wide-ranging collection of jokes centred around Bill Clinton and his sex life. Illustrations by John Jensen. Published by Chameleon Books/ André Deutsch. UK 1998.

4 'DUBYA4U2001', joke 200-dollar bill which pokes fun at George W Bush. USA 2000.

2

3

MORAL RESERVE NOTE
UNITED STATES · THE · OF AMERICA
200 · 200
THIS NOTE IS MORAL LEGAL TENDER TO PRESERVE THE U.S. CONSTITUTION
THE RIGHT TO BEAR ARMS
DUBYA4U2001
WASHINGTON, D.C. DQ200
Fₐ
IR66 DQ200
LONG LIVE
TALK RADIO
© 2000 A. ROSS
DUBYA4U2001
Ronald Reagan Political Mentor
GEORGE W. BUSH
SERIES 2001
200
George H.W. Bush Campaign Advisor & Mentor
200 · TWO HUNDRED DOLLARS · 200

4

1 Prime Minister John Major carrying the Conservative party manifesto, drawn by Steve Bell. UK 1993.

2 John Major and his wife Norma adorn a special edition jigsaw puzzle on sale at a Conservative party conference during the campaign for the UK general election of 1991.

3 The artful caricature and malicious humour of *Spitting Image* puppets. This bevy of early 1990s UK political party leaders are: (left) Paddy Ashdown, Liberal Democrat; (centre) Neil Kinnock, Labour; (right) John Major, Conservative; and (bottom) the Reverend Ian Paisley, Northern Ireland Democratic Unionist. UK 1993. Photograph by John Lawrence Jones.

UK politics: satire and photo-opportunities

After the overwhelming experience of Conservative leader Margaret Thatcher, John Major's relatively bland appearance (and politics) had cartoonists resorting to wonderfully far-fetched depictions of him. For example, political cartoonist Steve Bell often drew John Major wearing his underpants on top of his business suit in a Superman parody and as a sign of his 'uselessness'. Tony Blair, however, offered no such image problem. 'Tone' came to the general election of 1997 equipped with a new party called New Labour (which many deemed old conservatism), an image-building machine of non-stop photo-opportunities and an impressive set of teeth.

Blair's Cheshire cat smile became a ghostly visual trademark – rather like Margaret Thatcher's hair, which made a comeback in the general campaign of 2001 as a reminder that she had never really gone away. In the eyes of many, her attitudes and policies lived on through others – including Mr Blair. Another area for Blair ridicule was the UK's – or Blair's – 'special relationship' with the United States and President Bush, visualized in a variety of ways as dysfunctional or even dangerous.

The grand British tradition of satire and political lampooning continues to be upheld by cartoonists such as Steve Bell and Martin Rowson, as well as satirical magazines such as *Private Eye*, founded in 1961. The greatest casualty of the 1990s was the weekly TV programme *Spitting Image*, launched in 1984, which employed caricature in the form of latex puppets, originally created by Peter Fluck and Roger Law for magazine and book illustrations (see page 82). Politicians and celebrities alike were abused in hilarious style. Mrs Thatcher was known to have said that she didn't ever watch 'that programme'. *Spitting Image* continued to show no mercy until it reached the end of its run in 1996.

1

2

3

4 Front cover of the *Sunday Times Magazine* (25 January 1998) which refers to Tony Blair's need to 'tame' or clean up alleged corruption within long-established Labour local authorities in the west of Scotland. Pictured are, from left to right: Chancellor of the Exchequer Gordon Brown, Prime Minister Tony Blair and the Secretary of State for Scotland, Donald Dewar. Illustration by Jonathan Wateridge. UK 1998.

5,6 'New Labour, New Danger', controversial campaign posters known for their 'demon eyes' portrayal of Blair. Created by M+C Saatchi for the Conservative party prior to the 1997 election. Tony Blair and his party, New Labour, won the election by a landslide. UK 1997.

5

4

6

1 Poster for the Virus Foundry announcing the release of the typeface 'Newspeak' – the name of the official language of propaganda in George Orwell's *Nineteen Eighty-Four*, and a reference to Tony Blair's political spin and rhetoric as well as his intolerance of criticism. Designed by Jonathan Barnbrook. UK 1998.

2 Conservative party poster for the May 2001 general election showing Prime Minister Tony Blair as a pregnant man – a spoof of the classic Saatchi ad shown on page 16. It aimed to highlight Labour's failure to improve public services during its first term of office.

3 Front cover of Britain's leading satirical magazine, *Private Eye* (22 March – 4 April 2002), showing Tony Blair and George W Bush in conversation about the War on Terrorism. UK 2002.

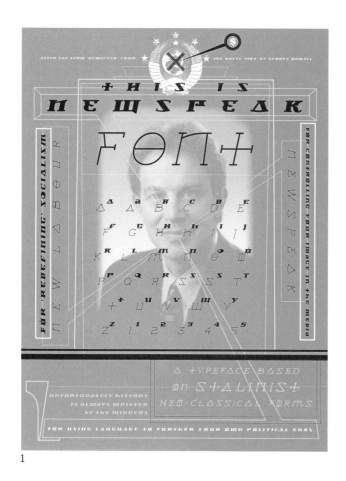

4 Billboard for the May 2001 general election which combined Conservative candidate William Hague's face with Margaret Thatcher's hair, suggesting to Labour voters that her legacy would live on through Hague (so they should get out and vote against him). Created by ad agency TBWA for the Labour party. UK 2001. Photograph by Jeremy Barr.

4

1 'Stalin's Funeral', poster by Yuri Bokser for a film directed by Yevgeny Yevtushenko. The poster image suggests the ongoing presence of Stalin (even after death) and an inability to be released from the horrors of the past, shown by the blood-red roses surrounding him. Russia 1991.

2 'East Side Story', poster by Yuri Bokser that plays with one of the most celebrated monuments to the spirit of communism, the sculpture known as the 'Industrial Worker and Collective Farm Woman' (designed in 1937 by Vera Mukhina). USSR 1990.

3 '1917–', poster by Yuri Bokser. The increasing 'openness' of the USSR meant the uncovering or discussion of dark issues from the past, such as the brutal application of Lenin's policies committed against intellectuals and the clergy. USSR 1989.

Post-Soviet Europe: cynicism and sarcasm from the East

Once the rush of revolutionary euphoria had passed, throughout the 1990s many of the former Iron Curtain countries of Central and Eastern Europe found the acquisition of democracy and the road to free market capitalism a mixed blessing. The work shown on pages 108–13 employs both subtle and sour graphic language to convey the social, economic and political disillusionment of countries including Russia, Poland and the former Yugoslavia.

Nowhere did greater social and economic problems occur than in Russia itself. The new freedoms and the opening of federal and provincial archives uncovered terrible truths of former regimes and purges. Some of the Russian posters are tinged with the bitterness of ghosts of the past, such as Lenin or Stalin, returning to haunt the present. The posters of Yuri Bokser, who died in 2002, in particular adopted a cynical yet sometimes playful tone about the USSR's attempts to rewrite history, embrace change and (unsuccessfully) forget past events and horrors. Those shown

here, produced in the early 1990s and on the brink of a new political era, resonate with recurring nightmares.

Other Russian work deals with events and actions after Mikhail Gorbachev met his downfall in August 1991. Alexander Faldin's poster (see opposite) points to 10 December 1994 and shows President Boris Yeltsin, successor to the deposed Gorbachev, threatening Grozny, capital of the breakaway rebel republic of Chechnya. The following day Yeltsin sent the Russian Federal Army to invade Chechnya by both air and ground attack. But by the end of the month, public opposition had forced him to call a halt to the air strikes and the army consequently suffered heavy losses. Despite a ceasefire, the Chechens themselves started a second military campaign in 1999 which grew into a savage war by the year 2000. Yeltsin's successor, the twenty-first century Russian President Vladimir Putin, initially came to prominence over his brutal military campaign to crush the rebellion in Chechnya. (At the time of writing, the conflict remains unresolved.)

Other posters emanating from Poland, Hungary and Moldova are

weighed down by the political situations and social problems developing in their post-communist societies. Cynicism rules: stalwart enemies form new political alliances, the subject of the mafia maintains a large graphic presence and in some cases the communists are voted back.

2

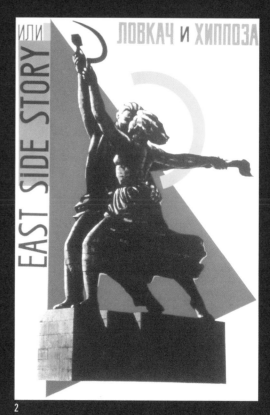

3

1

5

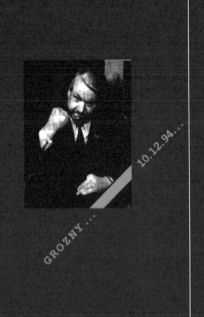

GROZNY … 10.12.94 …

JANUARY 22, 2001

TIME

PUTIN'S RUSSIA

As he grows ever more authoritarian, the President's popularity rises

2001

7

www.timeeurope.com   AOL keyword/TIME

4 'Gorbachev calendar', poster and calendar by Yuri Bokser showing Mikhail Gorbachev, the international figure who brought economic reforms to the USSR, in a satirical, cuddly photomontaged portrait — unheard of in previous years of hard, official portraits. USSR 1989.

5 Russian wooden dolls, bearing the likeness of political leaders and yet another indication of heavy links with the past. From large to small: Vladimir Putin, Boris Yeltsin, Mikhail Gorbachev, Yuri Andropov and Leonid Brezhnev. (The elderly, short-lived Konstantin Chernenko has been left out.) Russia 2001.

6 'Grozny … 10 December 1994', poster by Alexander Faldin showing President Boris Yeltsin threatening Grozny, capital of the rebel republic of Chechnya. Russia 1994.

7 Front cover of *Time* magazine (22 January 2001) showing Russian President Vladimir Putin — successor to Boris Yeltsin and former member of the KGB. USA 2001.

1 'Don't Be A Mafia Commodity!', billboard in Chisinau, capital city of Moldova – a former republic of the Soviet Union which declared its independence in 1991. The message is delivered by the US Department of State and the International Organization for Migration (IOM). Photograph by Stephen Buckle. Moldova 2002.

2 'Metabolism 89–99', poster by Marcin Wladyka commenting on the 10 years following Poland's free elections. Poland 1999.

3,4 'Comrades, Adieu!', poster created by István Orosz in 1989, the time of the pro-democracy revolutions in Central and Eastern Europe, when the occupying Soviet Army was withdrawing from Hungary. In 1995, when the communists were voted back into power in Hungary, Orosz produced a sequel entitled 'I Am Back Again'. Hungary 1989 and 1995.

1

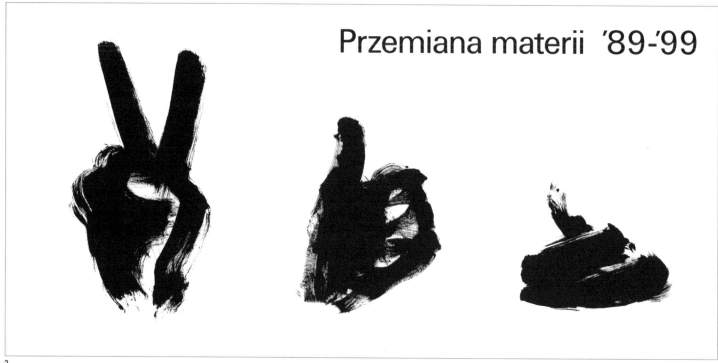

Przemiana materii '89-'99

2

3

4

5 'If You're Bored With Politics –
Choose Posters Instead!', poster by
Péter Pócs for an exhibition of his
work. The banana and orange
(having sex) are each symbols of
Hungarian political parties, once
opponents but now allied and
engaged in political lovemaking
in the post-communist scenario.
Hungary 1995.

5

1 'Enough!', original poster by the FIA Art Group (Nada Rajicic and Stanislav Sharp) displayed in the streets of Belgrade for their anti-war campaign. Yugoslavia 1992.

2,3 Two of more than 20 different interventions or modifications (to the poster 'Enough!') by Serbian artists, included as part of the exhibition of the FIA Art Group's anti-war campaign. Yugoslavia 1992.

4 Exhibition of the anti-war campaign entitled 'Enough!', conducted by the FIA Art Group. It included the original poster 'Enough!', created by the FIA Art Group, as well as interventions to the poster by other Serbian artists. The exhibition was held in the Belgrade Cultural Centre. Yugoslavia 1992.

Post-Soviet Europe: against the alienation of Yugoslavia

While pro-democracy revolutions brought an atmosphere of freedom to much of Central and Eastern Europe in the early 1990s, the artists and designers of Yugoslavia watched the break up of their country and its descent into war between the constituent republics. Escalating nationalism poisoned relations between ethnic groups, fanned by the ambitions of leaders such as Slobodan Milosevic of Serbia.

In 1992, the UN Security Council passed a resolution declaring that it was considering a bombing campaign against Serbia, because of the involvement of Milosevic's regime in the wars in Bosnia and Croatia. University students in Serbia engaged in anti-war demonstrations for two months.

At this time an artistic anti-war campaign was conceived by the Belgrade-based FIA Art Group, whose members – Nada Rajicic and Stanislav Sharp – conduct ambitious projects in photography, design, publishing and video with a large team of associates. The anti-war action bore the slogan 'Enough!', protesting against the war and alerting the public to the devastation that the bombing of Serbia would cause. They created a series of posters saying 'IMPOSSIBLE?! ENOUGH!' and 'WHY ARE YOU BLIND?', displayed throughout Belgrade in the summer of 1992. An exhibition was held in the Belgrade Cultural Centre, where over 20 well-known Serbian artists participated by adding interventions to the poster 'Enough!'. The slogan '(Im)possible, Enough!' was printed on T-shirts, folders, cards and mugs, and a series of anti-war radio jingles were broadcast (free of charge) by stations in Belgrade.

Another important project of the war years of 1990s Serbia – intended to combat creative isolation and lack of information from outside Serbia – was known as 'The Calendars of New Art and Contemporary Life', created by the FIA Art Group and published by Publikum printers in Belgrade (see overleaf). The first calendar on the theme 'Impossible' was launched in 1993 – a year of poverty, hyperinflation, war and the brain drain – the mass exodus of many of Serbia's brightest people to other parts of the world. It nostalgically presents photographs of artists, musicians and public figures from the carefree, creative life of 1980s Belgrade, with a nod to the rich tradition of the Serbian avant garde of the 1930s.

Since then a calendar has been published every year on a theme reflecting the turbulence and difficulties of Serbian society. Each calendar is launched by a promotion or spectacle in an unusual place – for example, a vacated museum dedicated

1

2

3

to former Yugoslav dictator Tito or an amusement park. The promotions have become eagerly awaited cultural events: the artists perform, the public joins in.

The third calendar, 'Surrealisme & Optimisme', created in 1996, was a collection of public figures and anonymous people who, in spite of the surreal events taking place in Belgrade in the 1990s, 'had the courage to be optimists'. The promotion was symbolically held in a photographic studio originally built as an atomic bomb shelter. Equipped with specially made 'Glasses of Optimism', the audience was involved in a performance of mass radiating of optimism.

In the spirit of creating positive energy and open communication with the world, the calendars have been distributed to artists, cultural institutions and the media throughout Serbia and – as much as possible – the world. The most ambitious was the 2001 calendar entitled 'Antiwall', which was concerned with the idea of breaking down barriers or walls within different types of media, within Serbian society, and between Serbian people (especially artists) and the world. Although the previous calendars had involved the photography and art of Serbian artists, the 'Antiwall' calendar embraced works by renowned international artists. Interestingly, the most acerbic and bitter comment came from Russia. The image shown on page 113 is a detail from a photo installation by the AES Group, a trio of Moscow-based installation artists (founded in 1987) – Tatiana Arzamasova, Lev Evzovitch and Evgeny Svyatsky, often collaborating with photographer Vladimir Fridkes. Their photo installation, entitled 'The Prince and the Beggar' (1995), was a comment on Russian life over the past 10 years. Both the prince and the beggar consume the golden egg – a symbol with many socio-political readings – with horrifying results, as shown on the calendar page.

4

1,2 Cover and September page from the New Art Calendar entitled 'Impossible', designed by the FIA Art Group with photographs by Stanislav Sharp. Yugoslavia 1993.

3 Special cardboard 'Glasses of Optimism' used for the 1996 New Art Calendar promotion in which the audience engages in mass radiation of optimism.

4,5 Cover and July page from the 1996 New Art Calendar entitled 'Surrealisme & Optimisme', created by the FIA Art Group. Design by Slavica Dragosavac, photographs by Stanislav Sharp. Yugoslavia 1996.

3

1

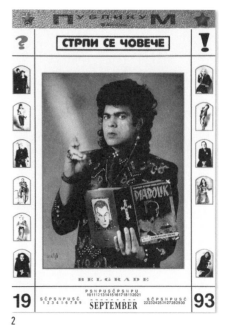

2

4

5

АНТИЗИД

КАЛЕНДАР НОВЕ УМЕТНОСТИ И САВРЕМЕНОГ ЖИВОТА

ΛΝΤΙШΛLL

CALENDAR OF THE NEW ART AND CONTEMPORARY LIFE

6

АЕС Група
ΛES Group

7

6 Cover (casing) of the New Art Calendar 'Antiwall'. Calendar concept and production by FIA Art Group, design by Mirko Ilic (New York). Yugoslavia 2001.

7 August page from the 2001 'Antiwall' calendar showing a detail from a photo installation entitled 'The Prince and the Beggar' (1995). Produced by the Moscow-based AES+F Group.

1 Signature poster by Alejandro Magallanes, used in actions by the group Fuera de Registro.

2,3,4 Members of Fuera de Registro document people's reactions to the booklet *No Anunciar*. Photographs taken in Mexico City's main square. Mexico 2000. Photographs by Erick Beltrán.

Anger and hardship from the South: the graphics of Fuera de Registro

The politics of Latin America, and particularly its politicians, leaders and dictators, often conjures up images of tension or anger. The images shown here are from a project produced by the group Fuera de Registro (Off the Register) — Alejandro Magallanes, Erick Beltrán and others — just before an election day in July 2000.

They photographed political campaign posters in Mexico City exactly as they found them — drawn on or mutilated by people in the street. They then compiled and produced a book entitled *No Anunciar* (literally 'No Announcement' or, in this context,

'Don't Bother Campaigning'), which was freely distributed to passers-by in the Zócalo (Mexico City's main square) and elsewhere, while a video was made documenting people's comments and reactions. Members of the group identified themselves by wearing Fuera de Registro's signature poster. Copies of the book were also sent to newspapers and other media, political parties and candidates — and even the President's office. More than a little unsettling, the book is a strong indictment, showing the public's general attitude to its politicians and their (lack of) competence.

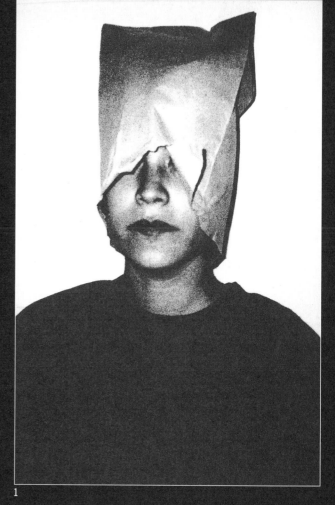

1

2

4

3

5,6,7 Front cover and inside spreads from the booklet (and project) *No Anunciar*. The project was a production of Fuera de Registro with the collaboration of Eduardo Barrera, Erick Beltrán, Ana Bertha Madrid, Alejandro Magallanes, Héctor Montes de Oca, Claudia Prado, Sebastián Rodríguez Romo, Leonel Sagahón and Mauricio Volpi. Mexico City, June 2000.

5

7

6

1 Mural depicting Elian Gonzalez and his journey to the United States, painted by Humberto Gonzalez (in Florida) at the height of the affair. USA 1999. Photograph by Tony Gutierrez.

2 'Helms Burton', poster by Alejandro Magallanes protesting against the US economic embargo against Cuba. Mexico 1996.

3 'Democracy!', poster by Ruth Ramírez of El Cartel de Medellín in which the US mouse and Cuba (depicted as a crocodile) stare each other out. Mexico c. 1996.

Anger and hardship from the South: social comment from Latin America

The relationship between the United States and Latin American countries has been an ongoing theme for artists and designers. For example, in the mid-1990s Mexican artist Alejandro Magallanes made a brash poster comment about the Helms-Burton Bill, a 1996 protraction of the US economic embargo against Cuba. Ruth Ramírez depicted the age-old presence of Cuba (the main island of which is often described as crocodile-shaped) eyeing up the excitable little American mouse. Also on the Cuban theme, a complex mural painting shows the turbulent powers at play while describing the extraordinary story of the six-year-old Cuban boy Elian Gonzalez whose mother attempted to migrate with him to the United States in 1999. Their boat sank, the mother was drowned and the boy was found by fishermen, floating in an inner tube of a tyre off the Florida coast. His survival and accommodation in Miami with relatives who wanted to keep him sparked off a diplomatic crisis — his father, a large mass of Cuban demonstrators and Fidel Castro wanted him back in Cuba (where he eventually ended up). The six-month controversy was a dramatic showing of the tension that still exists between the United States and Cuba.

Other important Latin American themes relate to dictatorships of the past that continue to haunt the present. A photomontage created by Steve Caplin in 2002 shows the former UK Prime Minister, Margaret Thatcher, in the uniform of former brutal dictator General Augusto Pinochet of Chile, alluding to their friendship and influence on each other. Mrs Thatcher remained loyal to Pinochet over the years due to his assistance to Britain throughout the Falklands War. In the late 1990s, the controversy surrounding his arrest and enforced stay in London (due to European allegations of human rights abuses) brought to light other features of the close relationship between the two countries. Throughout Margaret Thatcher's premiership discreet links existed between the two administrations, and Pinochet's free-market policies of the 1970s (resulting in Chile's 'economic miracle') were said to have been an influential model for the later Thatcher monetarist revolution in Britain. Although not a comment from Latin America itself, the photomontage shown hints at the long-established, discreet ties between the UK and Chile.

Images are also shown by the Argentinian design group El Fantasma de Heredia (Gabriel Mateu and Anabella Salem) relating to the ongoing search for 'disappeared' or missing people and their children — a product of their own country's bloody

1

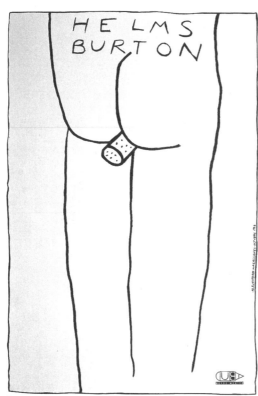

2

3

military dictatorship, which lasted from 1976 to 1983. The ghosts of this dark period are still present: members of the activist group Abuelas de la Plaza de Mayo (Grandmothers of the Plaza de Mayo), founded in 1977, continue to search for their children and grandchildren, kidnapped or born in detention centres during the military dictatorship. For years they walked the square in daily protest, and they still meet there on certain commemorative days, such as the anniversary of the coup. But their tactics have now become highly professionalized, involving the use of a team of lawyers, doctors and psychologists and a dedicated website for locating the missing children and disputing and re-establishing identities through the Argentine courts.

For this reason, identity remains an important theme in Argentina (see leaflet for a National Programme of Identity, below). But identification is also a necessary issue for immigrants and poor people who, without papers, are unable to find a job in humane conditions.

Alejandro Magallanes' poster for the Mexican film *Pachito Rex* (2001) alludes to yet another form of violence in politics. Set in the future, the film revolves around an assassination attempt on the egotistical presidential candidate of an imaginary Latin American country. But it can also be seen as a metaphor for the circumstances surrounding the assassination of the ruling party PRI presidential candidate Luis Donaldo Colosio in March 1994 in Tijuana, at a time when the PRI stranglehold on the country was beginning to weaken.

4 Illustration by Steve Caplin which appeared on the front cover of the *Guardian Weekend* magazine on 4 May 2002 in the UK. It depicts former Prime Minister Margaret Thatcher in the uniform of General Augusto Pinochet of Chile.

5 'Pachito Rex, It's Not Over Until It's Over', poster by Alejandro Magallanes for a film directed by Fabián Hofman – an experimental, interactive thriller using inventive digital effects. Mexico 2001.

6 Poster and leaflet by El Fantasma de Heredia promoting a National Programme of Identity as a primary concern for children's rights. Many of the 'disappeared' victims of the last military regime, as well as their children, remain unlocated. Argentina 2001.

7 '25 Years Since the Coup d'État – Memory, Truth and Justice', poster by El Fantasma de Heredia announcing an action to mark 25 years since the last coup d'état, which left 30,000 arrested/missing people. Argentina 2001.

4

5

6

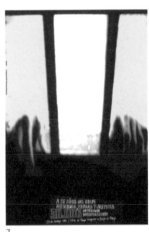

7

In the countries of the West, our experience of war in the 1990s was gained through an intermediary — mainstream media — that packaged selected data and viewpoints as 'information', often with bewildering results. The familiarity of Cold War divisions and geography, the directness and bravery of the protests and slogans of the 1980s pro-democracy movements in Europe had all been left behind. Instead there followed a web of confusing conflicts and uncharted territory. Those trying to follow events found themselves in a world of digitized and censored information,

↗

unfamiliar and difficult-to-pronounce geographic names, and a media interpretation of events and conflicts where (particularly in the case of the Balkans) good or bad sides were indistinguishable or changing, and where dishonourable acts seemed to be committed on all sides.

Editorializing and accompanying graphic devices in the mainstream media helped to create distance between onlookers in the West and events taking place. This included, for example, the overload of high-tech imagery, both still and moving, that proliferated in mainstream 'information', or propaganda, during the 1991 Gulf War. Or the jumbled and confusing (and ultimately demonizing) depictions of the wars in the Balkans, where all Serbian people tended to be cast as evil. But wherever the conflict and whatever the mainstream view, there are always alternative voices trying to make themselves heard — from both inside and outside the conflict. Alternatives which, more often than not, incorporate and rely on graphic forms such as posters, comics and

Graphic artists depict two of the many disturbing aspects of modern-day warfare: the ineffectual role of global institutions such as the UN, and the use of children as soldiers and fighters throughout the world.

1 'Infant-ry', poster by Lippa Pearce highlighting the issue of child soldiers worldwide. Created for Witness — a charity that uses the tools of current technology to fight human rights abuses. Photograph by Erik Miller, Panos. UK 2001.

2 'UNable', poster by Yossi Lemel created for the UN's fiftieth anniversary and critical of its role in the Bosnian War. The shell of the tortoise is the distinctive blue helmet of a UN (peacekeeping) soldier. Israel 1995.

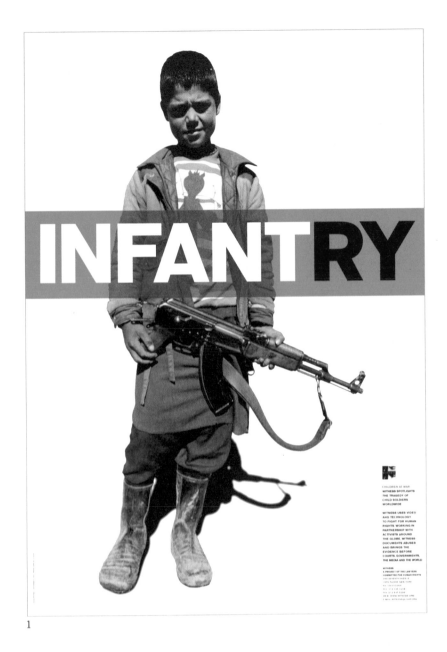

1

2

A wide variety of sources, both mainstream and underground, have provided information, commentary and protest related to conflicts from the early 1990s to the present.

1 Billboard intervention in Leeds during the 1991 Gulf War. By Saatchi & Someone (David Collins). The original billboard was advertising the *Sunday Times* newspaper and read, 'The Gulf. The coverage, the analysis, the facts' followed by the newspaper's logo and name at the bottom. The Saatchi & Someone logo can be seen on the lower right. UK 1991.

2,3 Images of modern warfare (missiles at night) on the front covers of *Despatches from the Gulf War* edited by Brian MacArthur, published by Bloomsbury, UK 1991, and *Virtual War: Kosovo and Beyond* by Michael Ignatieff, published by Chatto & Windus. UK 2000.

leaflets – and are becoming increasingly driven by the possibilities of new technology and the internet.

High-tech illusions

All modern wars and their reporting have involved censorship, and the reshaping or reinterpretation of information. Because of the limitations of capture and satellite technology of the time, the Vietnam War – the 'television war' – was shot on 16mm film which was shipped from the front back to news agencies, and highly edited along the way. Other alterations as well as editing could take place. Film used in current affairs coverage was sometimes physically degraded by programme makers – it was rubbed along a desktop to produce scratches and tramlines – to create the illusion of being rougher or more on-the-spot. (It was assumed that viewers wouldn't believe pictures that looked too clean.)

The 1991 Gulf War became known as 'the information war', a label that summed up the many forms (and faces) that information assumed. It was the first war to use real-time satellite news-links for television. But although the notion of 'real-time' seemed to promise instant clarity and fly-on-the-wall visuals, instead it gave way to a clean, technology-obsessed visual representation of war, constructed by designers, the media, governments and the military. The Gulf War became best remembered for its portrayal of bloodless, sanitized warfare.[1]

After war broke out (under the label of Operation Desert Storm), television audiences were bombarded with massive amounts of 'fighting' footage, largely of night bombings of Baghdad resembling fireworks displays. There were 'live' reports from correspondents billeted in multi-storeyed hotels and comment and analysis (that is, speculation) from

academic, political and military experts, substituting for real information.

All news material was subjected to 'a controlled information environment' by the coordinated efforts of both the military and governments of the Coalition countries involved. Although a coalition of 36 countries, it was led by the US military, with large British and French contingents. The management system devised by the Coalition forces for releasing information to the media involved, in essence, pools of reporters (Media Reporting Teams) attached to armed forces at the front. Non-pooled journalists were provided with official briefings by the military, or public relations officers. All reports were subject to government and/or military censorship, undermining any notions of 'live' on-the-spot broadcasts. The military kept a tight rein on journalists' movements and activities.

1

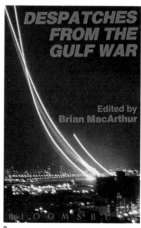

2

3

Few pictures emerged of wounded or killed Iraqi soldiers and civilians: the horrors of war failed to appear. Graphics, particularly information graphics and maps, were often substituted for real photography. Aerial photographs and videos – shot from cockpit cameras – showed bombed-out Iraqi airports, buildings and aircraft far below, looking like crushed toys, and continued the bloodless fantasy. But by releasing video footage of techno-wizardry and air strikes, accompanied by 'we are winning' hyperbole and expert speculation, the military distracted attention from the lack of hard facts emanating from its sources. The focus was on projecting a 'desired view' of what was going on. Control was subtle but effective. Audiences were kept occupied by the videogame entitled 'The war as portrayed by the media'.[2]

The Gulf War was also the first war to use stealth aviation technology[3] and to centre its PR around the use of state-of-the-art 'smart' weaponry, with declared capabilities that seemed to grow to mythic proportions – such as smart bombs that could allegedly go around corners, seeking out their prey. At this time, on the personal computer front, CD-ROM drives were just entering mainstream use and Nintendo and Sega were battling for cartridge and joystick supremacy. J C Herz, author of *Joystick Nation*, describes Operation Desert Storm as 'the greatest thing to happen to the interactive entertainment industry since Sonic the Hedgehog. Everyone in America had seen missile footage through laser-guided sights on television. Now they could play the war on their very own home computers.'[4] She goes on to describe some of the games that were inspired by the Gulf War.

The false wonder of advanced communications media (watching it all as it happens) and the emergence of smart technology and weaponry, collided with the burgeoning fashion for high-tech hardware and video/computer games. The new, popular use of war language and terminology began to feed the high-tech fetish. 'Surgical strikes' and 'pgms' (precision guided munitions) promised impossibly high accuracy and the myth of no casualties. 'Collateral damage' or 'friendly fire' sounded remarkably clean and efficient, compared with 'dead civilians' or 'hit by one's own allies'. All these factors conspired to distance the public from any sense of reality and supported the jingoistic atmosphere of the time.

Maps, myths and 'no blood for oil'

The action was happening in parts of the world less familiar to the West, in far-off mythical places. The Iraqi invasion of Kuwait in August 1990, which started the 1991 Gulf War, left many people in the West grabbing for

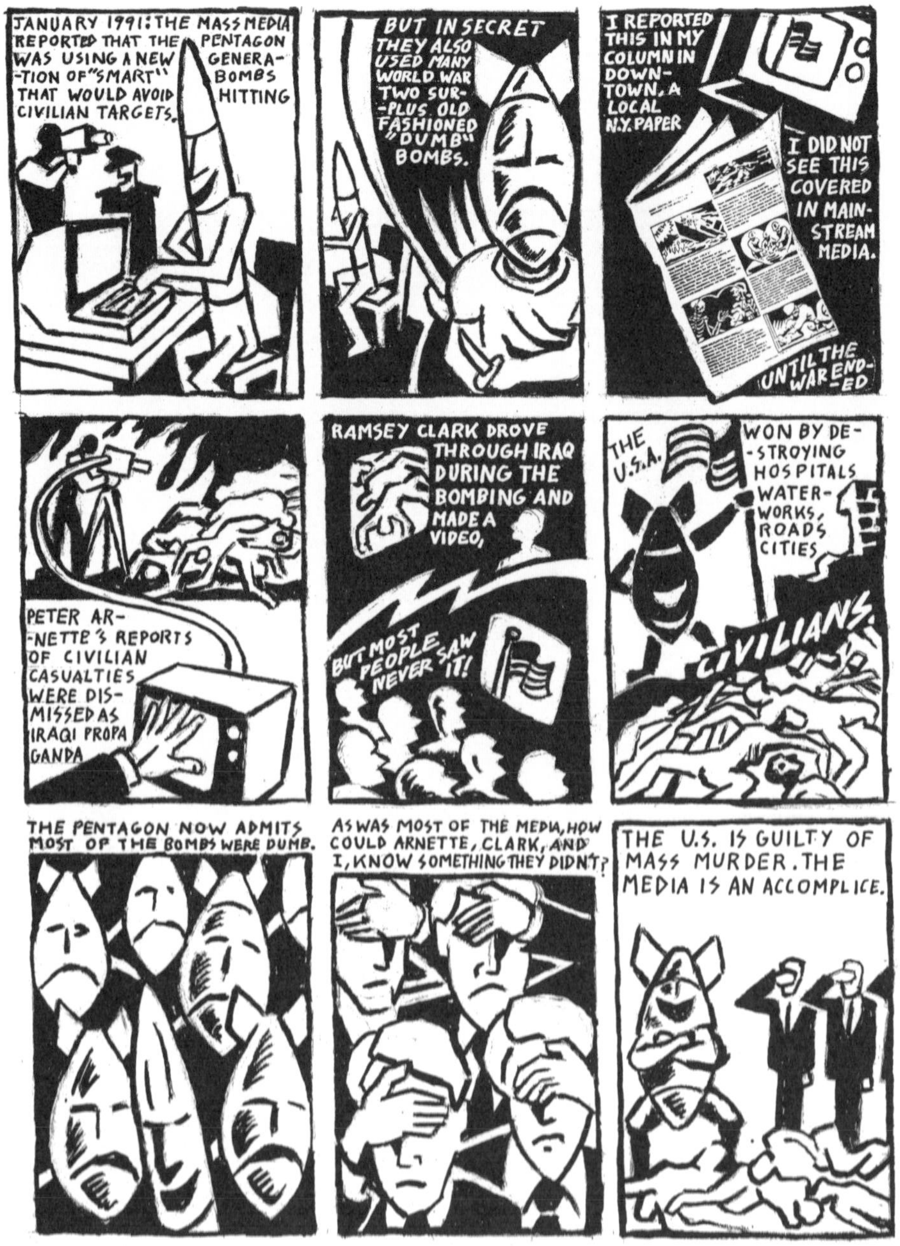

4

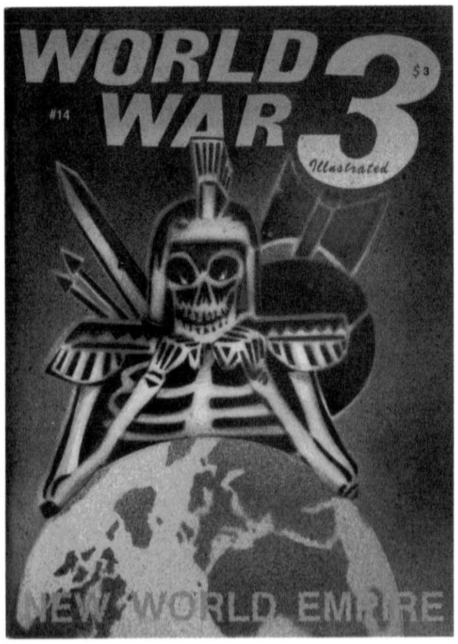

5

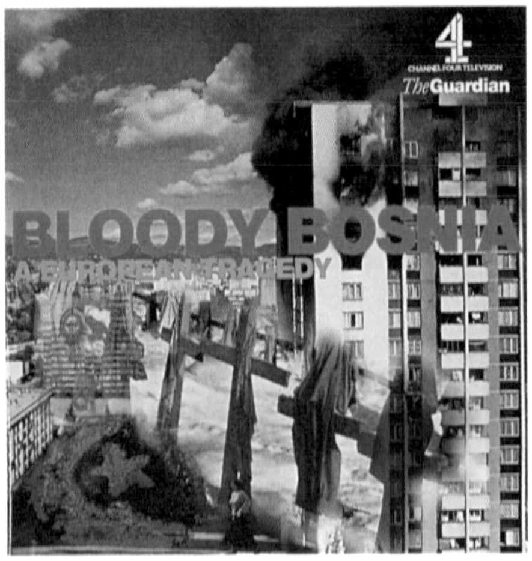

6

4 Part of the weekly comic strip produced during the Gulf War by Seth Tobocman for *Downtown*, a local New York City newspaper in which he highlights US military use of World War II surplus 'dumb' bombs. USA 1991.

5 Front cover of the long-running political/alternative comics magazine *World War 3 Illustrated* (Gulf War issue), co-edited by illustrators Peter Kuper and Seth Tobocman. USA 1991.

6 Front cover of an information brochure for the 'Bloody Bosnia' season of programmes on Channel Four television in the UK, broadcast August 1993. Cover designed by Jacek Depczyk.

The stories, accounts and images emerging from the war in Bosnia were marked by emotions ranging from anger and sarcasm to shock at the levels of cruelty and inhumanity.

1 Front and back cover, 30 November 1994 issue, of the privately owned, Sarajevo-based magazine *DANI* (Days), launched in 1992 and known for taking on controversial news subjects – in this case, NATO. Nine months after this issue, 37 people were killed by a Serb mortar landing near the market square in Sarajevo. This finally prompted NATO to bomb Serb military targets throughout Bosnia in a two-week campaign, leading to the Dayton agreement and the end of the war.

a map. Maps also became an important part of the high-tech game. More and more of them (with hyper-active graphics) produced blow-by-blow coverage of events and, as shown on page 135, became part of the mainstream 'briefing pack'. The need to brief the audience on the game plan and the movement of the players was essential to the notion of 'the game'.

Graphics played an important role here. Briefings predominated, involving a deluge of maps: televised electronic zoom-in maps and room-sized model maps (with model characters to push around);[5] dramatic printed maps complete with thrusting, demonstrative arrows, updated daily. There were endless lists and charts of hardware and gadgetry, apparently intended to instruct viewers about events. Even the small selection of editorial graphics shown on pages 134–5 gives the visual impression of protection and invincibility.

This fantasy ended abruptly with the photograph of the burnt Iraqi soldier that appeared in the UK national newspaper, the *Observer*, in early March 1991 (see page 136). It became obvious that this war was as horror-filled as any other war and people were being killed. Even the smart technology was

not a reality. At the end of the war, it all began to unravel – some sources said that 80 per cent of the bombs dropped were the old, freefalling 'stupid' variety. It remains, in the end, a cautionary tale of the role that graphics can play in reporting, romanticizing and maintaining the entertainment value of war, particularly during the conflict.[6]

And what of the anti-war protest movement and its graphics? Many in the graphics field, expecting to see the far-reaching visual variety of the Vietnam War protest movement repeated, were sorely disappointed. Some said there was no protest movement. The truth is far from it. A new form of visual anti-war protest was developing that continues today.

Lasting over a decade, the Vietnam War caused a profound outpouring of highly visual gut protest. The anti-war movement encompassed a wide variety of methods, including use of symbolism and horrific images (napalmed children, massacres and battlefield carnage). All were generated by certain realities – death and destruction overseas, bodybags coming home – that the ever-weakening arguments of politicians could not counter. The imagery, the horror, was everywhere.

The Gulf War gave birth to a more grassroots-based, information-centred protest, influenced by AIDS activism and other highly visual, street-orientated, direct action movements. It was less about the horrible realities of war – which were hidden from the public in any case – and more about digging around for the motives of war (with petro-dollars turning out to be the prime suspect). It combated the myths about smart weaponry; attached images of horror to the high-tech terminology; demonstrated the plentiful failings of the US government in power; highlighted the oil issue; and supplied drawings, paintings and photocopies in place of the real images that were missing (see pages 136–9). It held protest marches, which were often unreported in the media. It littered streets and walls with posters, flyers and other handmade messages. It sometimes lived in cartoons and collections of comics and illustrations, such as *Nozone* comics or *World War 3 Illustrated*. Above all, it was a grassroots movement that saw the controllers of mainstream media as part of the problem. Peter Kuper, illustrator and co-editor of the political comics magazine, *World War 3 Illustrated*, said in an article written at the time that he wanted 'to alert a graphics

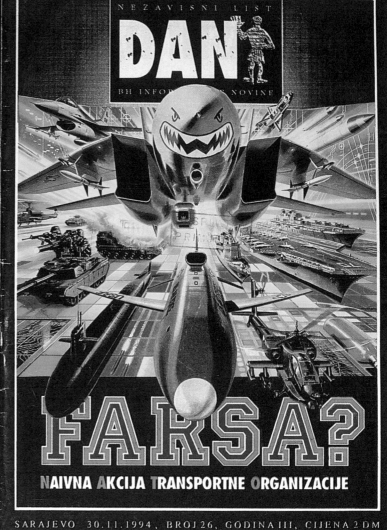

1

community that may feel frustrated by the difficulty of finding outlets and sources for activist graphics. They are as available as your local copy shop and as visible as graffiti on the walls.'[7]

Although the war ended on 28 February 1991, after a mere 42 days, the protests continued for a long time after, as did the bombing of Iraqi targets and sanctions against Iraq, which continued for more than a decade. So too did the sentiments that defined the mainstream media as a law unto itself, and activism as best placed in the street or in independent, alternative formats such as comics and, later, the internet.

The Balkans: the view from outside
The crises in the Balkans – the wars in Bosnia[8] (1992–5) and Kosovo (1998–9) and the bombing of Belgrade (1999) – brought their own perception and distance problems. If the Gulf War caused many onlookers to reach for maps, the Balkans had them reaching for history books as well. A poor sense of geography and history in current generations was partly to blame. The politics and history of the Balkans, an area of many past border changes and occupations, have always been complicated. Media myths abounded. There was talk of civil wars, and of deep-seated hatred between ethnic and religious groups who had been 'at it' for centuries. The UK's 'Bloody Bosnia' season on Channel Four in August 1993 comprised a week of programmes that attempted to show the social tragedies taking place (neighbour turning against neighbour, and so on). It also showed a three-part primer – three 15-minute slots – entitled 'Bloody Bosnia: The Essential Guide'. Described as 'television history for the MTV generation', it was an attempt to educate people about Bosnia's location, history and crisis – using exotic split-screen, visual layering to appeal to those who want their on-screen crises delivered with style.

But it did little to clear up prevailing confusions: its delivery was flashy and fast-paced and largely echoed sentiments current at the time that conflict was all rather expected and a product of the area and its nationalistic tendencies. Such views were also echoed by a press which was looking for something to hold onto. (Even in the year 2000, an article in the *Guardian* newspaper referred to 'the horrors in a complex Balkan War few could understand'.)[9]

It was only with hindsight that the real culprit began to emerge in the form of President Slobodan Milosevic of Yugoslavia.[10] In a spirit of political opportunism and a desire for constructing a Greater Serbia, he fanned existing nationalism and launched an offensive against Slovenia (1991), which quickly managed to declare its independence and fend him off. Then he attacked Croatia, bringing the sabre-rattling Croatian nationalist Franjo Tudjman into the fray and creating a cycle of battles and purgings of ethnic groups. This then set off the powder keg in Bosnia, with nationalistic Orthodox Serbs (Bosnian Serbs), Bosniacs (Bosnian Muslims, the largest group) and Catholic Croats warring against each other for territorial domination and exercising the strategy of 'ethnic cleansing' (the purging of 'unwanted' ethnic groups from areas they wanted to control). After the Dayton Agreement brought the end of the war in Bosnia in 1995, a shaky peace was enforced by NATO. But in 1998 Milosevic then turned his attention to Kosovo – a region with a Serb minority that was significant and holy within Serbian history and Orthodox religion – and claimed it for himself, waging war on the resident ethnic Albanians. Much of this chaos, from 1991 onwards, was driven by Milosevic's excellent performance as puppetmaster. He had not only purged the Yugoslav army to create a Serbian army loyal only to himself, but also legitimized, financed and controlled paramilitary forces, gangsters and warlords, which he used to bolster the rising power of Serb nationalism.[11]

The view from the outside (by onlookers from the West) during this decade of events was distressing. The conflict seemed incomprehensible. There were no briefings. Battle lines could not be neatly drawn out on maps, and in fact there seemed to be no proper battles at all, but continual damage inflicted by sieges, sniping, secret massacres and other appalling acts. If the Gulf War appeared sanitized thanks to information graphics, Bosnia was incomparably messy. Much of what was learnt about that war (at that time, in action) and the following Kosovo tragedy came from the stories of victims, the documentaries of social tragedy, the depictions of the after-effects of rape and carnage. Piecing it all together into a coherent whole seemed impossible, and even commentators were prone to despair. (Peter Howson, sent to Bosnia as an Official War Artist by the Imperial War Museum, returned to the UK traumatized – unable to make sense of the distress and atrocities he had witnessed, and certainly unable to paint them.[12] He later courageously went back to the scene, and on his second return produced paintings full of insights as well as horrors – but ultimately deeply disturbing to view.)

The West did not come out of it well. Western strategy in the area seemed riddled with mistakes, many of them catastrophic. A UN early enforcement of an arms embargo on Bosnia meant Bosnia could not defend itself from outside forces. The UN's lack of action and decision-making made it an ongoing witness to massive displacement of civilians, detention camps and war crimes – unable to take action or help. Its credibility hit rock bottom in July 1995 when Bosnian Serb forces marched into Srebrenica and massacred around 8,000 men and boys, while Dutch UN forces watched and did nothing (inhibited by UN instructions). Moreover, the West had dealings with Milosevic – elected president, fast becoming a ruthless dictator – and did nothing to support democracy in Serbia. While the Kosovo War raged, NATO (in the guise of US President Clinton) sent air strikes to Belgrade and bombed its citizens.

Much Western protest material targets the painfully slow response of the UN and its inability to stop massacres such as Srebrenica, the blue helmet becoming a symbol for indecision. NATO is pummelled from different directions: an Albanian protester tells it to go ahead and bomb Belgrade with the cynical appropriation of the Nike phrase 'just do it' (see page 124); Belgrade protesters tell it to stop, sticking targets to themselves (see page 167). Televised news provided its visual icon. The footage and reports of starving Bosnian prisoners stuck behind the wires of a Bosnian Serb detention camp in 1992 gave us the still image that encapsulated the horror of that war. In 1997, the ITN journalists responsible were accused by *LM* (formerly *Living Marxism*) magazine of fabricating the story. In a cloud of controversy and fury, ITN News took *LM* to court for libel – and won.

Perhaps carrying the most pertinent image for the horrors of the following Kosovo War is an American poster for refugee aid made later in the decade (see pages 156–7) that is devastating in its quiet compassion and impatience. It conveys the ineptitude, dithering and political prevarication that characterized so much of the West's response

2 Front cover of Christmas card from the UK news organization ITN in December 1997 showing a cheerful, healthy-looking man named Fikret Alic, photographed in Hjorring, Denmark in that month. See next page for inside of card.

Fikret Alić Hjørring, Denmark December 1997

2

to the Balkan crisis: 'meanwhile' people lose their homes, 'meanwhile' people die, 'meanwhile' we observe and pick through the sad piles of junk and clothing in the poster. To think of their fate is simply too much to bear.

The Balkans: the view from inside

The inside story of the Balkans only emerged much later, as the distances started to break down. For the creative communities, the artists and designers of most of the countries involved in the wars in the Balkans, a key issue was isolation, both from the rest of the world and from other artists. Feelings of injustice or being forgotten were often understandably present, as well as a desire to rejoin the world and get on with life.

Croatia was the first country to be hit badly. Although the worst of the Serb–Croat War lasted barely a year, the conflict was extremely brutal, and fighting continued throughout the Bosnian crisis. Its strong and well-organized graphic design community (with agencies and design associations based in Zagreb), poured out posters full of grief and anger at the damage inflicted on its people and its cultural heritage, including the terrible destruction of historical architecture and monuments.

In Bosnia, people soldiered on, despite shellings and destruction. The design group Trio (see page 144) carried on throughout the siege of Sarajevo. Using absurdist wit and black humour, they produced postcards that placed Sarajevo's fate as one element within a large number of modern icons – including pop art paintings, Marilyn Monroe and Absolut Vodka – turning Sarajevo into a modern icon itself. Other postcards made ironic visual jokes about the Olympic Games. In 1984 Sarajevo had hosted the Winter Olympics and drawn big international crowds. In Sarajevo 1994, the crowds just weren't interested, and seemed more than happy to abandon the city to its fate.

Posters played an important information role in Bosnia throughout the war. They spouted the politics of a large number of political parties, spoke out against nationalism and against Milosevic, memorialized particular people or acts of destruction (such as massacres), called for recruits to the army of Bosnia-Herzegovina, called attention to damage to buildings and cultural heritage, and conveyed other stark realities of war. Even after the war, posters continued to carry a great deal of public information, often related to reconstruction, such as warnings against landmines (for children) and calls for testimonials against war crimes.

Tales of the horrors of the Bosnian War found their way into comic book form (see pages 152–3). One example is drawn by a US-based artist who travelled to Bosnia to document the war; another is also by a US artist and conveys the story of Bosnian friends who lived through the siege of Sarajevo (and faxed messages out). Both comics operate as personalized storytelling or journalism (similar to Art Spiegelman's *Maus*, see pages 18 and 22) and offer a very different view of events from news reports or television. Like film documentaries or theatre, they allow a human story to unfold – of ordinary people caught up in the horrors of war. Their ability to involve readers with their characters or deliver horrors through association or symbolism (the sight of bloody shoes or a crazed look) allows them to pound a tragic message closer to our hearts and force us to look. Very different from mass media, such as television, which either censor out ugly truths or, by the nature of the programming or context, make it easy for us to look away. (Although they do provide a powerful form of storytelling in documentaries.)

Other interesting features of the comics shown are their different visual techniques. One emanates stylistically from the world of slick action comics with suitable renderings of people and emotions; the other is more a hand-drawn journal. In each case, technique affects the way the story is told, making them very different experiences for the reader. Both make emotions and horrors longer lasting and more memorable – often more effectively than other media.

For yet another visual reality of the siege of Sarajevo, it is necessary once again to consult a map. The map of the siege of Sarajevo produced by FAMA (see page 150) is a revelation: it shows almost at-a-glance how the layout and location of Sarajevo conspired to turn it into a sniper's haven. The city sits within a valley surrounded by hills and conveniently placed tall buildings – all perfectly sited for raining shells upon the desperate civilians of the town.

The story of Belgrade and its frustrations and fears under Milosevic is a tale that has unfolded over time. With Milosevic exercising an iron grip on the state media and threatening or demolishing independent media, little was known of the resistance within Serbia (and few were looking, as all Serbs had already been declared the 'bad guys' in the Western media).

After watching pro-democracy movements sweep Europe, the people of Belgrade soon found their newly elected president moving in the opposite direction,

2

Fikret Alić Trnopolje, Bosnia August 1992

Peace and Goodwill

tightening his control of the media and whipping up nationalist feeling. While the various wars ensued, Belgrade lived in an atmosphere of war-mongering and pro-nationalism. Many years of change and protest followed. There was, for example, a massive anti-Milosevic street protest in 1991, with violent clashes between protesters and the police – and in the end, the tanks rolled in. There were many anti-war protests throughout Milosevic's wars in the form of desertions from the army or draft dodgers.

The now renowned Radio B92 in Belgrade was central to the underground resistance movement. It showed outrageous defiance in the face of Milosevic's attempts to silence independent media. A highly irreverent, even abusive, voice in the middle of an era of regressive thinking, Radio B92 delivered alternative music – from grunge and Punk to indie rock and hardcore rap – as well as political satire, news and pranks to flummox both authorities and listeners. It became a creative centre for anti-war campaigns, anti-nationalism and other movements. It published books of anti-war stories, made films, released records and attempted to keep Serbia from becoming isolated from events – such as the ugliness of the wars being waged in its name – and from Europe. It was shut down or banned a number of times – first in 1991 (but it soon resurrected itself), and then again more forcefully in 1996, so it started publishing news bulletins over the internet. It was reinstated under international and public

pressure, shut down again in March 1999, and resurfaced again as B2-92 after the NATO bombings. Again it was closed, in 2000, but following the ousting of Milosevic at the end of that year, B2-92 rose again as B92, a voice that would not die and that still survives. Its continued presence on the internet provided a vital link between Belgrade (as well as the Balkans) and the world.

After the Bosnian War, Belgrade students and citizens took to the streets between November 1996 and March 1997, demonstrating for change. They marched through the streets, creating a shrill din with whistles, and conducted daily surreal stunts in Republic Square. They joined marches organized by the opposition coalition, during which a few protesters pelted the offices of the state daily newspaper *Politika* with eggs – an exercise that went on for days and became dubbed 'the Yellow Revolution'. Individuals would drive their cars into the city centre and feign a breakdown, causing gridlock chaos.

In the evenings, people would bang pots and pans to drown out the propaganda of the state TV (Radio Television Serbia) news bulletins. Meanwhile, Radio B92 would add to the chaos by transmitting all of the noise.[13] 'Women in Black', the peace protesters, were also active in these demonstrations and were already known for their weekly 'silent protests' (silent demonstrations and performances) against violence, against ethnic cleansing and against crime on all sides of the conflict. Nevertheless, by 1997 it was obvious that Milosevic had survived it all.

In 1998 a new spirit of revolt took hold in the form of the student movement Otpor! (Resistance!), founded by Belgrade University students. Otpor! set its sights on the democratic overthrow of Milosevic and on shaping Serbia's political future. Its members were young (averaging 20 to 21), and it targeted young people to vote for change. Its numbers grew quickly, encouraged by networking, graphic promotions, a website and visible protests: by March 2000 it counted 17,000 activists in over 70 Serbian towns; by July, it claimed 40,000. Its symbol – the clenched fist – appeared all over Serbia.

Although Otpor! was essentially a leaderless, non-hierarchical network, it operated a highly efficient marketing campaign with sophisticated, well-designed graphics more akin to an advertising agency. Its clenched fist – white on a black background – was handled like a corporate logo and printed on posters and other ephemera in an attempt to draw people together and give them the courage to act. Such image-building was important: their confident graphics looked like a powerful force at work, not some little street movement destined to fail. Confidence and humour gave Otpor! huge popularity and a political edge.

Otpor! protests often took the form of performance art: activists would appear in downtown Belgrade dressed as scientists and, down on their hands and knees, inspect the pavement with oversized magnifying glasses in search of any microscopic signs of civic involvement among the apathetic local

3 'Windows '99 – Natosoft', the famed black humour of the Balkans shown on a postcard on sale in Belgrade.

3

Playful comments and humorous, satirical performances happened in the 1990s amid Belgrade's atmosphere of defiance – against the Milosevic regime, NATO and violence in general.

population. On Milosevic's birthday, Otpor! delivered him a birthday card in town squares throughout Serbia. The cards thanked him for the childhood he had taken away from them, wished him a 'Happy Birthday, Mr President', and hoped that he celebrated the next one on a deserved 'holiday in The Hague' (the location of the International Criminal Tribunal for the Former Yugoslavia). In other pranks Otpor! members created an effigy of Milosevic and offered anyone with a dinar (penny) a chance to punch him, they painted his footsteps leaving Parliament in red to represent blood, they 'watched a falling star named "Slobotea" through a cardboard telescope'.[14]

Otpor!'s most important move came with the 'He's Finished!' campaign in the run-up to the presidential elections of 24 September 2000, with the byline 'massive turnout + ballot control = victory'. The opposition led by Vojislav Kostunica won, and although

Milosevic didn't go easily (a revolt on 5 October finally ousted him), by the end of 2000 he was well and truly finished, and now enjoys his 'holiday in The Hague'.

Closing the distance
The separation of the Baltic States from the USSR is represented here by the bloody tragedy in Lithuania, which produced a spate of murders, mourning and memorials in January 1991, just as the Western media was turning its spotlight on the Gulf War. The graphics and visual memorials describing the events are dark and defiant; the events themselves marked the start of the dismembering of the Soviet Union.

The Palestinian–Israeli crisis has built up a cycle of violence that threatens to cause irreparable damage to the peace process. Although Israel has an active peace movement which believes in both peoples living together, its activities have been undermined by the

ongoing occurrence of suicide bombings. The Palestinians' call for their own state, meanwhile, remains strong. With no diplomatic solution yet reached, one can only look at the extraordinary messages that have emanated from this country over the past decade and hope for the future.

The political graphics of both sides represent two richly coloured visual cultures. Israel has a strong graphic design tradition – particularly poster-work and corporate design – that has been a vital presence throughout much of the building of the proud, new state created in 1948. Designers David Tartakover and Yossi Lemel have each produced a large body of exceptional work rooted in political statement. A number of other well-known Israeli designers, such as Dan Reisinger, have over the years produced extraordinary posters on cultural or historical themes, making social comment, or for the cause of peace.

1

2

On the Palestinian side, the graphic imagery produced across the period of two *intifadas* (uprisings) in 1987 and 2000 owes much to the Palestinian painting tradition. Posters have often taken the form of reproductions of paintings that are imbibed with symbols and metaphors of national pride or daily experience, which to the non-Palestinian observer appear to describe ordinary domestic scenes and thereby avoid the anger of the Israeli authorities. The painting tradition also prompts young Palestinians to paint outside walls in graffiti and imagery with revolutionary slogans or murals and memorials to the dead. The skill and artistry of both Israeli and Palestinian artists and designers are displayed in the brave book *Both Sides of Peace* (see page 174), as are the fears expressed by both sides of the effects of violence on both societies.

Such fears of violence also existed in Zimbabwe, although designer Chaz Maviyane-Davies used the internet to close any distance between his country and the world. His protests against the power-hungry president, Robert Mugabe, before the Zimbabwean general elections of June 2000 cried out for support with the daily posting of electronic posters and an agitprop website. President Mugabe retained power and Zimbabwe's society and economy remained in flux. But Maviyane-Davies repeated the exercise in the 2002 elections. He continued his obsessive daily mailings, writings and passionate graphics (often accompanied by Ken Wilson-Max's comic strip *Shango*, carrying a different take on Zimbabwean culture), and produced an extraordinary atmosphere of community. It was as if many people around the world were reading the daily newspaper with him or sitting across the table

holding discussions with him. The energy and electricity were irresistible. Distance was closed – miraculously and forcefully.

The United States, meanwhile, so used to viewing war and conflict from a distance, suddenly had it all up close. The tragedy of 11 September 2001 left New York City traumatized, and the whole of America on alert. Interestingly, it was comic artists who once again provided artwork for relief funds and told the personal stories of what people were doing on that day, how their lives have been affected, what they believe now. Artistic expressions of sympathy came from everywhere, and tributes to heroic acts by firefighters, police and other public servants brought into view many renditions of statuesque angels, gods and goddesses, which probably owed more to comic superheroes than religious paintings. Comic art in its role as popular art seems

3 Members of Otpor! address the public.

4 'Resistance! Wake Up!', sticker from the student/people's movement Otpor! (Resistance!) showing its trademark clenched fist. Yugoslavia c. 2000.

5 'Resistance! To Him! – Our Target', leaflet from Otpor! showing the head of Slobodan Milosevic.

Violence and tensions escalated within Israel as the 1990s progressed. Once into the new century, the United States became the focus of violence with 9/11 and began to prepare for retaliation – despite calls for restraint.

1 Image from the splash page of designer Yossi Lemel's website. The map of Israel is shown within an animated, flickering flame, symbolic of its volatility. Israel 1998.

2 'Happy New Fear', poster produced in September 1995 by David Tartakover for the Jewish New Year (Rosh Hashanah), as a comment on the presence of violence in Israeli society. Within two months Prime Minister Yitzhak Rabin was assassinated by Yigal Amir, who fired three gun shots into his back. Israel 1995. Photograph by Oded Klein.

3 'Make No Mistake', poster by THINK AGAIN (D Attyah and S A Bachman), referring to the Bush administration's War on Terrorism. USA 2001.

4 Anti-war poster by Micah Ian Wright which comments on how the need for oil necessitates the waging of war, and particularly targeting owners of petrol-guzzling SUVs (sports utility vehicles) in the United States. Created at the time of the 2003 War in Iraq, it is a reworking of a US World War II poster by Harold Schmidt which originally stated 'Have you *really* tried — to save gas by getting into a car club'. USA 2003.

somehow appropriate. Calls for restraint (and no retaliation) also came from a number of directions. As fears loomed that Arab-Americans would be demonized, people began to contemplate the loss of civil rights that would affect everyone if the country made a protectionist and isolationist response.

The examples of the protests shown in this chapter, and the role that graphics has played in them, should make one thing clear. Closing the distance between what we see, what we can understand, and how we can help may in future mean taking a more questioning view of what we see through the channels of the mainstream media. To quote Michael Ignatieff in his book *Virtual War: Kosovo and Beyond*, 'Truth is always a casualty in war, but in virtual war, the media creates the illusion that what we are seeing is true. In reality, nothing is what it seems. Atrocities are not necessarily atrocities. Victories are not necessarily victories.

Damage is not necessarily "collateral". But these deceptions have become intrinsic to the art of war. Virtual war is won by being spun. In these circumstances, a good citizen is a highly suspicious one.'[15]

The global communications media is set to play an increasing role in our perception of the rest of the world, its peoples and its conflicts. Within this context, it is surely more important than ever to seek out alternative media, access different kinds of account (through the internet, comics journalism and personal chronicles, for example) and keep alternative views and the personal art of protest and commentary alive and well in us all.

.Happy NEW שנה טובה Fear.

2

FLAMMABLE

1

MAKE NO MISTAKE, OIL GLUTTONY MOTIVATES THIS WAR.

Hey George, rather than patroling the globe protecting oil, how about subsidizing renewable resources?

CHALLENGE THE PREVAILING NARRATIVE.   WWW.PROTESTGRAPHICS.ORG

3

THE MORE GAS YOUR SUV USES
THE MORE FOREIGNERS I HAVE TO KILL!
NOW DO YOU GET IT?

4

1 'January 13. Their Sacrifice for Lithuania – (Is A) Sacred Mandate for Us. Achieve, Believe, Endure!' Poster showing photographs of the events of 13 January. Artist unknown. Lithuania 1991.

2 'The European Way is the Continuation of the Baltic Way', poster expressing the Baltic States' desire to leave the dark, enter the porthole and join the light of the European Community. Lithuania c. 1991.

3 'Lithuania, the One for Me!', poster of the ever-popular image of a girl waving the tricolour of free Lithuania (illegal at that time) over the heads of Soviet troops during a mass demonstration in 1988. Lithuania c. 1991. Photograph by Zinas Kazenas.

4 'Vilnius 13 January 1991', poster focusing on civilians being crushed by tanks, artist unknown. Lithuania 1991.

Independence for the Baltic States: Lithuania's 'Bloody Sunday'

Operating in the shadow of the 1991 Gulf War, the Baltic States – Lithuania, Estonia and Latvia – made their bid for independence from Soviet rule.

Since the advent of the USSR reform policies of *glasnost* and *perestroika* in the mid-1980s, increased signs of revolt had spread through the Baltics in the form of nationalist demonstrations, anti-Soviet protests, and the reappearance in public of the old national flags and national symbols.

Lithuania declared its independence in March 1990, although this was suspended as

Gorbachev ordered Soviet forces to crack down on Lithuania's institutions and government buildings in the capital city of Vilnius. Months of tension came to a head in early 1991. On the night of 12–13 January in Vilnius, the Soviets unleashed a military assault. Unarmed citizens attempting to protect the centres of radio and TV broadcasting from takeover were killed by Soviet gunfire and crushed by tanks, leaving 14 dead and hundreds injured.

As the Soviets then occupied the radio and TV station, people travelled to Vilnius from all over the country and beyond to surround and protect the parliament buildings, erecting barricades and digging anti-tank

ditches. Some 80,000 people formed a human chain of resistance and protection around the parliament buildings. Art, political posters, children's drawings, items of Soviet propaganda and citizenship and portraits of Soviet leaders were all stuck to the Parliament House walls and barricades to confront further advances by Soviet troops. World opinion was outraged by the violence and killings, and Gorbachev brought the Soviet operation to a stop.

Political posters were made to commemorate the distressing events of that time and honour the sacrifice of the Lithuanians involved in what is now known as 'Bloody Sunday' (13 January 1991). Sections of barricades and

graffitied walls surrounding the parliament buildings have remained as a memorial for study by school trips and other visitors.

Estonia and Latvia also suffered tensions, demonstrations or human losses around that time. But by August 1991 all three Baltic States had declared their independence and received diplomatic recognition by the European Community.

1

2

3

VILNIUS 1991·01·13

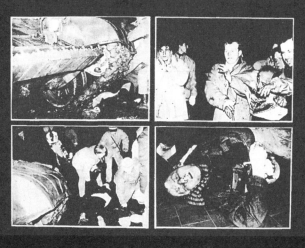

4

5

three boys view graffiti that says 'Gorbi – we are on top of your tanks' (we are not afraid of your tanks). Photographs on this page by Stephen Buckle, 2001.

7 Corner view of a remaining section of the barricades surrounding the Lithuanian Parliament buildings in Vilnius, now serving as a memorial to the events of 13 January 1991.

8 Side view of the barricade.

6

7

8

The 1991 Gulf War: 'the information war'

Iraq's invasion of Kuwait in August 1990 led to the start of the Gulf War in January 1991, waged against Iraq by a UN-backed coalition of 36 countries led by the US military with large contingents from the UK and France. The Gulf War was dubbed 'the information war', known for its highly censored portrayal of bloodless warfare. Video footage of air strike techno-wizardry; the mythic capabilities of 'smart' bombs and precision guided weapons; the media and press briefings with step-by-step, zoom-in zoom-out maps; and endless charts showing dazzling arrays of hardware all fed the fantasy of a videogame conflict, with armchair consoles ready for battle to commence in every viewer's living room (see pages 134–5). Non-messy, technology-clad words—such as 'surgical strikes' and 'collateral damage'—entered popular vocabulary as part of the game play and have remained in the public domain ever since. Graphics played a seminal role in maintaining the entertainment-value of the war, while purporting to provide information.

In the realm of popular graphics, individual countries exorcised their own ghosts. Britain unashamedly displayed its jingoism and unerring love of a good fight. The United States mustered popular support and bedecked itself with yellow ribbons, a powerful symbol of heartfelt support tinged with past regrets.

Although it can be traced back to a 1949 John Wayne cavalry film, the more recent meaning of the yellow ribbon was derived from a pop song from the Vietnam War era, where it signalled a lover's welcome for a returning soldier.

The turbulent reality of that unpopular war, however, was often lack of public support for soldiers (many of them drafted) both while serving overseas as well as on their return home. When the Gulf War started decades later, many Americans wanted to ensure that however much politicians may be blamed, US soldiers should not feel abandoned (as they did in Vietnam) by their country and the folks at home. The yellow ribbon was adopted as a symbol of support and remembrance, and remains so today.

THIS ISN'T THE HOLY WAR I HAD IN MIND!

SUPPORT OUR TROOPS
IN DESERT STORM

2

2 US bumper sticker from the Gulf War of 1991.

3 Fax message for Saddam Hussein from *Sun* readers, appearing on an inside page of the British tabloid newspaper the *Sun*. UK 16 January 1991.

4 Front page of the *Sun* newspaper, 16 January 1991.

5 Ribbon with star (pin) and badges sold in the USA during the 1991 Gulf War.

TO: Saddam Hussein

FROM: Sun Readers

● WANT to give Iraqi tyrant Saddam Hussein a piece of your mind? Now you can, thanks to The Sun fax service.
● Fill in your personal message to the potty president on the special fax letter below—then send it via the Iraqi Embassy. Let's show the mad dog that we're all rooting for our boys in The Gulf.

WRITE YOUR OWN FAX MESSAGE

Iraq Embassy Fax No: 071-584 7716

To whom it may concern,

Please pass this message on as a matter of great urgency to Saddam Hussein.

3

4

5

1 Cartoon by Michael Heath, cartoonist for the *Independent* newspaper and the *Spectator* magazine, commenting on the proliferation of maps and information graphics at the time. UK 1991.

2 'Showdown in the Gulf' was one of the popular catchphrases of the Gulf War, shown here in the CBS News logo for Desert Storm with approved title for TV coverage. CBS News graphics were by special events producer/director Eric Shapiro, art director Ned Steinberg, and graphic designers Louis Palisano, Liz Kennedy and Stephen Vardi. Originally broadcast on The Evening News with Dan Rather over the CBS television network. USA 1991.

3 Cover page and spreads from *The Sunday Times*, 'War in the Gulf, 16-page Colour Briefing', 27 January 1991, UK. Special section in a leading British newspaper on the Gulf War machine, including people, places (maps) and technology (equipment).

4 Fold-out map of the Gulf War area (37 x 50 cm, 14 ½ x 19 ¾ inches), by *Time* magazine which achieved fame for its use by US President Bush during the Gulf War. Designer Nigel Holmes, artists Steven Hart, Nigel Holmes, Joe Lertola and Paul Pugliese, researcher Deborah Wells. USA 1991.

5 The F-15 E 'Strike Eagle', displayed in CBS News weapons graphics, USA 1991. Originally broadcast on The Evening News with Dan Rather over the CBS television network.

6 The Patriot missile, displayed in ABC News weapons graphics. USA 1991.

7 A visual listing of major Allied and Iraqi weapons shown on the back of *Time* magazine's fold-out map. Designer Nigel Holmes, artists Steven Hart, Nigel Holmes and Joe Lertola, researcher Deborah Wells. USA 1991.

"LET'S GET OUTTA HERE, IT'S A GRAPHICS ATTACK!"

1

2

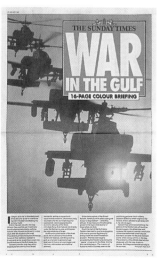

3

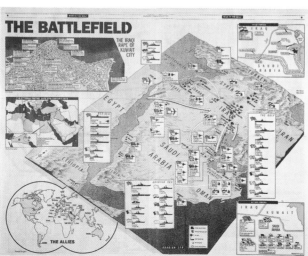

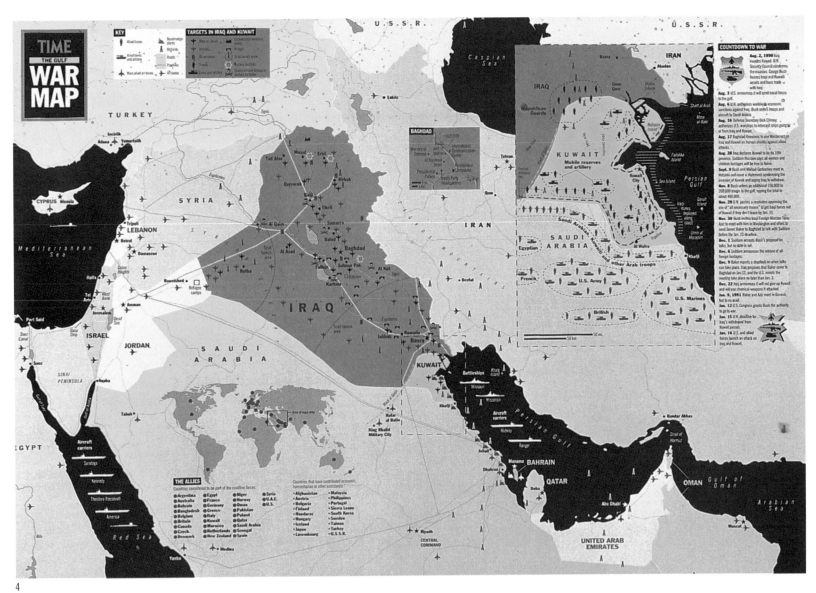

4

5

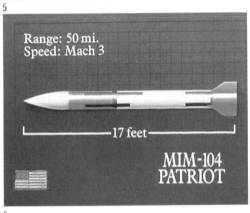

6

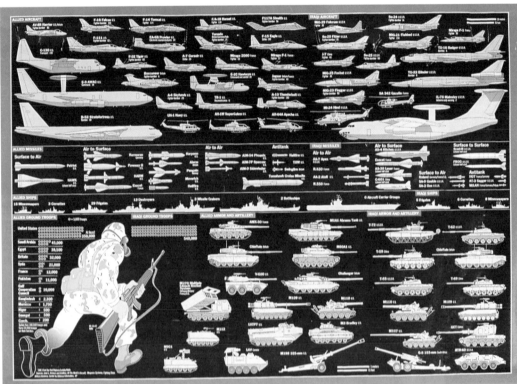

7

1 'Collateral Damage', street poster by Scott Cunningham, which makes use of a military term very much in evidence then and now. Collateral damage refers to unavoidable damages, such as civilian casualties. USA 1991.

2 'New World Odor', screenprinted poster by Mark Vallen. The title is a pun on 'New World Order', the phrase used by US President Bush to describe the socio-political reconfiguration of the world after the fall of the Iron Curtain. USA 1991.

3 Page from the *Observer* newspaper (3 March 1991) showing the photograph of a burnt Iraqi soldier associated with the end of military action in the Gulf War. UK 1991. Photograph by Kenneth Jarecke, Reuters.

4 Front cover of *Yahoo* No 5, by comics artist Joe Sacco (lips by Claudia Basrawi), carrying a portrait of the Commander-in-Chief of the Coalition forces in the Gulf, General Norman Schwartzkopf aka 'Stormin' Norman'. USA 1991.

The 1991 Gulf War: images of protest

A contrast to the high-tech information display of the war and its events was supplied by the anti-war protest movement, which fought fire with fire, offering its own version of information. Protest graphics combated the myths of smart weaponry; brought issues such as oil into the discussion; argued the failings of the US administration in power; and dragged blood and death back into the equation through drawn or painted imagery (due to lack of any real photographs). Posters emanating from other countries (shown on pages 138 and 139) provided wide-ranging anti-war sentiment or brought desperate situations to the world's attention – such as in Israel, where the population lived in fear of chemical attack from Iraq. The protest movement also fostered a mistrust of mainstream media – the vehicles of official propaganda – and that mistrust remains a vital part of grassroots protest today.

It is not surprising that a real, photographic blood-and-guts image is often associated with the end of the war. It is a single, still image of a charred Iraqi soldier – one of the human corpses found on the highway to Basra where allied aircraft decimated the main Iraqi retreat from Kuwait City at Mutla Ridge around 27 February. It is the action – and by association, the image – that was alleged (by commentators of the time) to have pressured President Bush into stopping the war when he did (28 February 1991).

Some still argue that President Bush should have allowed the military to continue to Baghdad and finish the job of toppling Saddam Hussein. Others argue that the ensuing butchery and consequent public reaction would most certainly have destroyed Bush's political career. As it was, the photograph appeared in the UK national newspaper the *Observer* in early March 1991 and provoked intense shock and outrage, which resonated subsequently throughout the world's media. The fantasy of the high-tech war was redressed in one primitive blow of photographic reality.

1

2

3

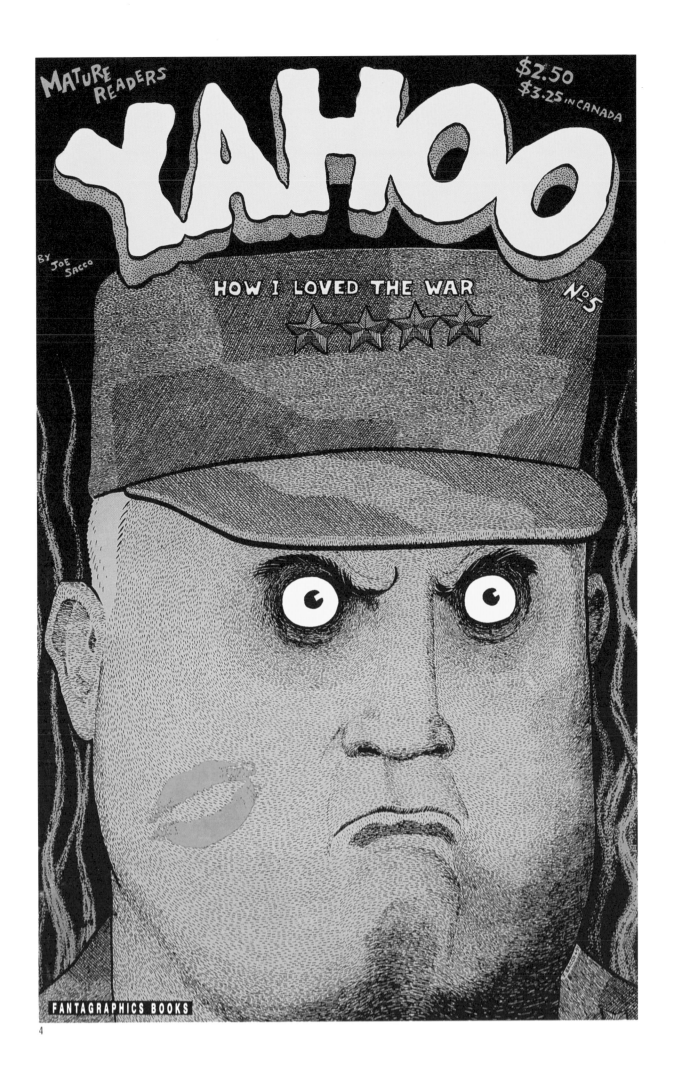

1 'On Your Face' (slang for 'a bad situation'), poster by Yossi Lemel created six months before the Gulf War – a prediction of things to come. (The straps of the gas mask form the Star of David.) Israel 1990.

2 'No Blood for Oil', poster by Keith R Potter and Steven Lyons. Published by the Emergency Campaign to Stop the War in the Middle East. USA 1990.

3 'Jonathan's Teddy Bear', poster by Eytan Hendel showing the gas mask his six-year-old son drew to keep his teddy bear safe under attack. Israel 1990.

4 'We're Going to Win!', poster by Nous Travaillons Ensemble (We Work Together) published after the Gulf War. France 1991.

5 'No War', silkscreen poster by David Lance Goines. Self-published and distributed free to peace groups. USA 1991.

1

2

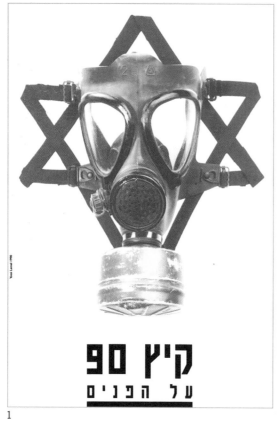

3

4

5

6 'Uncle George Wants You',
poster by Stephen Kroninger.
Self-published and distributed
by the *Village Voice* in Manhattan,
then distributed by the *Progressive*
magazine in Madison, Wisconsin,
and redesigned as T-shirts in New
York City. USA 1991.

6

1 'SOS Croatia', poster by Ranko Novak which makes use of the pattern of the 'sahovnica', the distinctive red-and-white checked medieval shield – Croatia's heraldic emblem. Croatia 1991.

2 'Krvatska!', a war poster using wordplay, combining *krv* (blood) and *Hrvatska* (Croatia), by Boris Ljubicic. Croatia 1991.

War in Croatia: posters of devastation and loss

The election of the nationalist Franjo Tudjman as President of Croatia in 1990 reflected the country's desire for independence from the federation of Yugoslavia. Tudjman resurrected the red-and-white chequerboard Croatian coat of arms in the national flag. An emblem from the Middle Ages, it had been banned by Yugoslavia's postwar leader Tito because of its more recent historical associations with nationalist massacres of Serbs and other minorities in the 1940s. Not surprisingly, the Serbian population in Croatia grew to fear the idea of Croatian independence under Tudjman.

Another crucial factor came into play: the rising power and aggressive, land-grabbing nationalism of Serbian leader Slobodan Milosevic. His ruthless desire for Serb domination of Yugoslavia or the creation of an independent 'Greater Serbia', as well as the brutal campaign he launched in 1987 to take over the Yugoslavian provinces of Kosovo and Vojvodina, caused fear in the other republics of the federation. Slovenia and Croatia declared independence from Yugoslavia in June 1991. Milosevic's loyal Yugoslav People's Army (JNA) and paramilitaries struck at Slovenia but met fierce resistance and withdrew after only 10 days. They then turned and attacked Croatia.

Over the following year, the viciousness of the Serb–Croat War shocked everyone. The Croatian border town of Vukovar was levelled, with 5,000 dead; the ancient port of Dubrovnik was held under a long siege. Throughout the war there were massacres of innocent people on both sides; both Serb and Croat militias ran wild. It was also in the Serb–Croat War that the phrase 'ethnic cleansing' was first used to describe the ethnic purging of areas either side wanted to control.

By January 1992, Slovenia and Croatia were being recognized by other countries as independent states, marking the death of the old Yugoslavia. The ensuing scramble by politicians for power

and territory – along with fears by minorities for their own safety – has been identified as the spark that set off the Bosnian War.

Croatia has a long, proud tradition of graphic design; its creative community is known for its organized international exhibitions and societies. Zagreb has long been a centre for arts such as film and writing. The graphic design community, reeling from the shock of the war, still managed to carry on with the ZGRAF 6 international exhibition of graphic design in November 1991. Soon after, the Zagreb Arts Fund initiated an exhibition entitled 'For the defence and renewal of Croatia' and encouraged the creation of propaganda posters.

1

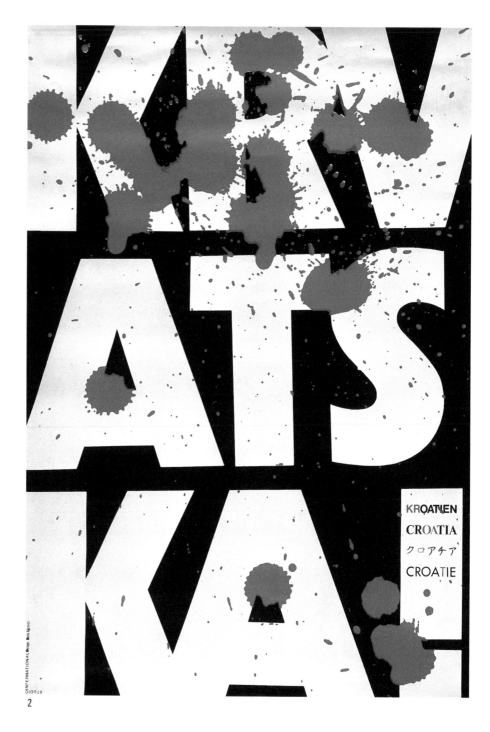

2

140

A wide range of posters appeared. Internationally renowned designer Boris Ljubicic produced posters that derived their strength from symbolism and wordplay. His poster on the opposite page uses the word *Hrvatska*, meaning Croatia — and contained within it, *krv* which means blood. His poster-broadsheet 'Read Between the Lines' (see page 143) provides an account of the destruction of Vukovar. Other symbolic statements include Boris Bucan's painterly rendition of Dubrovnik, and Predrag Dosen's abstract association between the sands of time and sandbags — both part of a state of siege. The series 'Documenta Croatica' (see page 143), with a print run of 26,000, was widely distributed for use in charity campaigns. It presents a more literal listing of devastation, by attempting to chronicle the loss in human, ecological, religious and cultural heritage terms.

3 'Stopped Sands of Time', poster by Predrag Dosen where the sands of time (symbolizing progress and life) are stopped to become the sandbags of war. Dosen's town Osijek, in the eastern part of Croatia, was shelled heavily by Serb forces for nearly five months. Croatia 1992.

Predrag Došen
A.D.C.Z.
ZAUSTAVLJENI PJEŠČANI SAT

3

1 'Stop – For the Sake of Peace, Croatian Artists 1991', poster by Nenad Dancuo. It incorporates the sign of the Hague Convention (displayed on churches, monasteries, palaces and other cultural monuments) with a target, to show that even 'protected' buildings were neither safe nor places of sanctuary. Croatia 1991.

2 'Dubrovnik', poster by Boris Bucan. Dubrovnik, a beautiful old fortress and tourist attraction on the Adriatic coast of Croatia, was attacked and shelled during the Serb–Croat War. Here a tourist poster image becomes a war image, with heraldry around the border, trees resembling smoke and a gun fighter arising ghost-like from the fortress top. Croatia 1992.

3 'International Museum Day', poster by Boris Ljubicic alluding to a past of classic beauty and proud heritage – as well as bloodshed. Croatia 1992. Photograph by Boris Ljubicic and Damir Fabijanic.

4,5 'Documenta Croatica', posters by S Henigsman and M Tudor, used in charity campaigns and printed in two sets of colour. A red set dealt with the Croatian people's suffering; a green set dealt with environmental effects. Croatia 1991–2. Photography by R Ibrisevic and G Pichler. From the Croatian History Museum, Zagreb.

6 'Read Between the Lines', poster-broadsheet by Boris Ljubicic which pulls viewers in to read the story behind the large print – an account of the devastation of Vukovar, a town in East Croatia which was levelled. Its people fled or were killed. Croatia 1994.

1

2

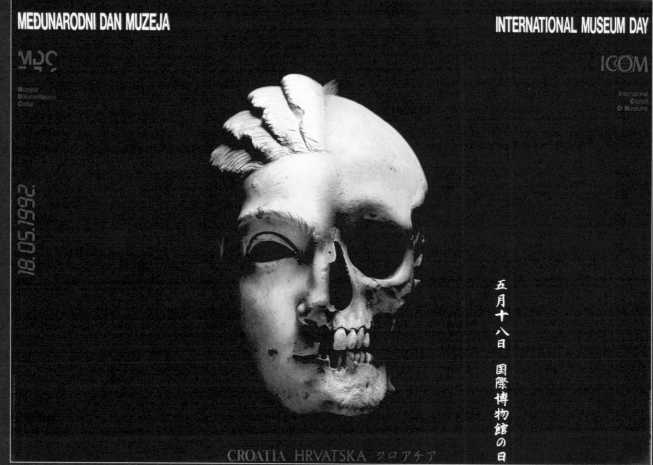

3

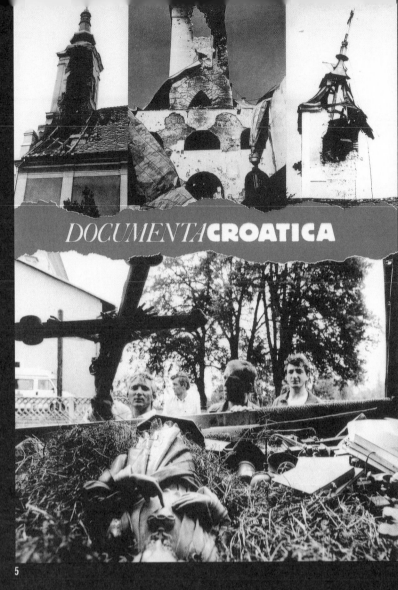

DOCUMENTACROATICA

DOCUMENTACROATICA

4

5

6

1 'Enjoy Sara-jevo' postcard by Trio design group working in Sarajevo during the Bosnian War. Bosnia 1993–4.

The Bosnian conflict: Trio design group and others

Prior to the wars in the 1990s, it was common for artists and designers in the Balkans to travel to different cities and nearby countries to work on projects, attend competitions and network with the thriving creative communities. The isolation and immobility brought by war is difficult for the creative soul to bear. What is never in question, however, is the desire and commitment to carry on, to tell the story of events, despite dangers that range from sniper bullets to explosions in the local café and difficulties like lack of electricity and paper shortages. In Bosnia, posters have always played a significant information role and they played an important part in telling the war story.

The Sarajevo-based design group Trio was formed in 1985 by Bojan and Dalida Hadzihalilovic (husband and wife) and Leila Hatt-Mulabegovic, who later emigrated to Zurich. The group was later joined by other associates and helpers, including Bojan's father Fuad (shown in photograph). With the start of the Bosnian War, Sarajevo went under siege in April 1992. The siege lasted three and a half years until February 1996. Bojan and Dalida decided to stay in Sarajevo and ran a commercial office throughout the war. The office was computerized, with early versions of Coreldraw, Pagemaker and Photoshop, when electricity supplies allowed. When not, they worked by hand with tempera and inks. They designed product packaging, graphic identities – for the National Railway company of Bosnia-Herzegovina among others – and a wide range of newspapers and magazines, including many covers for the controversial privately owned magazine *DANI* (Days) which often handled confrontational topics such as the corruption of political leaders or government incompetence.

The work that has gained them international renown is the personal work they produced on the plight of Sarajevo. An extremely prolific team, Bojan and Dalida produced a flood of posters and postcards during the war years, imbibed with their characteristic sense of irony and black humour. When paper became short, they printed on existing items such as maps. When electricity became short, they hand-painted their work, then printed it later in smaller postcard format. A common subject was the Winter Olympic Games staged in Sarajevo in 1984. Trio used it as a sardonic symbol of how a city can be in popular focus one minute, and forgotten by the world the next, when in danger or need. An added bitter twist of reality was the shelling and burning to the ground in 1992 of Sarajevo's Olympic Museum, including its contents and artefacts.

Coca-Cola logo redesigned by "Trio" Sarajevo

1

Trio's most famous work was a series of postcards produced between September 1993 and February 1994 in which Sarajevo's fate became the satirical theme of reworked cultural and pop icons, including the Coca-Cola logo and Absolut Vodka. The postcard format was chosen so that they could be transported out of the city and communicate with the outer world, and also because of shortages of paper and ink, again the subject of a cynical joke printed on the back of the postcards ('... printed in war circumstances. No paper, no inks, no electricity, no water. Just good will'). (Trio still works in Sarajevo as part of the ad agency Fabrika, meaning 'factory'.)

More visual stories of the war have been depicted in poster form by other exceptional artists such as Cedomir Kostovic, part of the graphic design team for the 1984 Winter Olympics in Sarajevo. He moved to the United States in 1991 but continued to produce posters that act as commentaries on the Bosnian situation, and are sometimes subtle, sometimes blatant in their display of anger or despair. Asim Djelilovic conceived another poster series during the war, although they were not produced until after it. His graphic style – highly illustrative, cheerful and cartoon-like – carries a dark and sinister edge, especially when used to present events or disasters about to take place.

2 Distributed as photocopies, this photograph is of the 'War Studio' in Sarajevo where Trio worked, showing Bojan and Dalida Hadzihalilovic (centre and right) and Bojan's father Fuad (on the left). Bosnia 1993.

2

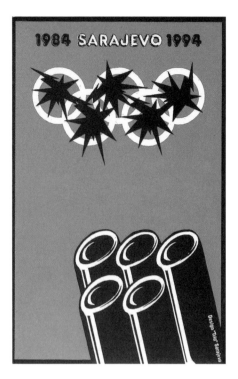

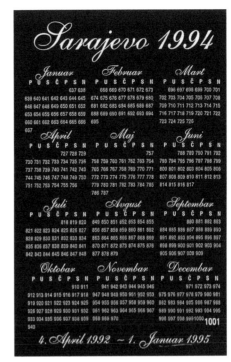

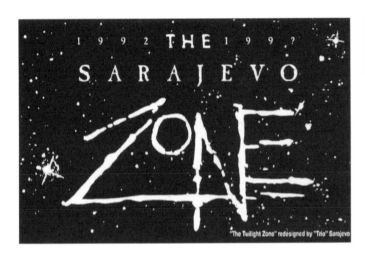

1 'Disunited Nations of Bosnia and Herzegovina', poster and postcard by Trio. A reworking of the UN logo which comments on the Vance Owen Plan of 1993, a failed peace plan with disastrous results that proposed dividing the country into ethnic territories. Bosnia 1993.

2 'Brotherhood and Unity', poster by Cedomir Kostovic which carries the slogan of Tito's Yugoslavian state as a dark, ironic comment on the divisions and brutalities that followed in the Bosnian War. USA 1994.

3 'Open your eyes. Tell us what you saw. The families of missing people need your help. The Red Cross needs your testimony.' Two versions of a poster designed by Trio for the Red Cross, which is asking people for testimonials of crimes or abuses witnessed during the war. Bosnia 1999.

1

2

3

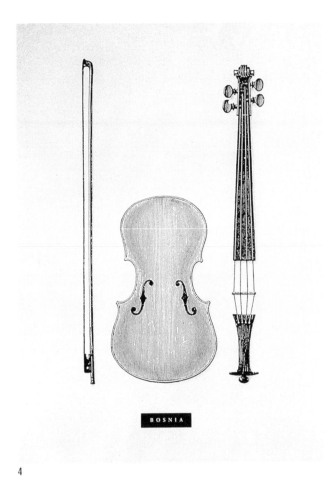

4

5

6

7

4 'Bosnia', poster by Cedomir Kostovic, commenting that a violin divided into parts (unable to make music) is like a country separated into three ethnic parts – Muslim, Serb and Croat. USA 1995.

5 'Ciao!', poster by Asim Djelilovic that refers to the death of Tito, the leader/dictator who held the federal state of Yugoslavia together. His departure allowed many suppressed difficulties to surface. Bosnia 1996. From a series of 27 posters by Djelilovic telling the story of the Bosnian War.

6 'Perfect!', poster by Asim Djelilovic showing a spectacled sniper taking aim, symbolizing the role of Serb intellectuals in starting the Bosnian War. Also inspired by the death of Suada Deliberovic, shot on a bridge by a sniper during a peace demonstration in 1992 – the first violent death in Sarajevo. Bosnia 1992. One of a series of 27 posters.

7 'End of War!?', poster by Asim Djelilovic which visually expresses the sound of a machine gun – and the scepticism many felt about the 1995 Dayton peace agreement. ('Rat' is the Bosnian word for 'war'.) Bosnia 1996. One of a series of 27 posters.

1 Detail of the FAMA 'Sarajevo Survival Map' (see caption below), showing particular danger zones (due to snipers) within the city. Bosnia 1996.

2 'Sarajevo Survival Map 1992–5', commemorating the siege of Sarajevo. Produced and published by FAMA International. Author Suada Kapic, illustrator Ozren Pavlovic, photographer Drago Resner, designer Emir Kasumagic. Bosnia 1996.

The siege of Sarajevo: the story told in a map

An alternative graphic rendition of the siege of Sarajevo is presented in the commemorative map shown on these pages. The siege lasted from April 1992 to February 1996, during which time the Yugoslav People's Army and local militias blockaded, shelled and demolished the city (hit daily by around 4,000 shells). The map was produced and published in 1996 by FAMA International, a Sarajevo-based media publishing house devoted to preserving the memory and experience of the Siege of Sarajevo for educational, cultural and collective healing purposes. It was conceived and authored by Suada Kapic and illustrated by Ozren Pavlovic.

The map is a beautiful item — artistically drawn, warm in colour — that presents harrowing information. The large pink blobs mark 'danger zones' (prone to shelling); the targets and little running figures mark sniper areas; and the stick-like shapes around the drawn edge represent 260 tanks, 120 mortar launchers, and numerous anti-aircraft guns and snipers. Suddenly, the beautiful but deadly geography of Sarajevo is revealed: a city snuggling in a valley surrounded by mountains — on top of which sat a vast array of artillery, ready to pound it into dust or pick its inhabitants off one by one. Cynically speaking, Sarajevo was made for a siege. Endless news footage could never convey piecemeal what this map shows in one graphic blow.

On the back, details of buildings, streets and other areas are explained, forming the long story of the siege. It describes the devastation of the city and its buildings, often burned to the ground, as well as the devastation of daily life: the loss of telephone lines, phone boxes and postal services; the massacres in markets; the loss of water and electricity; the incessant shellings and snipings. It relays moments of hope: how newspapers continued to be produced and distributed, and how — despite the continued shelling of maternity wards and clinics, no matter how often they moved to avoid fire — the local radio station every morning announced how many baby boys and girls had been born in the previous 24 hours. It also carries harsh, cynical comments aimed at, for example, foreign correspondents' cameras sited around the bridges (usually dangerous sniper zones), 'waiting for the "live" shot of death which would bring them money or awards'.

The map ends its story with the final figures: 10,615 people killed — 1,601 of them children — and 50,000 wounded. It was the longest siege in modern history — 1,395 days: over three and a half years. Appropriately, a copy of the map is said to be displayed in the International Criminal Tribunal offices in The Hague.

2

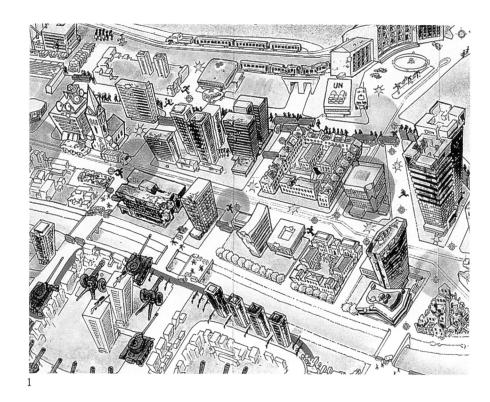

1

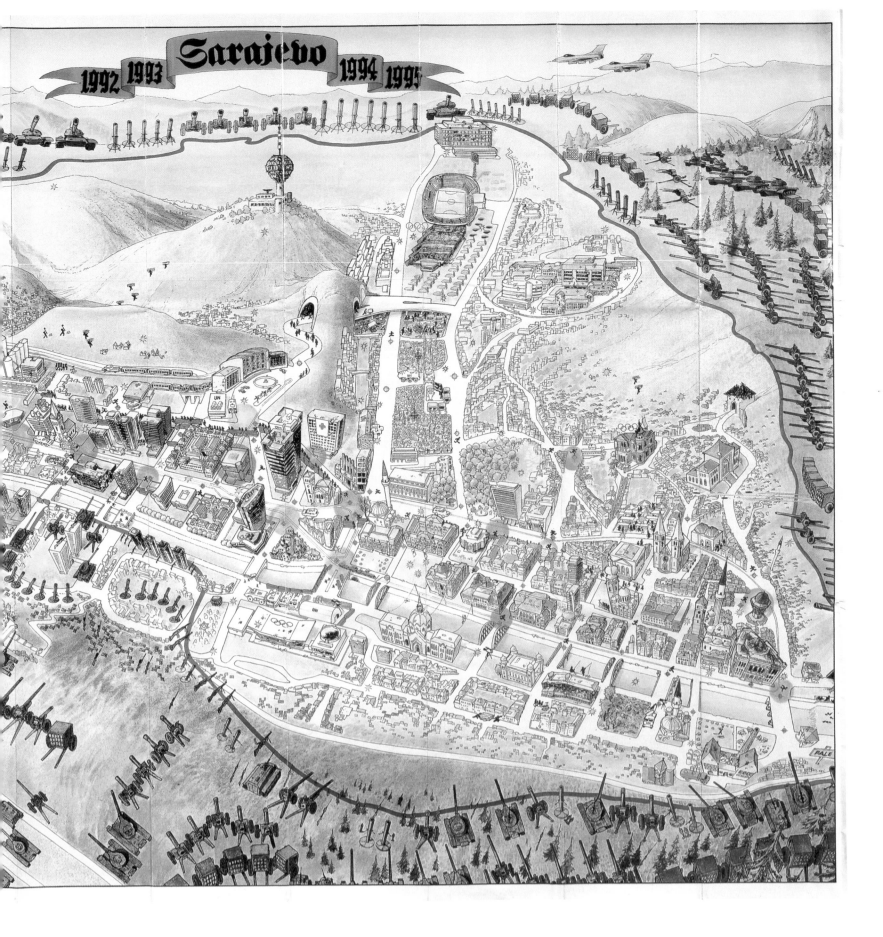

1,2,3 Front cover and inside pages from the book, *Fax from Sarajevo: A Story of Survival*, by Joe Kubert. Published by Dark Horse Comics. USA 1996.

4,5,6 Front cover, detail and spread from the book, *Safe Area Gorazde: The War in Eastern Bosnia 1992–95*, by Joe Sacco. Published by Fantagraphics Books. USA 2000.

Personal tales of survival: the Bosnian conflict in graphic novels

In the years after the war in Bosnia, stories of conflict and survival began to emerge in media ranging from painting and film to comics. Two excerpts of comics journalism are shown here, both extraordinary examples of storytelling but very different from each other in approach.

Comics artist Joe Kubert's graphic novel, *Fax from Sarajevo: A Story of Survival*, is the story of his friends, Ervin Rustemagic and his family, and their (successful) attempt to survive the horrors of the siege of Sarajevo and ultimately escape to freedom and safety. During their ordeal, Ervin's only communication with the outside world was through faxes to Kubert and others. It is this collection of Ervin's reported experiences and on-the-spot

reactions to horrifying events that Kubert has put together into a graphic novel. It is drawn in the familiar style of BLAM! POW! action comics, which somehow heightens the notion that life and reality is stranger (and potentially far more horrifying) than fiction. Kubert also supplies background material and snapshot photographs of the family involved, which strengthen the connection between reality and fiction.

Comics journalist Joe Sacco visited the UN-designated 'safe area' of Gorazde, a largely Muslim town isolated in Bosnian Serb territory in Eastern Bosnia, four times in late 1995 and early 1996. *Safe Area Gorazde: The War in Eastern Bosnia 1992–95* is the story in comics form of the friends and people he met and lived with there: their recollections of the events and terrible human losses of the past few years, their

desperate need for everything from medical supplies and food to electricity and water; and their desire for contact with the outside world. It is also the story of the horrific ethnic cleansing that took place as Serb forces, behaving with murderous cruelty, expelled the Muslim population from the towns and villages of that area, right under the nose of the international community and the prevaricating UN.

The story is told with the controlled tone of a documentary, comprising a large number of testimonials strung together and supplemented with Sacco's brutal honesty in questioning his own and other outsiders' roles in visiting the area. His drawings are an equally extensive chronicle of events – once again, controlled and measured, even when describing the horrific aftermath of atrocities. This is perhaps its strongest quality – the ability to

convey both the beauty and the insanity through drawings, as well as the ability to see with calm and sympathetic, but exact and accurate eyes.

Although both publications are stories of survival, they offer very different perspectives on the war. One is the story of a family in Sarajevo: a desperate battle to survive and a subsequent attempt to flee the country. The other is the story of people who live in a town – an enclave – that views Sarajevo as the Western 'media darling' (receiving all the attention). They will probably never leave their country, but slowly move from their trapped and endangered existence to a degree of mobility and a slightly more hopeful future. Both projects are about hope, with the subtleties and complexities of that emotion shown through the ever-fascinating genre of comics.

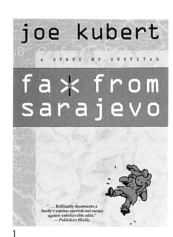

1

2

3

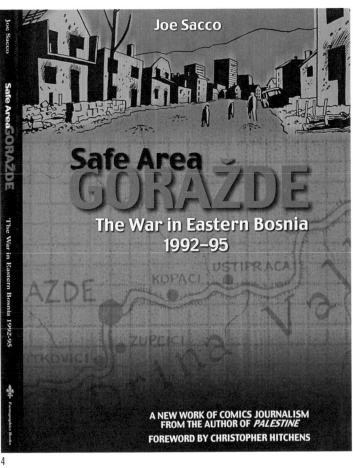

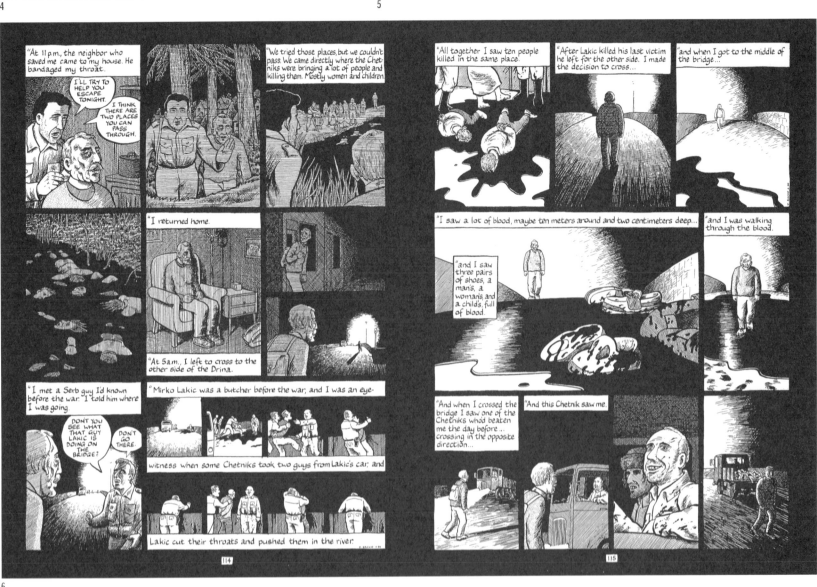

1 '10 with Onions, 10 with Troubles' ('10 with Onions' refers to a popular Yugoslavian dish of 'fingers' of meat). From the New Embroideries project by Skart, Belgrade, summer 2000. Text for all pieces by Skart and the Single Mothers' Association 'WOMEN', Zemun (near Belgrade). Image by Dusica Tomic (40), single mother refugee from Kosovo. Embroidery by Lenka Zelenovic (47), single mother from Zemun. Photograph by Andreja Leko.

The war in Kosovo: the movement of populations

The war in Croatia and then another in Bosnia failed to bring Milosevic the territorial expansion – or 'Greater Serbia' – he craved. So after 10 years of exerting repressive control in the republic of Kosovo, he launched a military campaign there in February 1998 to drive out the Albanians and restore Kosovo to the Serbs. This would involve attempts to eliminate the Kosovo Liberation Army, which was fighting for independence from Serbia, and driving out or eliminating the (majority) ethnic Albanian population, many of whom were Muslims. The fighting that ensued by both armies was savage; the ethnic cleansing of innocent people brutal.

After months of failed negotiations by NATO, which was enforcing UN demands for both sides to stop fighting, Serb forces launched another massive offensive in March 1999. Ethnic cleansing escalated: by this point 20,000 Kosovo Albanians were leaving Kosovo each day, displaced to refugee camps in surrounding Albania, Montenegro and Macedonia. The overwhelming numbers began to de-stabilize the receiving countries.

NATO started the 78-day bombing campaign against Serbia (24 March to 9 June) that eventually brought the war to an end as NATO troops entered Kosovo. Milosevic withdrew. At home in Serbia, he claimed victory. Outside Serbia, he was charged with war crimes.

The prevailing image of the Kosovo War is therefore one of moving or displaced populations. Many went to refugee camps and were then ordered back home; many fled to the mountains and forests; thousands were sent abroad to other countries; and still others – particularly large numbers of men – disappeared. The poster 'Meanwhile' (see page 156–7) by Nicholas Blechman, Christoph Niemann and Paul Sahre – designed to raise money and awareness for the refugees of Kosovo – encapsulates in a horrifying image the prevarications of the politicians, as well as questioning the fate of those now missing from the photograph.

Overwhelming issues such as missing persons, mass graves, confronting the past – are all part of reconstructing lives. A project is shown here from the Belgrade art and design group Skart (Scraps), founded by Dragan Protic and Djordje Balmazovic, which involves an embroidery project undertaken with a single mothers' society (including single mother refugees from Kosovo and Bosnia) on the break up of Yugoslavia, as part of their process of grieving.

The embroideries were started in the summer of 2000 and 30 different embroideries were exhibited in a street show in Belgrade, a week before the September elections that voted Milosevic out. Posters of the embroidery '10 with Onions, 10 with Troubles' – an elaborate and beautiful way of stating '10 years of sheer hell' – were distributed during the 5 October demonstrations and revolution in Belgrade.

1

Тамо далеко, више нема нико!

2 'There, Far Away, No One Else Can Stay', a 'before' and 'after' image with text from a Serbian World War I song. From the New Embroideries project by Skart, Belgrade 2000. Embroidery by Borka Ciganovic (65), refugee from Krajina, Croatia. Photograph by Andreja Leko.

3 Work in progress: Svetlana Lacic (36), single mother refugee from Kosovo and her son. From the New Embroideries project, Skart, Belgrade 2000.

4 'If I Say It's Darkness, Darkness Will Eat Me Away. While Embroidering Pretty Flowers, Forever Safe I Will Stay.' From the New Embroideries project by Skart, Belgrade 2000. Image and embroidery by Milka Orlic (68), mother of a 'missing person', and a refugee from Kosovo. Photograph by Andreja Leko.

Overleaf 'Meanwhile', poster created in aid of Kosovo refugees (showing a Kosovo refugee camp in Macedonia). Designed by Nicholas Blechman, Christoph Niemann and Paul Sahre. USA 1999.

Ako kažem da je mrak, poješće me mrak, zato vezem lepo cveće pojesti me niko neće

MEAN

Deserted Kosovar refugee camp, Macedonia. Call: 1 (800) HELP-NOW

WHILE

1–6 Logos created at various points in Radio B92's turbulent history:
(1) First Radio B92 logo by Slavimir Stojanovic.
(2) B92 was ousted from its offices in March 1999, and its frequency and name taken over by the state. The station resurfaced on a different frequency and in different premises later that year under the name B2-92, using this logo designed by Sinisa Rogic.
(3) Logo used for the Free B92 campaign after the state takeover. Design by Sinisa Rogic and Olivera Batjic.
(4) Another logo used for the Free B92 campaign after state takeover. Design by Sinisa Rogic.
(5) Redesign of the Free B92 logo for use by the post-revolution Radio B92, back on its original frequency. By Sinisa Rogic. 2000.
(6) Logos for B92.Net and TV B92. 2001.

Resistance in Belgrade: Radio B92

Radio B92, the voice of underground resistance in Belgrade, has become legendary for its show of defiance when Milosevic was tightening his grip on independent media; for its eclectic mix of alternative music along with news, political satire and pranks; for its role as a central hub for anti-war, anti-nationalist and other campaigns and publishing experiences; and for its sheer will to survive. It was shut down—not once, but four times in a decade, and never failed to bounce back.

Founded in 1989 at a time when Milosevic's repressive media policies were just starting to kick in, Radio B92 embarked on a turbulent decade, steered by editor-in-chief Veran Matic. Along with a challenging music policy that incorporated cutting edge sounds from grunge to hardcore hip hop, Radio B92 also had an ultimately serious mission: to produce news bulletins that told 'the truth' about what was really happening in Serbia (and in its surrounding wars) and broadcast them throughout Serbia and the world. It remained true to this mission, pioneering the use of the internet to combat media repression. When faced with shutdown, it made its news bulletins available via the internet and a satellite link. During the time of the NATO air strikes on Belgrade, B92 was shut down but its news bulletins were on the website in English and Serbo-Croat, receiving over a million hits per day.

The most comprehensive survey of B92's history is Matthew Collin's book *This is Serbia Calling* (2001), a highly readable account of what was happening to ordinary people in Belgrade while their leaders were wreaking havoc. It builds up a picture of how dangerous B92 really was to the authorities, containing an account, for example, of how an editor at a TV station in Eastern Serbia was accused of provoking unrest and sentenced to a year in prison for the crime of displaying the Radio B92 poster 'Free Press—Made in Serbia', shown here.

B92 still exists and has grown into an umbrella association of activities including radio, television, internet, film production, publishing, a music label and more—but its campaign for freedom of expression remains, in its own words, 'unshakable'.

1

B₂92

2

3

6

4

5

Resistance, the story of Belgrade
radio station B92, by journalist
Matthew Collin. Cover designed
by Keenan. Published by Serpent's
Tail, UK 2001.

8 'Free Press for Free People',
controversial poster for Radio B92
with art direction by Igor Avzner of
Focus Communications, Belgrade.
Designer Marica Kuznjecov,
photographer Nenad Kojadinovic,
copywriter Ivana Avzner.
Yugoslavia c. 1999.

Matthew Collin

THIS IS SERBIA CALLING

ROCK 'N' ROLL RADIO
AND BELGRADE'S
UNDERGROUND RESISTANCE

As heard on **B B C** RADIO 4

free press

made in serbia

1 'Human Rights Are Yours' – You too should read the full Declaration of Human Rights', one of a number of posters aimed at teenagers. It was produced at a time, around the end of the Bosnian War, when Serbian society was suffering ever greater losses of freedom and rights under Milosevic's rule. Designed by Manja Stojic and Miljenko Dereta for Civic Initiatives. Yugoslavia 1995.

2 Cardboard 'walking glasses' worn in the 1996–7 walks held by the opposition coalition, Zajedno (Together). Top: front view of one pair, bearing the word Zajedno. Middle: front view of another pair. The logo-type on the left (behind the egg) is from *Politika*, the daily state newspaper and unofficial property of Milosevic. On the right is the word *Diary*, the daily newspaper of the city of Novi Šad, next to a figure or monument known to be the symbol of Belgrade. On the far right is the word *Day*, title of another Yugoslavian newspaper. Bottom: back view of glasses.

The Yellow Revolution: Belgrade's mass protests of 1996–7

At the end of the Bosnian War, Serbia faced federal and local elections in November 1996. Although Milosevic and his wife Mira, and their respective political parties, claimed victory in the federal elections, the local elections yielded very different results. Surprisingly, they were won in many cities, certainly all major cities, by an array of oppositional parties and groups who had banded together into a coalition entitled 'Zajedno' (Together). As a quick solution to an obvious problem, Milosevic simply annulled the election results, smashing any hopes for change.

People poured out their anger in protests and demonstrations from November 1996 to March 1997. The opposition coalition Zajedno held 'walks'; students demonstrated with imaginative daily stunts and surreal spectacles; actors performed a metaphorical style of resistance theatre in the streets; and the Centre for Cultural Decontamination held performances, exhibitions and discussions. People marched in the streets blowing shrill whistles; at 7:30 in the evening for 10 to 15 minutes, leaning near open windows regardless of freezing weather, they would bang pans together in order to drown out the state news broadcast on RTS (Radio Television Serbia).

Zajedno 'walks' would noisily wind their way past targeted institutions such as the parliament building, the offices of the pro-regime daily newspaper, *Politika*, and the offices of the RTS. At one point on one of these walks, someone took out an egg and threw it at the building. For a long time afterwards, eggs were thrown at these institutions, splattering goo and eggshells everywhere in what became known as 'the yellow revolution'.

The 'walking glasses' on these pages hail from one of these colourful protests. They're a souvenir 'fun object', for the walks were to a great extent about keeping everyone's spirits up: they became a social occasion. The glasses were a call to get out and participate, making visual references to the power of the eggs (in one pair of glasses shown here, the egg on the left pushes the logo for *Politika* into the background). They also flashed their feel-good colours, as if to say 'put on your shades, and walk out in style – it's cool to be against the government'.

In early 1997, Milosevic clamped down on protests and ugly scenes developed where protesters were assaulted by police and with water cannon. Milosevic was eventually forced to accept the results of the local elections. But by June 1997 the opposition coalition Zajedno was collapsing and in July Milosevic acquired the new title of President of Yugoslavia. In a pattern familiar throughout much of the 1990s, mass protests brought first hope and then frustration and disillusionment as the regime remained unscathed. Their time had not yet come. But the mass protests were not in vain, for out of that spirit would grow Otpor! (see page 162).

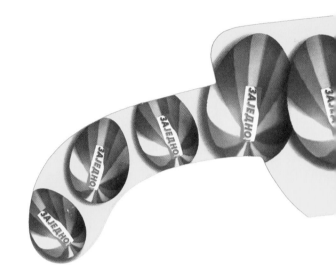

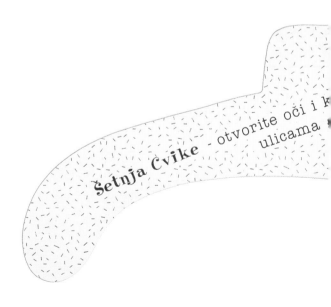

1

2

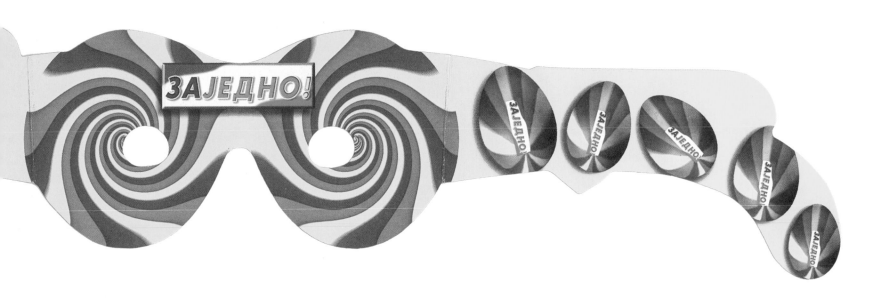

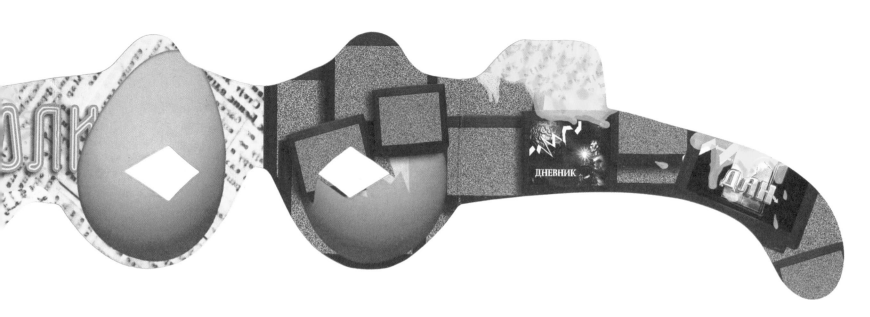

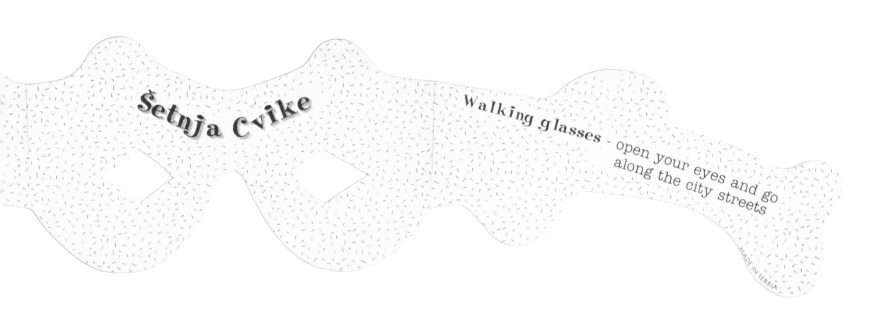

Šetnja Cvike

Walking glasses - open your eyes and go along the city streets

1 Front cover of the *New York Times Magazine* showing three members of Otpor!, 26 November 2000.

2 'Renewal!? — Stamp on the System! Long Live Resistance!', leaflet by Otpor!. The text on the image of Milosevic says 'Novi Sad' (a city in Serbia) and the date. Yugoslavia 1999.

3 'Bite the System', the first leaflet produced by Otpor!. Yugoslavia c. 1998.

4 'It's time … Resistance!', Otpor! sticker featuring the hallmark fist.

5 'Think — Resist!', leaflet by Otpor!. Yugoslavia c. 2000.

6 'Free Yourself — Resist!', leaflet by Otpor!. Yugoslavia c. 2000.

7 'Defend Yourself — Resist!', leaflet by Otpor!. Yugoslavia c. 2000.

The student resistance movement: Otpor!

Out of the spirit of the mass protests of 1996–7 grew the student movement Otpor! It was conceived in October 1998 by a group of Belgrade University students during a three-month protest that resulted in the departure of a Milosevic puppet dean and the return of purged departments and professors. Emerging victorious, Otpor! then turned its sights on Milosevic, aiming to topple him by voting him out.

The movement's youthful fearlessness and energy proved to be among its greatest weapons. Otpor! thrived as a leaderless network with an average membership age of 20. (With no leader or ringleader, the authorities never knew who to hit.) It spread like wildfire: in less than two years there were 40,000 members operating across Serbia. Its members accused Milosevic of stealing their childhood and offering them nothing but horrors and war experiences in return. Otpor! saw its mission as motivating the public to get out and vote, and it particularly targeted young people who had just reached the voting age of 18 or who felt alienated by politics.

Armed with the symbol of a clenched fist — a sign of initiative and power — Otpor! operated a marketing strategy which was strong, sophisticated and corporate in appearance. Its authoritative white lettering on black and the heavy use of the fist symbol on everything from flags and T-shirts to matchboxes exuded the confidence of a campaign that could not fail. Its first leaflet, entitled 'Bite the System', was a powerful introduction to a body of graphics that conveyed a heavy sense of theatre and drama.

Appropriately, another of its chief weapons was a sense of humour and of the absurd. Otpor! combated people's fear of the regime through jokes, little mocking protests and absurdist performances, bearing such titles as 'Hey Chief, when are you going to the Hague?', a mock-birthday celebration where protesters (2,000 of them in the town of Nis) got the chance to convey their sarcastic best wishes to Milosevic on a big birthday card. A sign that Otpor! was not ignored, but was instead considered deeply irritating and a real threat to Milosevic, was seen in the numbers of detentions and beatings of Otpor! members by the police — approximately 190 over six months from late 1999 to early 2000. There were many attempts to label the activists as terrorists funded by the CIA.

By the year 2000, Otpor! wished to appeal to a broader voting base and renamed itself The People's Movement, Otpor! Its most notable move was delivered with the 'He's Finished!' campaign, aimed at the federal and presidential elections on 24 September 2000. Its formula for the regime's defeat — 'Massive turnout + ballot control = victory' — did the job, and Milosevic would soon be on his way out.

1

2

Grizi Sistem

3

ВРЕМЕ ЈЕ ОТПОР!

4

МИСЛИ

ПРУЖИ ОТПОР!

www.otpor.com

5

ПРУЖИ ОТПОР!
www.otpor.com

6

БРАНИ СЕ

ПРУЖИ ОТПОР!

www.otpor.com

7

1 A member of Otpor! pins a badge on a man in the street and gains his support. Yugoslavia c. 2000.

2 Otpor! T-shirt.

3 Otpor! merchandising: mug, matchbox, badge and calendar cards. (One of the cards says 'Otpor! Until Victory!')

4 '2000 – This is the Year', poster by Otpor!. Yugoslavia 2000.

5 '"The Patriot" is Finished!', leaflet by Otpor!. ('The Patriot' was a sarcastic term for Milosevic.) Yugoslavia 2000.

6 'Mission Possible, One More Month and He's Finished!', leaflet by Otpor!. Yugoslavia 2000.

7 'He's Finished!', sticker from renowned Otpor! campaign relating to the election of 24 September 2000 in Yugoslavia.

8 'He's Finished!', Otpor!'s sticker in action, covering Milosevic's face on a poster. Yugoslavia 2000.

"ПАТРИОТА"
ЈЕ ГОТОВ!

24.09.2000.

5

24.09.2000.

MISSION POSSIBLE

JOŠ MESEC DANA
GOTOV JE!

6

ГОТОВ ЈЕ!

7

8

1,2,3 Posters from the 'target protest' on the Strike On Yugoslavia website (created by anonymous Belgraders), relating to the bombing of Belgrade and the anti-NATO demonstrations. 1999.

4,5,6 Photographs from the target protests and peace concerts in Belgrade, 28 March 1999.

7 Belgrade residents hold candles and target signs while on night watch at one of the city's main bridges (Brankov) on 7 April 1999. They are acting as a human shield to protect the bridge from NATO air strikes. Photograph by Dimitri Messinis, Associated Press. 1999.

NATO bombs Belgrade: the target protest

Five months of failed negotiations between Milosevic and NATO had allowed ethnic cleansing and carnage to run riot in Kosovo. In order to get Milosevic to withdraw his military forces from Kosovo, NATO – led by the United States – went to war with Serbia. It bombed Serbia and Serb forces in Kosovo in an air war that lasted 78 days (24 March to 9 June 1999).

The NATO air strikes started on the unprepared population of Belgrade on 24 March. Radio B92 was shut down, but continued to report the war via news programmes and public service information on its website. The people of Belgrade came out to protest against the bombings, which they viewed as an attack on them personally. They organized anti-NATO concerts in Republic Square, which were attended by thousands of people. 'An invitation from Belgrade' – a peace initiative written anonymously on behalf of the people of Belgrade – called for a stop to the demonization of the Serbs (created by 'irresponsible journalism on all sides') and was posted on the web. It called for peace and invited people to visit Belgrade and have direct contact with the people of Serbia. It also carried photos of the protests, peace concerts and a number of protest signs with targets.

While attending the Republic Square concerts, demonstrators pasted paper targets on their foreheads, their bodies, even their children – as a show of defiance to NATO. Residents on night watch even held target signs and candles in a long line of people that stretched across a bridge, thus providing a human shield to protect the bridge from NATO air strikes. In the following weeks, the target symbols kept reappearing – and gradually spread to protests as far away as Montenegro and Macedonia.

All right.
Drop those bombs.
Launch those missiles.
Let the flame be your partner
and let the flame alone be the witness
that

WE STILL LOVE YOU.

Belgrade, Serbia

TARGET

1

SAY NO! NOT NATO

TARGET

2

Mom, am I somebody's

yes
no
yes
no
yes
no

TARGET

Come to Belgrade and find out

3

4

5

6

7

1,2 'It is time for spring cleaning of Serbia for Europe – Only changes can put us back in Europe', both Cyrillic and Roman alphabet versions of an election poster (intended for towns throughout Serbia, not just Belgrade). Created by Miljenko Dereta, Ivan Valencak and Saki Marinovic of Civic Initiatives. Yugoslavia 1999.

3 'Choose the Right Thing ... Become a Citizen', poster by Miljenko Dereta, Ivan Valencak and Saki Marinovic of Civic Initiatives introducing civil rights and citizenship to young people. Yugoslavia 2000–1. The messages/labels on the products read as follows (left to right). Row 1: Equality – equally sweet; Democracy – a drink for all times and all generations. Row 2: Dialogue – you can breathe freely; Integration – a friendly touch; Professionalism – a good taste; Being a citizen – freshness in every moment; Row 3: Responsible media – keeps you awake (alert); The right to choose – without health hazards (damaging influences); Tolerance – share a bite with somebody; Freedom – high definition (sharper focus); Row 4: Responsibility – a good old recipe; The right to choose – takes all the spots away (like cleanser); Human rights – fit everyone perfectly.

4 'If Not Elections, Then What?' (a quotation from the Declaration of Human Rights is cited at the bottom); poster created by Miljenko Dereta, Ivan Valencak and Saki Marinovic of Civic Initiatives, for the elections in 2000 which started the downfall of Slobodan Milosevic. Yugoslavia 2000. Photograph by V Miloradovic.

More calls for change in Serbia: human rights, elections and reforms

When Milosevic set three levels of elections – local, federal and presidential – to take place in Serbia on 24 September 2000, the People's Movement, Otpor!, was not the only group campaigning for change.

Examples are shown here of civic awareness posters and pre-election campaign materials produced by Građanske Inicijative (Civic Initiatives) and designed by executive director Miljenko Dereta, Ivan Valencak and Saki Marinovic. Civic Initiatives is an NGO (non-governmental organization) dedicated to the democratization of Yugoslavia. It works to help Serbian society, especially young people, become aware of the role and importance of citizens' participation in the democratic process. It also conducts educational programmes on human rights and citizenship issues.

In some of the campaign materials shown, both Roman and Cyrillic alphabets were used in a broad appeal to the various ethnic groups throughout Serbia. (Cyrillic is in fact the official alphabet of Serbia. It remains the first alphabet that many children learn at school and continues to be used for street names, official documents and so on. Both alphabets were accepted when Serbia became part of Yugoslavia. Cyrillic has also been exploited by the nationalists and is at times marked with nationalistic associations.)

Advertisements are shown on page 171 that call for political and economic reform. They were created by Igor Avzner of Focus Communications, based in Belgrade, for G17 Plus – a group of respected Serbian economists. Avzner was also responsible for the controversial 'Free Press – Made in Serbia' poster for Radio B92, shown on page 159.

The range of printed material here captures the now-or-never call for change which would eventually vote Milosevic out on 24 September. It would also spur on the force of popular resistance that would help to topple him from power in early October.

1

2

3

AKO NE IZBORI ONDA ŠTA?

"Volja naroda je osnova državne vlasti: ova volja treba da se izražava na povremenim i slobodnim izborima, koji će se sprovoditi opštim i jednakim pravom glasa, tajnim glasanjem ili odgovarajućim postupkom kojim se obezbeđuje sloboda glasanja"

"UNIVERZALNA DEKLARACIJA O LJUDSKIM PRAVIMA" član 21/3

4

7–10 Four instalments from a pre-election 2000 newspaper ad campaign for G17 Plus, created by Igor Avzner of Focus Communications, Belgrade. Yugoslavia 2000.
(7) 'We Are for Radical Reforms' (the man says: 'So Am I').
(8) 'We Are for Collaboration with Europe' (crowd: 'So Am I').
(9) 'We Are for Freedom of the Media' (crowd: 'So Am I').
(10) 'There Are More and More of Us on the Same Side – Vojislav Kostunica – President of Yugoslavia'.

7

8

9

10

1 'We Want Peace', sticker. Israel 1993.

2 Front page of one of Israel's main newspapers *Yedioth Ahronoth* (Latest News) showing the handshakes on the White House lawn between Israeli premier Yitzhak Rabin and PLO leader Yasser Arafat (with Bill Clinton) that accompanied the signing of the Oslo Peace Accords of 1993. The graffiti that mars the photograph is a sad premonition of violent future developments. (The PLO is the Palestine Liberation Organization.)

3 'Peace Agreement', poster by Dan Reisinger, which refers to the signing of a peace agreement between Israel and Jordan. Israel 1994.

4 'Talk Peace with the PLO Now', poster and logo designed by David Tartakover, issued by the Israeli peace organization Peace Now. Israel, early 1990s.

Tensions within Israel: the delicate balance of peace

Although the early 1990s seemed to bring a glimmer of hope for peace in the Israeli–Palestinian conflict, it was not to last.

The ratification of the Oslo Peace Accords of 1993 marked the beginning of a negotiated peace process. US President Bill Clinton slipped into the role of peace-broker; handshakes were exchanged on the White House lawn; and the Nobel peace prize was awarded to Yasser Arafat, Yitzhak Rabin and Shimon Peres. But as the decade moved on, events conspired nearly to destroy the peace process. One early tragic development, for example, was the assassination in 1995 of Prime Minister Yitzhak Rabin, respected to a great extent by both sides.

A strong peace movement has been present throughout, supported by the work of groups such as Peace Now, Gush Shalom (Israeli Peace Bloc), Yesh Gvul (There is a Limit)—active in support of the 'refuseniks' or soldiers who refuse to serve in the Occupied Territories—the international Women in Black and others. Their efforts have been made all the more difficult by escalating violence, suicide bombings by Palestinian and other militant groups, and lack of political or diplomatic solutions. As the new century dawned, diplomacy gave way to what some viewed as a showdown between Yasser Arafat, leader of the Palestinian Authority, and Ariel Sharon, hard-line Israeli Prime Minister—while the people of both sides feared for their national survival, and the killing went on.

The difficult progress of the Israeli peace movement, as well as some of its more hopeful moments, can be followed by viewing some of the posters and graphics shown here. In a region renowned for its tradition of poster art, a wide range of Israeli graphic designers have made momentous graphic pleas for peace. The prolific Israeli designer David Tartakover chose to focus on political issues over the years and has self-published a large number of posters on matters of personal concern which have achieved international renown. He designed the logo for the Peace Now movement in the 1970s, and since then has produced powerful graphics that often question and confront the actions of the state, and always call for all people within Israel to live together in peace.

Yossi Lemel has also grown to be a central figure in Israeli, and international, political poster art with his equally prolific turnout of work. If Tartakover's posters derive their strength from the use of Jewish cultural symbols and traditions, Lemel's posters extract their provocative force from manipulation of the signs and symbols of the here-and-now (such as the indignity of UN forces in the Balkans depicted as a tortoise squirming on its back; see page 119). They also bear the hallmark of beautifully polished still photography, used to make stunning images with often controversial political messages.

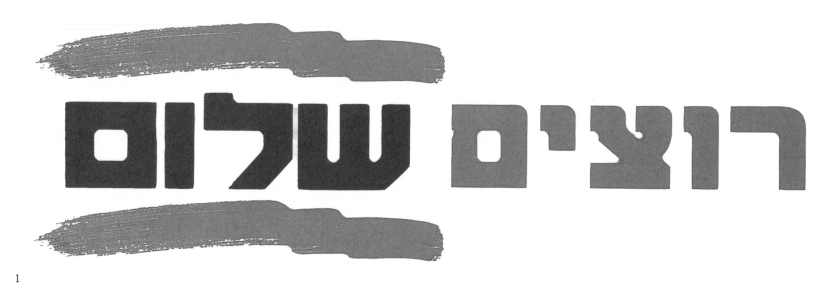

1

2

3

4

5 Poster by Yossi Lemel
commenting on the continuing
breakdown of the peace process.
Israel 2000.

6 David Tartakover's despairing
New Year's card for 2003, in which
the *sabra* (cactus) takes on the
appearance of a skeleton or demon
during a long period of continued
violence and suicide bombings.

7 'Bring the Settlers Home',
self-published poster by David
Tartakover stating that Jewish
settlers should leave the Occupied
Territories (areas disputed as
Palestinian). Israel 2000.

8 A Palestinian boy rides past
intifada graffiti in Jabalia refugee
camp in the Gaza Strip, 2003.
Photograph by Ahmed Jadallah,
Reuters.

9 Posters demonizing Yasser Arafat
as a negotiating partner for peace.
Israel 2001.

5

2003 - ANOTHER HAPPY NEW FEAR

DAVID TARTAKOVER - TEL AVIV

6

BRING THE SETTLERS HOME

7

8

9

1 Front cover of the 1996 book *Both Sides of Peace: Israeli and Palestinian Political Poster Art*. Book design by Dana Bartelt, USA, cover design by Yossi Lemel, Israel. Each *sabra* (cactus, symbolic of the area) is tied to the other by strings the colour of the Palestinian and Israeli flags. The closer they get, the more they hurt each other. Published by the Contemporary Art Museum, Raleigh/University of Washington Press.

2 'Roots', poster by Ben-Ami Ratinsky. The Israeli flag is used to express the idea that although the state of Israel was declared in 1948, its roots reach back thousands of years. Israel 1991. From the book *Both Sides of Peace.*

3 *The Visitor*, a painting of the daughter of a Palestinian prisoner, by Palestinian artist Issa Abeido. The painting has coded meanings: the girl acts as a reminder of those held in Israeli prisons; her pendant bears an image of the Dome of the Rock (a symbol of unity for Palestinians); and the grapes in the background say she is from Hebron. Probably reproduced as a poster or postcard. From the book *Both Sides of Peace.*.

Tensions within Israel: posters of peace and violence

In 1996 designer Yossi Lemel was one of the driving forces, along with US writer, designer and curator Dana Bartelt, of a book and exhibition project entitled *Both Sides of Peace: Israeli and Palestinian Political Poster Art*. In this project, poster art was collected and displayed from both sides of the conflict, with accompanying explanation of the context, the symbolism and the motives behind the imagery produced by both sides. Its very production was a feat of logistics and understanding for that point in time, and its continuing relevance remains undiminished. Four curators were involved: Dana Bartelt of New Orleans, Yossi Lemel of Tel Aviv, Sliman Mansour of East Jerusalem and Fawzy El Emrany of Gaza City. The book is certain to provide a cultural learning aid for designers and others for many years to come.

As time has moved on the situation involving 'both sides' has dramatically worsened, as graphically described in Yossi Lemel's poster 'Bloodbath' (opposite), an image of common humanity and destruction. It relates to the cycle of violence, enveloping both Israelis and Palestinians, that was prompted by suicide bombings carried out by Palestinian and other militant groups in 2002–3. The title 'Bloodbath' can be taken to simply mean 'massacre'. But Lemel himself suggests further interpretations. The first is that of suicide (cutting one's wrists in the bath), as if both sides are committing suicide together. In a second, the bathtub is roughly the shape of Israel, and they are all bleeding into Israel together. In a third, the bathtub is reminiscent of a morgue where all will end up on a cold slab, with dripping drains and cold, hard surroundings. It remains an intense and harsh statement from a country that desperately needs to find its way to peace.

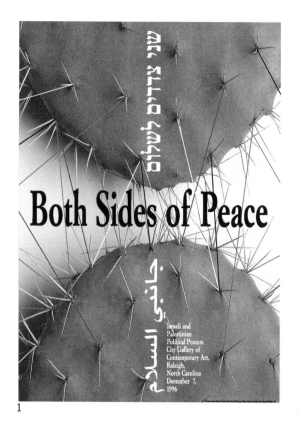

1

2

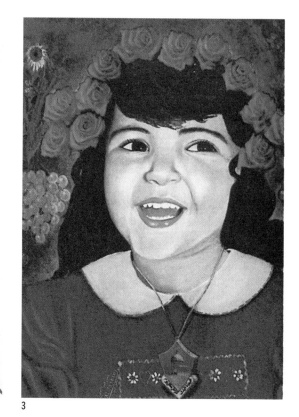

3

ISRAEL PALESTINE
ישראל פלשתין 2002

Yossi Lemel

4

1 Rabin Memorial: a spontaneous show of graffiti, paintings and other statements of respect which appeared at the site of Rabin's assassination in Tel Aviv in 1995. Photograph by Sandra Jacobs.

2 'We'll Never Forget and We'll Never Forgive', poster by David Tartakover, commemorating the second anniversary of Prime Minister Yitzhak Rabin's assassination. Israel 1997. Photograph by Gadi Dagon, and of Netanyahu by Chen Mika.

3,4,5 'The Murder of PM Yitzhak Rabin: 2000', three posters by Israeli designer Yossi Lemel, created in 2000 to commemorate Rabin's murder in 1995. (3) shows the *sabra* (cactus) used as a symbol for 'the ultimate Israeli' (Lemel's words); (4) shows the bottom of a bullet; (5) shows a *yarmulka* to symbolize the murderer, Yigal Amir.

6 'United Colors of Netanyahu', poster by David Tartakover, referring to Binyamin Netanyahu, Prime Minister of Israel 1996–9. Israel 1998. Photograph by David Karp.

Tensions within Israel: the assassination of Yitzhak Rabin

The moderate Israeli Prime Minister Yitzhak Rabin was assassinated by Israeli extremist Yigal Amir in 1995, more or less bringing an end to hopes of strengthening the peace process at that time. Although Rabin was considered by some factions to be 'selling out' to the Palestinian Authority, he was widely respected. A spontaneous reaction to his death occurred in the area where he was killed in Tel Aviv – Israelis covered all the concrete walls of the site with graffitied messages of love and respect (below). His memorials, including poster commemorations, have been many over the years.

A different type of comment is reserved for Rabin's elected successor Binyamin Netanyahu (Prime Minister, 1996–9), known to have an extreme disregard for the peace process and an aggressive attitude towards the idea of an independent Palestinian state. David Tartakover's commemoration of Rabin's assassination plainly contrasts the two men. His Benetton pastiche, however, looks more at the neuroses that may prevail when violence breeds ever more violence. Netanyahu is shown with enough bodyguards or 'suits' to fill a fashion catalogue, with far-reaching implications for society if it doesn't work for peace.

1

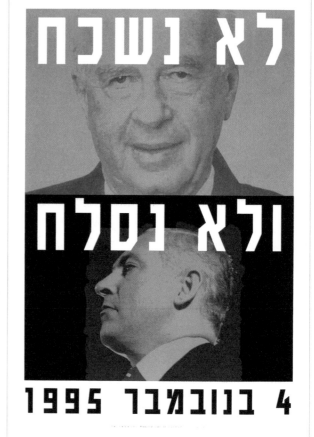

2

176

3

4

5

UNITED COLORS
OF NETANYAHU.

6

Zimbabwe's elections: the Graphic Commentaries and Shango

Zimbabwe approached the new century in an atmosphere of violence and intimidation, largely due to the power politics of President Robert Mugabe and his ruling party, Zanu-PF. In the countdown to the year 2000 elections, renowned graphic designer Chaz Maviyane-Davies embarked on '30 days of graphic activism'. At a rate of one or more images per day, he produced around 50 Graphic Commentaries – electronic poster images – emailed daily to individuals and civic rights groups around the world. They were accompanied by Maviyane-Davies's written texts, many quotations and African proverbs, links to additional sites such as the Save Zimbabwe site containing a petition to the UN to mediate the elections, as well as a comic strip entitled *Shango*.

As part of the same call for solidarity, a request was made by Maviyane-Davies to graphic designers around the world to send images and join in the creation of an agitprop exhibition/website based on the theme of freedom of expression. The cyberspace exhibition, called 'Agitnet' (www.article7.org), was launched on Africa Day, 25 May 2000, and eventually housed all of the Graphic Commentaries. This daily barrage of emails and websites produced a rolling powerhouse of information, graphics, discussion and solidarity – all designed to chronicle and highlight the issues, power abuses and realities prevalent in Zimbabwe at that time.

In the end, the ruling party prevailed, and the atmosphere in the country grew steadily worse. Less than a year later Maviyane-Davies felt it necessary to take his family abroad and took up an educational position in the United States. But in the run-up to the next general election in March 2002, Maviyane-Davies decided to undertake a further 30-day 'marathon of activism', as Zimbabwe faced yet another election plagued by intimidation, a flawed electoral process and, by all accounts, a terrorized opposition. This month of activism was called 'The Portal of Truth' and was again accompanied by writings, letters and the comic strip *Shango*.

This constant flow of imagery and text over the internet generated an overwhelming response and messages of solidarity from around the world – a model of hope and faith in the future, despite the inevitable disappointment of the election outcome. The comic strip *Shango* made a substantial contribution to the momentum of the marathon. Its main character represents an uncontrollable force – both good and evil. Here *Shango*'s artist and writer Ken Wilson-Max tells the story of the comic (in 2002):

'There are many accounts of the life and death of this Yoruba King and god, the "God of Thunder". He was a complex man, equally good and bad in many respects and he seemed the ideal character to attempt to put the awful situation in Zimbabwe and Africa into perspective.

'*Shango* was inspired by real events, reports from newspapers, opinions and the word on the street that came to me in the four-week period leading up to the voting. The daily strip was to be optimistic, to help get people to vote. This was the most difficult thing to do because things weren't (and aren't) optimistic at all. Eventually though, I read about ordinary people who were prepared to risk their lives to vote for change and this became the underlying theme of *Shango*: that people can make a difference if and when they are ready. And that their choice should not be guided by tradition, nor should it be forced by the powers that be.'

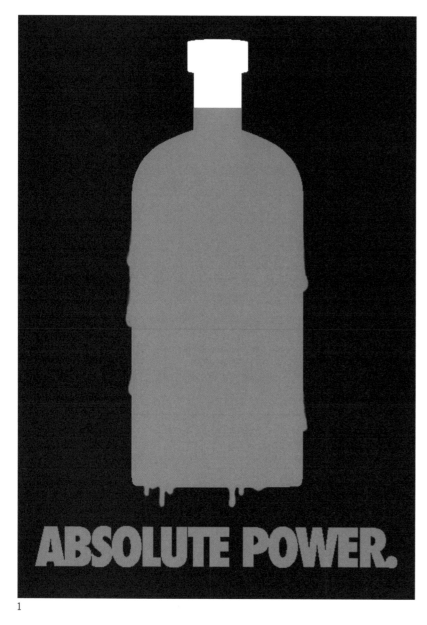

1

2

3 Episode One of the comic strip *Shango* by Ken Wilson-Max, in which Shango is introduced as a shadowy figure in the background. This and further instalments accompanied the Graphic Commentaries prior to the June 2000 elections.

4,5 *The Return of Shango*, Ken Wilson-Max's comic strip returns to accompany the second 30-day 'marathon of activism' on the internet created by Chaz Maviyane-Davies and entitled 'The Portal of Truth', 2002.

6,7 Two electronic posters from 'The Portal of Truth', by Chaz Maviyane-Davies, 2002. They protest against intimidation surrounding the 2002 elections and other developments in Zimbabwe.

THE RETURN OF SHANGO

TWO YEARS HAVE PASSED. ALL OVER THE LAND THERE IS
DEATH AND DESTRUCTION. THE EMPEROR, ONCE WEAK, IS NOW
STRONGER THAN EVER. AND DETERMINED TO MAKE HIS PEOPLE
PAY FOR TURNING AGAINST HIM.
HE HAS FOUND A WAY TO STAY STRONG AND TO SUSTAIN HIS
ADDICTION TO POWER. IN HIS INNER SANCTUM HE HAS
INVENTED A MACHINE THAT SUCKS THE LIFE FORCE OUT OF THE
PEOPLE, MAKING HIM STRONGER.
THE PEOLE CALL OUT TO SHANGO, AND SHANGO HAS NOT COME...

BUT HE AND HIS AXE ARE THERE...

11 September 2001 and beyond: US popular art and graphics

The tragedy of 9/11 – when two jets flew into the twin towers of the World Trade Center, another into the US Pentagon and still another crashed in Pennsylvania – lingers on in the imagery created at the time, as well as the actions undertaken since. The images on this spread, many of which were collected in New York six months after the event, still show signs of a traumatized city and nation.

Also still very much in evidence were comic renditions of heroes. Comic book artists were quick to honour the courage of firefighters and other public servants as well as of the public itself, with comic art renditions of scenes from the events displayed in an exhibition presented by the NYC Comic Book Museum. 'Tribute' comic books were created, with collections of pieces from many different comics artists, providing poignant personal stories and reactions to

the events, and raising money for relief funds and other charities. In a land where comics are arguably the most important popular art form – and comic superheroes a vital part of growing up – it seems understandable that such imagery should provide a lasting memory of 9/11, and an important focal point for intense emotions and personal and collective grief.

OSAMA BIN LADEN

$5,000,000

REWARD

WANTED
DEAD OR ALIVE

The Unthinkable

New York, September 11th, 2001

ATTACK ON AMERICA
September 11th, 2001

WE WILL BE STRONGER

New York, September 11th, 2001

GONE BUT NOT FORGOTTEN

The Twin Towers, New York, 11th September, 2001

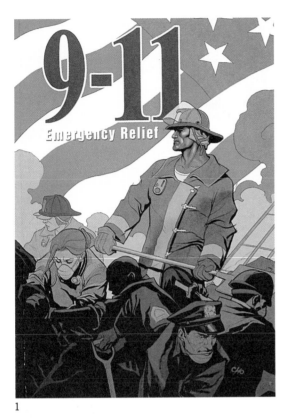

1

2

3

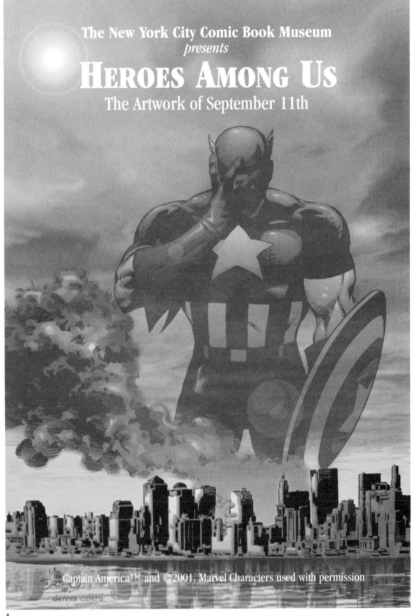

4

1,2 Stills from the flash-movie 'The Cycle of Violence', created after 11 September but before military action in Afghanistan and urging Bush to exercise sober restraint. By Free Range Graphics. USA 2001.

3,4 Stills from the flash-movie 'Protect Civil Liberties', which cautions against taking new, post-9/11 security measures too far. By Free Range Graphics. USA 2001.

5 'Bitter Pill', poster by art activist collaborative THINK AGAIN (D Attyah and S A Bachman). USA 2001.

6 'Innocent', poster by THINK AGAIN. USA 2001.

7 'How to Build a War Machine', poster by THINK AGAIN. USA 2001.

8 'Documentation: Protestgraphics by THINK AGAIN', protest in San Francisco against military action in Afghanistan. USA 2001.

11 September 2001 and beyond: calls for restraint

In the weeks and months following 9/11, notions of retaliation began to appear in the form of the Bush administration's global War on Terrorism, as well as fear of attacks on Arab and Muslim Americans. Calls for restraint began to emerge. THINK AGAIN, a US art activist collaborative founded by D Attyah and S A Bachman, produced no-cost demo graphics for activists' use in protesting against such retaliation, including the impending war in Afghanistan in 2001. In their words, they 'use images to challenge indifference' and have designed and distributed over 50,000 posters and postcards since 1997 on a wide range of political issues, from economic inequality to the relationship between television networks and the CIA, as well as creating major public actions or simply handing out postcards in the street. Their material is very powerful and very direct – when they say 'challenge the prevailing narrative' on their website, they mean it.

Other post-9/11 projects shown here include work from the US design studio Free Range Graphics – another important web presence – which has produced short flash-movies on themes such as the need to exercise restraint (and avoid military action) and the protection of civil liberties, endangered if security measures introduced after 9/11 go too far.

Protests against the war in Afghanistan took place around the world. Interestingly, a visit to the Indymedia website at the time showed an extraordinary number of protests taking place which never actually made it into mainstream news media.

1

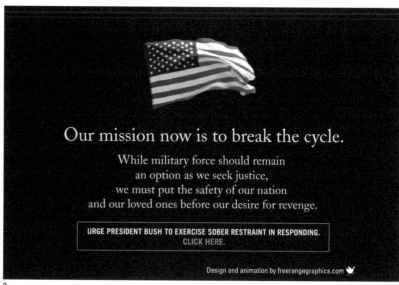

2

3

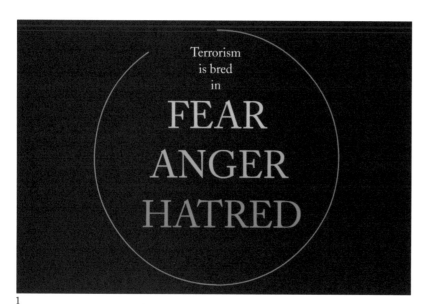

4

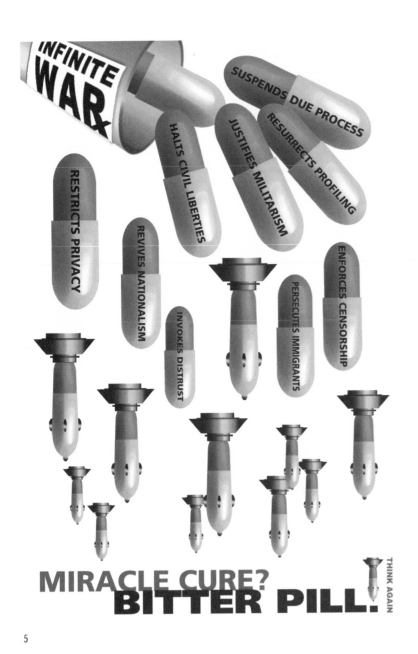

5

6

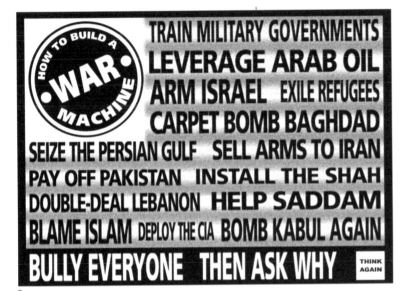

7

8

1 Anti-war protesters gather in London at the start of the history-making demonstration held on 15 February 2003 against the impending US/UK-led war on Iraq. Photograph by Peter Macdiarmid, Reuters.

2 'Make Tea Not War', poster from the 15 February march, aimed at Prime Minister Tony Blair. Created by members of Karmarama, a London advertising and design agency. UK 2003.

11 September 2001 and beyond: the war in Iraq

The next stage in the War on Terrorism was to bring even greater protest from around the world. On 15 February 2003 more than a million people protested in the streets of London against an American/British-led war on Iraq – the biggest demonstration in UK history. At the same time around the globe, millions marched in more than 300 cities and more than 60 countries, blaming the US and UK leaders (Bush and Blair), the politicians and the oil industry for the impending conflict.

When the war in Iraq finally took place, the military combat operations only lasted from March to May 2003. But subsequent attempts to rebuild the country and create a lasting peace saw Coalition troops, as well as UN staff, aid workers and Iraqi civilians attacked and bombed by resistance fighters. More US and UK troops died in the six months following the end of the declared war than during it.

The lasting graphic image of the war became the pack of playing cards issued by the US military to their troops in Iraq in April 2003 so that they could recognize targeted members of Saddam Hussein's regime, both during the military phase of the war and after. In the months that followed the war, the playing cards became a reminder that some of the personalities pictured still remained at large, and the playing card format was appropriated by those determined to keep questioning the political justification of the war.

The deposed Saddam Hussein, in hiding for eight months after the war, was finally captured in December 2003 by Coalition troops.

1

MAKE TEA NOT WAR

KARMARAMA

1 'Regime Change Begins At Home', a selection from a set of playing cards designed by Noel Douglas and produced by Bookmarks in response to the 'Iraqi Most Wanted' playing cards (see below). According to the creators, they show 'our most un-wanted individuals and organizations – the warmongers and profiteers within our own countries' who pose a threat to global peace and security. The title was a popular slogan of the anti-war movement. UK 2003.

2 'Iraqi Most Wanted', a selection from a reproduction pack of the playing cards issued by the US military to their troops as a means of recognizing the 52 'most wanted' Iraqi personalities in the War in Iraq. Created by The USA Playing Card Company. USA 2003.

A♠
GEORGE W BUSH
aka "Dubya"
President of the United States
"This is still a dangerous world. It's a world of madmen and uncertainty, and potential mental losses."

A♣
TONY BLAIR
aka "Bomber Blair"
British prime minister
"It's worse than you think. I really do believe in it" —on the neo-liberal project of New Labour.

A♦
JAMES D WOLFENSOHN
President of the World Bank
"20 million people are not going to get out of poverty"—explaining why the bank should focus on other issues.

K♥
ROBERT MALLETT
Senior VP Pfizer
"We do pricing by markets." Generic AIDS drug—30 cents. Pfizer equivalent—$1.70.

Q♠
DONALD RUMSFELD
US Secretary of Defense
"It has nothing to do with oil, literally nothing to do with oil." But then again... "In wartime, truth is so precious that she should always be attended by a bodyguard of lies" (quoting Churchill).

Q♥
ANDRÉ CALANTZOPOULOS
President and CEO of Philip Morris International
One of the world's largest tobacco corporations. #1 contributor to the US federal election. $5 billion annual profit. 3 million people die every year from tobacco-related illnesses.

9♠
CONDOLEEZZA RICE
US National Security Advisor
"The idea that you have to wait to be attacked to deal with a threat seems to us simply to fly in the face of common sense."
A former Chevron Oil executive so popular with the industry she had a supertanker named after her!

9♦
SIR PHILLIP WATTS
CEO Shell Oil
Shell is responsible for serious human rights abuses in Nigeria, arming and aiding the Nigerian military who executed environmental activist Ken Saro-Wiwa. Shell is now another key beneficiary of the war in Iraq.

8♦
LEE RAYMOND
CEO Exxon Mobil
"Unworkable, unfair and ineffective"—Raymond on Kyoto. Esso US federal election campaign contributions—$1.376 million (91% Republican, 9% Democrat). The US pulled out of the Kyoto protocols following George Bush's election.

4♠
HENRY KISSINGER
Former US Secretary of State
"The illegal we can do right now— the unconstitutional will take a little longer."

3♣
JOSÉ AZNAR
President of Spain
'Opportunists' and 'rancid isolationists'—Aznar describing his critics, while only 4% of the Spanish population backed his pro-war stance.

2♣
WERNER WENNING
CEO Bayer AG
Bayer manufactured chemical weapons throughout the 20th century. It held the patent and made huge profits from the anti-anthrax drug Cipro during the anthrax scare in the US.

1

A♠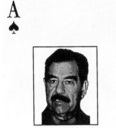
SADDAM HUSAYN AL-TIKRITI
President

A♣
QUSAY SADDAM HUSAYN AL-TIKRITI
Special Security Organization (SSO) Supervisor/Ba'th Party Military Bureau Deputy Chairman

A♥
UDAY SADDAM HUSAYN
National Assembly Member/ Olympic Chairman/ Saddam Feyadeen Chief

K♠
ALI HASAN AL-MAJID AL-TIKRITI
Presidential Advisor/ RCC Member

Q♥
BARZAN ABD AL-GHAFUR SULAYMAN MAJID AL-TIKRITI
Special Republican Guard Commander

Q♦
MUZAHIM SA'B HASAN AL TIKRITI
Air Defense Forces Commander

J♠
IBRAHIM AHMAD ABD AL-SATTAR MUHAMMAD AL-TIKRITI
Iraqi Armed Forces Chief of Staff

J♠
RAFI ABD AL-LATIF TILFAH AL-TIKRITI
Director of General Security (DGS)

9♦
TAHA MUHYI AL-DIN MARUF
Vice President RCC Member

8♠
TARIQ AZIZ
Deputy Prime Minister RCC member

8♣
WALID HAMID TAWFIQ AL-TIKRITI
Governor of Basrah Governorate

7♣
ZUHAYR TALIB ABD AL-SATTAR AL-NAQIB
Director of Military Intelligence (DMI)

7♦
AMIR HAMUDI HASAN AL-SADI
Presidential Scientific Advisor

6♠
AMIR RASHID MUHAMMAD AL-UBAYDI
Presidential Advisor/ Oil Minister

6♦
SABAWI IBRAHIM HASAN AL-TIKRITI
Presidential Advisor

5♠
HUDA SALIH MAHDI AMMASH
WMD Scientist/ Ba'th Party Regional Command Member

5♣
BARZAN IBRAHIM HASAN AL-TIKRITI
Presidential Advisor

4♥
HUMAM ABD AL-KHALIQ ABD AL-GHAFUR
Minister of Higher Education and Scientific Research

2

3

3 Anti-war poster by Micah Ian Wright commenting on alleged attempts by the Bush administration and mainstream media to stop debate on the necessity for war in Iraq, as well as misrepresenting the level of opposition waged by the anti-war movement. It is a reworked version of a British World War II poster (1942), artist unknown. It said 'Someone Talked! – [newspaper text] US Ship Sunk By …', warning of the damage the public could do by voicing or passing on information that could be acquired by spies. USA 2003.

4 Stop the War Coalition activists carry posters for use in demonstrations during the Hutton inquiry into the death of government scientist Dr David Kelly (chief advisor in the field of weapons of mass destruction) and more broadly, the government's justification of the war. The politicians pictured are, from left to right: Geoffrey Hoon, Secretary of State for Defence; Jack Straw, Foreign Secretary; and Tony Blair, Prime Minister. UK 2003. Photograph by Mykel Nicolaou.

4

1 One of ten posters created as part of a new collaboration between FIFA and UNICEF — featuring photographs of children playing football over four continents. Designed by Browns. UK 1999.

2 Logo for Witness, the organization that helps activists record human rights abuses and bring perpetrators to justice. Designed by Chiat Day. USA 1992.

3 This image by Physicians for Human Rights/Witness is used in information booklets describing the work of Witness. It is a video still showing the exhumation of a mass grave site near a church and surrounding sites in Kibuye, Rwanda, June 1996 — and recalling the genocide that took place in that country in 1994 which left up to one million people dead. Physicians for Human Rights is an organization that uses the medical and forensic sciences to investigate and prevent human rights abuse. USA 1996.

Hope for the future: facing up to history

After viewing many images relating to war, it helps to know that efforts are always being made to bring respect to victims of the past, help to those endangered in the present, and hope to those facing the future. Two graphic images of hope are offered here.

The first is from a series of 10 posters designed by Browns design studio, London, in 1999, to promote and celebrate a new relationship formed between FIFA (the Fédération Internationale de Football Association, which runs the World Cup competition) and UNICEF (the United Nations Children's Fund). Produced in five languages and distributed to over 60 countries for use in schools, hospitals, government offices and conferences, the series shows children playing football in varying situations across four continents. The posters in the series, particularly the one shown here, show how football can lift young people out of their circumstances. This poster also hints at the ability of the young to endure, to override their war-torn circumstances and to see a bright future full of football.

The second image is one used by Witness, an organization that has used current technology to 'change the human rights landscape forever'. It was founded in 1992 by pop musician Peter Gabriel, the Lawyers Committee for Human Rights and the Reebok Foundation. (The organization was originally inspired by the amateur video footage witnessing the beating of black motorist Rodney King by four Los Angeles police officers in 1991.) Since then Witness has supplied local activists scattered around the globe in over 50 countries with the video technology and field training they need to document human rights abuses and bring such evidence to courts, governments and the attention of the world. This work takes many forms. For example, it helps activists to secure video evidence of mass graves in order to corroborate allegations of genocide. It uncovers the appalling conditions of children forced to work as cheap labour or as child soldiers. It aims to stop abusive practices or bring the perpetrators of abuses to justice — all of which can be viewed on their topical and dynamic website, www.witness.org.

Although the image shown opposite might be seen as a depressing one, it can also be read as an image of great caring, conveying the notion that if mistakes are made, if abuses take place, we care enough to try to find out what happened and to claim back the identity and the dignity of the unknown victims. It is an image about facing up to history, and about taking on responsibility for what is presently happening in the world.

2

unicef
United Nations Children's Fund
FIFA

Pure football. Pure hope.

"Sometimes we play football with the soldiers. We beat them easily. They blame their boots."
Kemal (age 10), Sarajevo

1

3

Graphics have long played a powerful role as a social tool — they raise awareness, apply a critique and ultimately provoke change. Throughout the last century traditional graphic formats, including posters, banners, pamphlets, magazines and even cartoons and comics, were used for this purpose. Other formats have been appropriated for social purposes more recently. Badges, so popular in the 1960s and 1970s for political messages, attention-grabbing jokes and bold declarations of identity, have moved in and out of fashion ever since. T-shirts, on the other hand, have ↗

never really gone away, transmitting the energy of a slogan as well as the enthusiasm of the person wearing it.

The power-position of the advertising billboard has often been appropriated for social and political purposes. Billboards were taken over by campaigns, activists and community artists in the mid-1980s as a way of subverting their position of authority and domination of the environment. Even today, corporate advertising on billboards is subjected to intervention by graffiti or subvertising, often in the name of protest. New technology has also become a substantial force for promoting social causes. Websites are used by campaigning groups for spreading the word and for organizing protests, as well as creatively by artists to explore new ways of encouraging people to engage with issues.

As well as a widening range of graphic formats, the issues themselves are subject to change and mirror current concerns. New stereotypes are challenged; old enemies such as drugs or AIDS are

Social critique and social awareness found new directions in graphic expression in the 1990s, including the use of biting satire and wildly anarchic humour.

1 'Dressing the Poor', illustration/text by James Victore, taken from *Nozone* No5, the poverty issue. USA 1993.

2 'I take one everywhere I take my penis!!', safe sex poster by Art Chantry which humorously exploits the stilted conduct and language of US authority and public service in the 1950s. USA 1996.

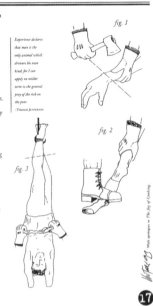

1

2

handled with ingenuity and optimism; ongoing taboos are broken; and expressions of identity and strength are reinforced.

Social critique: low-tech and high-tech

The 1990s spanned the spectrum of low-tech cut-and-paste to high-tech digital graphics, employed in social critique. Two projects are shown representing the opposite ends of a decade of technological change. Starting with the low-tech early years of the decade, *Nozone* (see pages 200–1), a sharp underground political comics-zine, was born in 1990 at the height of the conservative Bush (George, Sr) era, when protest culture in the United States seemed to be fighting against insurmountable odds. It was self-published and edited by Nicholas Blechman – aka Knickerbocker – in New York City, with each issue involving a troop of illustrators and comics contributors. Although inspired by the do-it-yourself zine culture of Punk (late 1970s and early 1980s), *Nozone* was more reminiscent of the underground press of the 1960s and early 1970s, because of its political outspokenness and its international reach. For *Nozone* made its way overseas and had an international following, despite its sporadic appearance (a year could lapse between issues) and a talent for changing its format and becoming unrecognizable.

Initially conceived as an 'ecological' comics-zine – hence the name – *Nozone*'s first eight issues appeared between 1990 and 1998. Issues covered air pollution and nature, war, utopia, poverty, crime, extremism and work. Most began with a sharply cynical word-and-image essay, and the comics content ranged from soft humour to blood-and-guts black humour to incomprehensible weirdness. It also acted as a showcase for a broad spectrum of comics and illustration talent: favourites such as James Victore and Peter Kuper could be found within its covers.

But *Nozone* was, in the end, a creature of the underground and therefore a tactile experience. The format of each issue varied radically, there was no masthead, the earliest issues felt as if they were printed on toilet paper, and various bits were stuck on by hand. By issue No 6, the paper had improved and the design was even high-tech, but it never lost its sense of fun. It remains a rare, eccentric voice of dissent from a highly conservative era in the United States.

At the end of the 1990s, a very different project used humour and new technology to explore the personal politics of poverty. Launched in 1999, 'NeedCom: Market Research for Panhandlers' (see pages 202–3) – a Web Lab project in association with PBS Online – continues to be one of the most innovative websites in turn-of-century cyberspace. Created by US artist Cathy Davies, with head writer Drew Gorry, NeedCom uses satirical humour and the corporate language of forms, polls and hyped-up ad phrases to engage us in 'market research for panhandlers' (beggars).

Visitors are drawn into the site with corporate sales-speak, then given the opportunity to check their attitudes towards panhandlers. They are invited to rate the 'sales pitch' of each of six panhandlers via an Effectiveness Survey. They proceed to additional sites and view photos of each panhandler, listen to their pitch again, examine their props (cups, crutches) and then vote on how much money to give them.

Once a visitor's vote – or virtual money contribution – is cast, they are then told how their generosity rates against other contributors to the survey. They can visit other sites to find out more about the panhandlers – their real circumstances, background history and so on – and read extensive interviews with the panhandlers themselves. According to creator Cathy Davies, 'Many of the panhandlers I interviewed were excited to talk about what they did: regarding it as a job, rather than a source of shame. I learned that most of the panhandlers' pitches were products more of necessity or habit or beliefs about poverty than tested strategy. Despite the clinical, factual questions I asked, the panhandlers often wanted to tell me about emotional and philosophical factors of their jobs.'[1]

For all its fast-talking hype drawn from the world of market research and measured responses, NeedCom is an immersive experience. The visitor interactions – polls, surveys, written responses – are all devices for the exploration of issues and attitudes. They confront us with our personal prejudices towards panhandlers and poverty in general, making us explore existing stereotypes of poverty (such as 'all panhandlers are bums or drunks' or 'why don't they get a job?'), while questioning our own daily strategies for dealing with people in poverty.

NeedCom is a true curiosity: a website that is not what it seems. Through the use of irony, satire and humour, NeedCom snares and involves its visitors in a process that makes them question attitudes and fears – and then sends them away affected or changed, and perhaps questioning their original stance. NeedCom is supported by Web Lab, a think tank that exists to encourage innovation on the web and which promotes experimental ways of using the web 'as a transformative force in people's lives and in society'.[2]

Social awareness in all shapes and sizes

The clothing retail giant Benetton brought us social awareness with retail and commercial aims attached, in the guise of a single, global brand. Oliviero Toscani's photography and creative direction produced a decade of provocative Benetton advertising, prompting some of the great image controversies of the 1990s. From 'the bloody baby' of 1991 and the death of AIDS sufferer David Kirby in 1992 to the 'Sentenced to Death' campaign in 2000 that proved to be Toscani's step-too-far, Benetton pounded the public with images that made them baulk. Discussions in the media, boycotts of shops and other protests followed. Rarely had the public become so engaged by the images around them. Editor Tibor Kalman's handling of Benetton's *Colors* magazine, issues 1 to 13 (1991–5) – a brilliant, educational and controversial approach to the project – and the sheer column inches published on Benetton imagery added to the impact and influence of Benetton's advertising on the world of graphic design and the public at large. The moral question of whether it is right to use such socially controversial campaigns to sell clothing remains an open one, to be revisited by designers and educators.

But if Benetton was the big 'social awareness' adventure of the 1990s, there were other equally adventurous small projects. The Lifeline Project in Manchester in the UK, for example, deals with the issue of drug use, and the Treatment Action Campaign in Durban, in South Africa, campaigns for affordable treatment for people in South Africa with HIV/AIDS.

If anything could be learned about approaches to the growing problem of drug abuse from UK graphic campaigns of the late 1980s, it was that broad-based public media campaigns using condemnatory tones and sensationalized scare tactics do not work – particularly on young people.

1

The government's drugs information strategy – with its ghoulish images of wasted victims or arms riddled with needle scars – probably did more to terrify parents than 'get through' to their kids. In the eyes-wide-open, sceptical climate of the 1990s, the images from those earlier campaigns, such as 'Skin Care by Heroin' showing a sore-ridden, sickly boy, were collected and treated by young people as iconic images of ridicule, to be pasted mockingly on bedroom walls.

The Lifeline Project in Manchester, by contrast, provided a graphic response to the explosion in recreational drug use in 1990s Britain. Founded in 1971 as a 'street'-based drugs charity, Lifeline has over the past decade produced publications aimed at different groups engaged in drug use, their parents or loved ones – or anyone not using drugs, but 'living in a world profoundly affected by drug use'.

It starts with the assumption that young people sitting in today's classrooms may have experimented with drugs or be taking them

regularly. Moralizing is therefore left behind. Hard information is the priority, and in a form that is not condescending or out-of-touch with 'the realities' of the young. Humorous comics are the chosen medium, because of their accessibility and acceptability.

The comics are conceived, edited and, for the most part, drawn by communications director Michael Linnell, with help from a few associates and support from a large contingent of researchers in the field. Audiences are carefully targeted and researched, on the basis that the more specific the research, the more appropriate or accurate the publication will be. Time is spent with users – their lifestyles, behaviour, patterns of speech, dress, language and even current jokes are all considered relevant. The results are analysed and then tested.

Lifeline's Publications Department has a prolific output of challenging material (good for at least four or five complaints a year in national newspapers), and they are self-financing. Describing itself as 'an independent

voice', Lifeline directly challenges the idea that behaviour can be changed through judgemental mass media campaigns.[3]

The threat of AIDS is another issue inherited from the 1980s. Late in that decade, ACT UP (see page 214) took to the streets of New York City and with powerfully visible live protests and graphic campaigns, challenged the US government and large drug companies to confront the escalating AIDS crisis in America. As well as spearheading a movement of public concern and protest, ACT UP showed the potential power of graphic design to push urgent social causes to the top of the political agenda. That power was expressed by demo posters and placards, safe sex posters, educational material and other awareness campaigns throughout Western countries and further afield.

By the mid-1990s, the West was exploring and benefiting from new drugs and treatment for the HIV virus, and being lulled into a false sense of security and complacency. Despite the continuing efforts of activists and HIV charities – still sounding alarms and continuing the fight – mainstream safe sex education began to wane. The quantity of AIDS awareness graphic propaganda in the West dwindled, amid vague assumptions that the battle was over. Meanwhile, a global disaster was brewing. By the turn of the century, AIDS was at the top of the global agenda, as the disease devastated countries in Africa, especially sub-Saharan Africa. The overall statistical

2 'Meet the Muffiosi. We Are Dyke Action Machine!', postcard by the two-person public art project known as Dyke Action Machine or DAM! (Carrie Moyer on the left, and Sue Schaffner on the right). USA 1998.

3 'We Have Brains – We Women Think Well, A Lot and Very Beautifully', poster by Margarita Sada of Las Muñequitas Contratacan (The Little Dolls Fight Back). Mexico 1997.

Racism or racist behaviour continues to be an issue in many countries of the West, often due to social problems such as unemployment or crime (blamed on ethnic minorities, immigrants or refugees) or antagonisms between other groups.

1 'RaCism', anti-racist poster by James Victore in which the word itself depicts how racial hatred can tear society apart or make it destroy itself. The poster was inspired by the race riots that broke out in Brooklyn, New York, in the summer of 1993 between Hassidic Jews and African-Americans. USA 1993.

snapshot: in December 2001, UNAIDS/WHO reported that 22 million people had died from AIDS-related diseases since its discovery about 20 years ago, with three million dying in 2000 alone. In 2001, more than 36 million were infected, 25 million of them in sub-Saharan Africa. In Botswana, 36 per cent of adults had the HIV virus; in South Africa, 20 per cent.[4]

Occasional rays of hope shine through the stories of misery and death, as defiance rises up from the streets. The Treatment Action Campaign, launched in Durban in 1998, fights for access to treatment for all South Africans with HIV/AIDS and to overcome the stigma of being HIV positive, and the attendant image of powerlessness and death. Its maximum visibility protests are directed largely at raising awareness, preventing the spread of the disease and persuading intransigent Western drug companies to bring down the price of anti-retroviral medication.

In April 2001, for example, Treatment Action Campaign was instrumental in forcing a humiliating legal climbdown by 39 of the world's largest pharmaceutical companies. Arguing an infringement of their patent rights, the drugs companies were on the brink of taking legal action against South African legislation that gave the government the right to import generic drugs at a fraction of the cost of branded drugs. In the face of international protest and damning cries of 'profits before people', they dropped the case to avoid a public relations disaster and damage to investor confidence.[5]

Treatment Action Campaign maintains its visibility through posters, pamphlets, meetings, street activism and letter writing. But in a society permeated with ignorance and fear of the disease, the T-shirt worn by

Treatment Action Campaign members – which says 'HIV Positive' – is nothing less than a badge of courage. It brings a taboo out into the open, confronts fearful truths directly in order to bring about changes in attitude, and challenges the power of the drug corporations.

Health activism and body politics continued to do battle with other stereotypes and taboos in the 1990s. Taboos surrounding breast cancer received a heavy challenge from the Fashion Targets Breast Cancer campaign. Ralph Lauren inspired the American fashion industry to launch the campaign in 1994, leading to the design of a symbolic 'target' T-shirt as a mark of support and identification. The highly successful campaign and its T-shirt crossed the ocean in 1996 to lend its support and fundraising power to Britain's Breakthrough Breast Cancer charity, aiming to raise funds for medical research. The British fashion industry rallied and since then thousands of T-shirts have been worn by high-profile celebrities, models and designers (making it a 'trendy' cause); the UK's first research centre was built and opened its doors in 1997; and the subject of breast cancer was thrown into the public domain and has been discussed openly ever since. It was a massive achievement for turn-of-century Britain, which shamefully had one of the highest mortality rates for breast cancer in the world.

Fashion politics continued to push its way into the media and battled with stereotypes of disability. Disabled actors and models (professional and not) found their way into TV commercials in the UK, and into cutting-edge fashion magazines such as *Flaunt* in the United States and *Dazed & Confused* in the UK. *Dazed & Confused* carried a high-profile

visual fashion essay in September 1998, created by fashion designer Alexander McQueen and photographer Nick Knight, which explored notions of beauty and disability – moving away from beauty as perfection to the beauty of imperfection. Compiled as a 'celebration of difference', people with different physical disabilities were chosen as models and paired with different fashion designers for customized clothing. The power of the resulting photographic essay came not only from the artistic forces at work but also from statements by the models about public attitudes and their experience of the project.

Violence, visibility and direct action

Growing occurrences of violence against babies, children and teenagers cast a heavy shadow on the 1990s. Perverse new forms of violence – such as massacres in schools or children shooting other children – have become America's new nightmare. The Columbine High School massacre in Littleton, Colorado, in 1999 (see page 210) was one example. The thoughtful graphic comments produced in response are disturbing and painful.

Equally disturbing are the skilful posters, leaflets and TV advertisements produced for campaigns against child abuse in the UK, rising to meet the heavy challenge of raising viewers' awareness and convincing them to take action. It is now recognized that child cruelty is one of the most widespread problems in the UK, with research suggesting that the greatest dangers for children are at home. A study on child deaths from abuse or neglect published by the National Society for the Prevention of Cruelty to Children (NSPCC) in 2001 cited the statistic that

1

one to two children are killed each week by parents or carers – although the reality is likely to be higher.[6]

Advertisements such as the baby injecting heroin by Bartle Bogle Hegarty, for UK charity Barnardo's, or the Saatchi & Saatchi animated cartoon child who after a beating turns back into a real child, for the NSPCC (page 212), are not going to make abusers stop their behaviour. The mission of such ads is broader – if a memorable ad raises awareness of definitions of abuse and its consequences, it may alert viewers to cases around them, and encourage them to take action or seek help.[7]

The energy that fuelled the liberation struggle for gays and lesbians was channelled into a consolidated movement of AIDS activism in the United States in the late 1980s. By the early 1990s the gay community had struck back through activist groups such as ACT UP, and would carry on fighting against the broadening global crisis. Artists such as Keith Haring (who died in 1990) and David Wojnarowicz (who died in 1992) left behind art-icons as a legacy of that time.

The 1990s was therefore about gays and lesbians making a stand for their rights, but also about pushing issues, demands and visibility further. In the United States, action against queer-bashing and other issues of survival and visibility prompted the founding of the activist groups Queer Nation (1990) and Lesbian Avengers (1992) in New York City, both using radical new protest methods such as 'kiss-ins' and flaming-torch marches;

branches of both groups popped up all over the country. In the midst of this supercharged New York atmosphere came activist art collaboration Dyke Action Machine (DAM!) – founded in 1991 by Carrie Moyer and Sue Schaffner – whose graphic campaigns and websites have used imagination and skill to promote lesbian activism and visibility for over a decade.

In the UK this radicalism came in the form of the queer rights group Outrage! (founded in 1990), who rejected the conformist politics of the mainstream lesbian and gay rights movement. Instead it engaged in 'protest as performance' including stunts such as kiss-ins, Exorcism of Homophobia and Queer Valentine's Carnival. The group's grittier actions – used to fight police harassment of gay and bisexual men from 1990 onwards – included invading police stations, busting police entrapment operations and deafening New Scotland Yard with foghorns and whistles. As a result police attitudes changed 'from persecution to protection' (against queer-bashers) and 'the number of men

convicted for consenting gay behaviour fell by two-thirds' between 1990 and 1994. Outrage! continue to claim the title of the world's longest surviving queer rights direct action group.[8]

In a broader sense, the 1990s brought a wide range of issues relating to women, such as taking back power that had been eroded by the conservatism of the 1980s, or creating a power image for a new generation of up-front feminism. It also meant asserting visibility, power and control through a wide range of media tools and direct action methods. The Women's Action Coalition or WAC (founded in 1992) in the United States focused on issues relating to women's rights – abortion, especially, alongside rape and other forms of violence against or harassment of women – by latching onto the power of mainstream media. It developed links with producers and reporters, often inviting them along to its protests, and thus appeared in newspapers, on magazine covers and on TV. It ran high-profile, multi-media protests, making use of the full range of communications technology

2 'Racism', screenprinted anti-racist poster by Lex Drewinski showing a foot stepping on a face – repeated in the colours of the German flag. Germany 1993.

3 'Immigrant', poster by Luba Lukova for the Immigrant Theatre Festival at Manhattan's Lower East Side theatre, which shows a positive image of an immigrant – not as an outsider but as one grafted to a society, soon to grow to be a part of it. USA 1997.

2

3

available at that time – from faxes and emails to telephone 'zaps' and video cameras – and of graphics for identity. If it spotted injustice in established legal or government practice, it had no qualms about confronting politicians, judges and other 'people of power' through the media.

Feminism continued to reinvent itself, communicating in media that ranged from the hand-drawn posters of Mexican designer Margarita Sada and the cartoons of UK artist Jacky Fleming to the web activities of SpiderWomen or the new technology explorations of US cyberartist and designer Diane Gromala (see pages 218–19). Examples such as these put to rest earlier notions that women were not as inclined as men towards the use of new technologies.

Women continued to create images of strength, attack age-old stereotypes and challenge new stereotypes and prejudices. In the post-9/11 climate, the veil (for example, the burqa, chador or hijab) became a powerful and potentially confusing graphic symbol with a range of meanings. It could be used to feed fears and prejudices associated with terrorism that were re-emerging at the time; it could be seen as a symbol of repression by fundamentalist regimes; or it could be a symbol of individual empowerment, commitment and religious belief. Such interpretations were present throughout much of the 1990s but became heightened by events such as the war in Afghanistan (when international forces ousted the Taliban regime in 2001) and other products of the ongoing War on Terrorism.

Racism and extremism (or fascism) have also become grave issues for twenty-first-century designers; they appear in different forms and guises from one country to another, as do protests against them (see pages 222–9). The difficulties inherent in multiracial society in the United States, for example, are highlighted in artist Aaron McGruder's controversial comic strip *Boondocks*,[9] as well as the posters of designer James Victore who has made racism one of his particular targets over the years. His bold artistic statements make uncomfortable viewing because of their directness. History and its injustices are being redressed through events such as Australia's National Sorry Day – a long overdue apology to the Aboriginal population – and renditions such as the book, *Latino USA: A Cartoon History*,[10] an account of the Latino role in US history, written by Ilan Stavans and expressed through cartoons by Lalo Alcaraz. A large number of anti-racist and anti-fascist protests and campaigns such as the Noborder Network, with accompanying websites and graphics,[11] are taking place throughout 'the New Europe', as its countries resist the mobile populations arriving at their door.

Immigrants and Euro-racism

Immigrants, migrant workers and asylum-seekers look set to be the scapegoats of the twenty-first century. In turn-of-century UK, for example, some of the tabloid media spoke of a 'crisis' attributed to the 'flood' of asylum-seekers 'invading' Britain. Such notions

seemed to be a creative product of tabloid editorials and the government's electoral worries. The reality in population terms, according to Kevin Toolis writing for the *Guardian* in May 2000, was very different. Averaging the figures for asylum applications over the four years from 1996 to 2000, it appeared that the British Home Office was asked to consider one refugee case for every 12,000 UK citizens. As there were likely to be many rejections, Toolis set the figure for successful applicants as 'probably 1 per 25,000 native head of population'.[12]

Nevertheless, this histrionic climate of 'invasion' had, and continues to have, consequences that should not be overlooked. Suspicion and blame of non-whites was enough to bring the far-right British National Party into the British political arena. In the 2001 local government elections, the northern town of Oldham saw the British National Party pick up more than 11,500 votes in its two constituencies – 16 per cent of the vote in one; 11 per cent in the other. In Burnley, a Lancashire town, it picked up 4,151 votes, or 11.2 per cent of the vote – its second best result of the election.

The reunification of Germany in October 1990 led to continuing economic and employment problems, contributing in turn to a rise in racism and nationalism, and to anger vented at migrant, refugee and immigrant populations. Germany's borders have become highly contested 'frontlines' of control, involving immigration or border police and civil disobedience campaigns.

LEX DREWINSKI

1

(The Eastern German border with Poland is said to be one of the most heavily guarded borders in the world.) Since 1998 anti-racist border camps have become an important political tool for anti-racist groups in Germany. Public actions, demonstrations and workshops are a part of these camps, drawing heavy media interest. Their aim is not only to disturb the perceived institutions of racism – such as existing deportation camps or border police – but also to draw attention to and counter everyday 'accepted' racism in German society.

Much of the work done by Berlin graphic designer and activist Sandy K (see pages 225–7 and 228–9) centres on the plight of Germany's migrant workers and immigrants, as well as confronting the culture of blame and the 'closed-borders' mentality. Prime examples are the posters he created for 'Kein Mensch ist Illegal' ('No One is Illegal'), an anti-racist campaign founded by artists, activists, radio practitioners, photographers, film-makers and others at the Documenta X exhibition in Kassel in 1997, that attempted to raise public awareness of the difficulties faced by illegal immigrants (i.e. those with no legal papers). The series of posters on pages 226–7 attempts to counter the dominant stereotype – presented by commercial media – of illegal immigrants as a large, faceless group with no individuality. Distributed throughout Germany, each poster carries an immigrant's 'story', focusing on the daily difficulties with work, health, education or just being in a public place without authorization papers.[13]

2

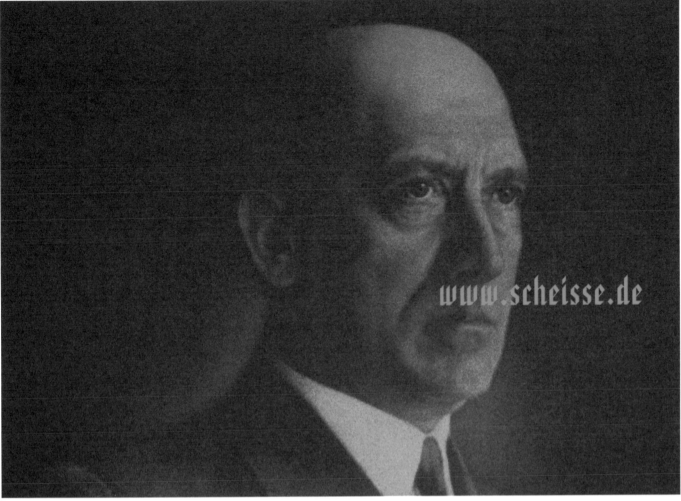

3

2 'A Job for Walter First', anti-fascist poster by Sandy K that opposes a phrase popular with neo-Nazis ('Jobs for Germans First'). Created for the elections in the county of Brandenburg, and in collaboration with anti-fascist groups in the area. Germany 1998.

3 'www.shit.de' (de is Deutschland or Germany), billboard by Uwe Loesch for the city of Mönchen-Gladbach, Germany, in protest against the propaganda put out by neo-fascists on the internet. It depicts Hitler as a modern-day skinhead. Germany 2000.

Despite social difficulties and health crises within their countries, the graphic designers of Southern Africa remained defiant and produced some of the most memorable and high-spirited graphics of the 1990s.

1 Spread from *i-jusi* No 11 (the type issue), designed by Garth Walker at Orange Juice Design. *I-jusi* magazine aimed to create a new design language inspired by 'the new South Africa'. South Africa 2000.

2 'Mandela for President', poster used extensively by the ANC (African National Congress) during the campaign for the first democratic elections in South Africa in April 1994. His victory marked the beginning of 'the new South Africa'.

Germany and the United States remain significant bases for neo-Nazi groups. In Germany estimates indicate 54,000 individuals aligned to the extreme right, compared with tens of thousands spread throughout the rest of Europe. Estimates of Americans involved suggest between 100,000 and 200,000, and the two countries run a close partnership. Despite Germany's outlawing of Nazi-inspired books, memorabilia and propaganda, such materials have been shipped from the United States to Germany for years. (In the United States they are protected by the First Amendment: Freedom of Speech.[14]) There is also a strong neo-Nazi presence on the web. According to the BBC, in December 2000 the German Interior Ministry claimed that around 800 (mainly) German-language sites were broadcasting racist and Nazi propaganda, and using the internet to circumvent German law. They also noted that 90 per cent of foreign-based neo-Nazi websites were actually set up in the United States, where – like books and memorabilia – they are protected by the First Amendment.[15] German neo-Nazi sites can be placed on American-based servers or internet providers, or German authors can simply transmit their material to American websites.

In April 2002, extreme-right-winger Jean-Marie Le Pen received a large first-round vote which carried him through to the second stage of France's two-stage presidential elections. Famous for his rants against immigrants, Le Pen and his National Front (NF) party had been a familiar but minor political presence in France for over two decades. Nevertheless, the first-round ballot victory alarmed much of Europe, even though the vote was interpreted by many to be a 'message' to the incumbent president Jacques Chirac, subject of many scandals, to clean up his act. The French took to the streets. An estimated 1.3 million people came out on May Day to protest against Le Pen. Chirac won a victory over Le Pen in the second stage vote on 6 May. But the experience left many in the European Union breathing a shaky sigh of relief – shaky because of the number of hard-right groups and leaders already in European governments. These included the Northern League (a far-right member of Silvio Berlusconi's coalition in Italy) and Jörg Haider's Freedom Party (part of the coalition government in Austria).

Linking the fears of European electorates with high levels of immigration has been one of the more successful strategies of the Right and has allowed it to gain ground over recent years. Popular resistance is answering the wake-up calls, like Le Pen's first-round victory, and creative artists and their protests remain determined to keep such forces at bay through their highly visible (and graphic) resistance. But if graphics can warn of difficulties ahead, as in the building up of a New Europe, it can also provide a call of hope from other parts of the world. Despite the devastation of AIDS and other cruelties in recent years, powerful expressions of identity and strength still emerge from Southern Africa. Designer Chaz Maviyane-Davies's 'Rights' calendar comprises dignified and proud images of African culture; *i-jusi* magazine, created by Orange Juice Design, reverberates with energy as it celebrates the visual language and vernacular graphics of post-apartheid South Africa. Both projects (pages 230–33) reflect Africa's eternal ability to bounce back, recover and find new hope and optimism.

Graphics continues to exert a powerful influence in the political realm, and its wide range of well-loved print formats are now extended and energized by the new technologies. For both are needed: banners and posters carried in the street offer raw strength and human contact; the new technologies offer global conversations and experimental opportunities for devising new ways of changing attitudes or showing defiance. The range is exhilarating: websites test our prejudices to poverty; hand-drawn cartoons rewrite history or complain about sexism; logos on T-shirts challenge taboos; planes write 'sorry' (for injustices) in the sky; computer-augmented (body) output produces morphing typefaces; SpiderWomen cruise cyberspace; posters condemn extremism; banners march against racism. This extraordinary mix of low-tech and high-tech, of old and new, has become the hallmark of twenty-first-century protest and will remain its great and enduring strength.

1 Front cover of the first issue of *Nozone*, the political comics-zine published, edited and designed by Knickerbocker (Nicholas Blechman). USA 1990.

2 Front cover of *Nozone* No 5 (the poverty issue), illustration by Mark Marek. USA 1993.

3 Back cover of *Nozone* No 5, designed by Knickerbocker. USA 1993.

4,5 Pages from *Nozone* No 5, designed by Knickerbocker. USA 1993.

Exposing truths, fighting against the odds:
***Nozone* comics-zine**

The 1990s was a groundbreaking decade for new graphic expressions in social critique and social awareness. The US underground comics-zine *Nozone*, self-published by Nicholas Blechman, was born and raised during the conservative Bush, Sr years of the early 1990s and acquired an international cult following for its political outspokenness. Its initial lifespan stretched to eight themed issues – the first was published in 1990, the last in 1998 (although it has since been resurrected) – yet it managed to rail against a large number of topics including air pollution, traffic, guns, the Gulf War, poverty, crime, extremism and the police.

Inspired by Punk's do-it-yourself culture, *Nozone* defied all corporate notions of identity or brand recognition. The format and style varied; the size varied; the title and the magazine itself were often hard to find. A different group of comics artists and illustrators filled each issue, and *Nozone*'s content was dynamic and varied. Doses of acerbic wit gave it political urgency. (See James Victore's contribution to *Nozone* No 5, 'Dressing the Poor', on page 191.)

Nozone was at its spikiest in issue No 3 against the Gulf War; and at its sourest in the poverty issue, No 5, hissing an anti-corporate stance (in 1993) that would easily have fit in with the anti-globalization movement of a decade later. (The publishing blurb reminded readers that *Nozone* was independently financed, and had no association with the 'corporate shits that run our economy and dominate our culture'.) *Nozone* painted a painfully funny if somewhat grim portrait of the United States in the 1990s and will be remembered as one of the more surreal political voices of our time.

1

2

3

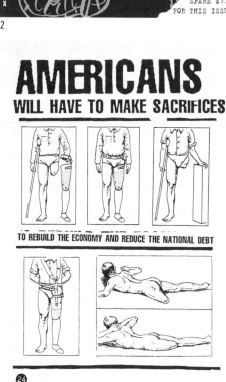

4

5

6 'Surgical Strike', centre-spread
illustration by Knickerbocker for
Nozone No 3. USA 1991.

7 Front cover of *Nozone* No 3
(the war issue), created at the
time of the 1991 Gulf War. Cover
illustration by Joost Swarte.
USA 1991.

6

7

Exposing truths, fighting against the odds: NeedCom website

In 1999, US artist Cathy Davies created the innovative website 'NeedCom: Market Research for Panhandlers'. The visitor is put through an extensive, market-research-style survey (pushed along by corporate sales-speak) and required to explore many different sides of begging: Who does it? Is one pitch better than another? How much do they earn in real life? Is their poverty genuine? Why do they do it? Eventually, the visitor is asked to make a fake electronic contribution to their chosen beggar. Then the crunch comes with the 'Results' page: the visitor's results are compared with other results, revealing his/her generosity or stinginess, and offering an opportunity to explore the issues further.

Many other opportunities exist for acquiring information during the course of the survey, such as researching the beggars' backgrounds or circumstances, or listening to their opinions. Visitors are invited to answer questions (through quick polls) about their own background or their general attitudes to panhandling, and are given opportunities to review their giving habits, and their attraction to certain pitches. They can even join a focus group and write their views about giving (panhandlers vs. charity), or divulge their assumptions about panhandling as well as reading other contributors' views. They can also read the results of a panhandlers' focus group, where panhandlers have commented on topics such as 'rich people' or discussed their attitude to their daily occupation.

It amounts to an experience that becomes a questioning of one's own prejudices and feelings, the real value of human life, and so on. What starts out as a game, ends up as a personal evaluation and perhaps a change of attitude. Both illuminating and disturbing, NeedCom is trail-blazing in its innovative use of new technology to explore issues and attitudes as well as its shrewd use of existing technology, without reverting to state-of-the-art special effects or other features.

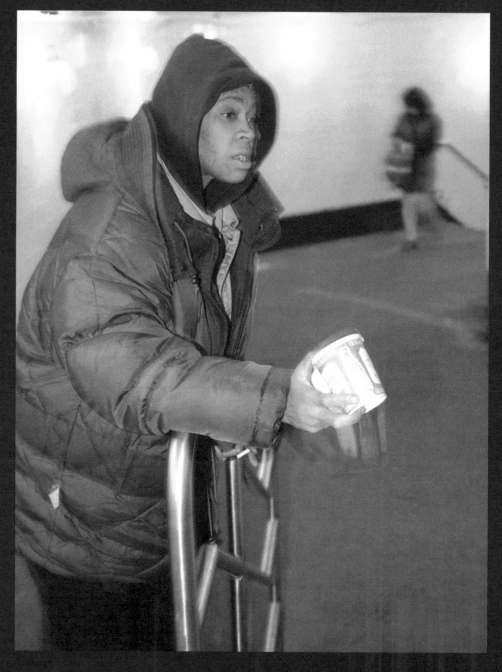

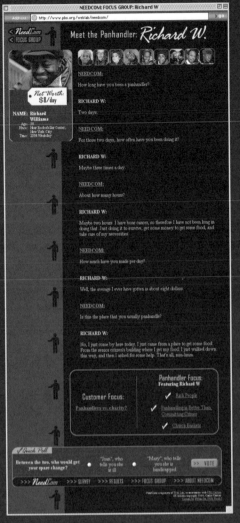

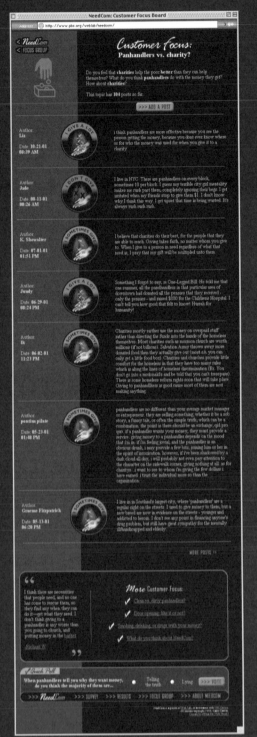
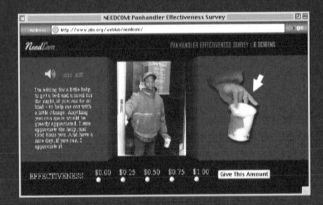
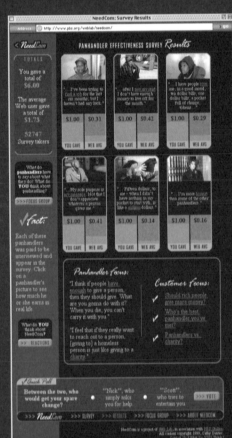

1 An example from the overtly political 'reality' campaign. The image of AIDS sufferer David Kirby on his deathbed brought boycotts and protests to the doors of Benetton shops. Concept by Oliviero Toscani, photograph by Therese Frare. Italy 1992.

2 The bloodied clothes of a soldier killed in the war in Bosnia – with a statement from his father, who donated the clothes and pleaded that his sons effects 'be used for peace and against war' (shown in an untranslated line of type at the top). Concept and photograph by Oliviero Toscani. Italy 1994.

3 A nun and a priest kissing, thereby annoying the Catholic Church. Concept and photograph by Oliviero Toscani. Italy 1991.

4 One of the early United Colors of Benetton ads, showing a newborn baby girl. It found itself banned in at least four countries and launched Benetton on a decade of social awareness and controversy. Concept and photograph by Oliviero Toscani. Italy 1991.

Exposing truths, fighting against the odds: social awareness as brand

In 1989 the clothing giant Benetton launched 'United Colors of Benetton' as the label for a single, global brand – and henceforth clothing disappeared from their advertising. The photographer and creative director Oliviero Toscani started delivering the overtly political messages that would define a decade of Benetton advertising. The early images were immediately provocative – a black woman breastfeeding a white baby, a priest and a nun kissing. But it was the 'bloody baby' of 1991 that proved to be one of the most controversial, swiftly followed by the campaign depicting the death of an American AIDS sufferer in 1992. A long line of images emerged over the decade that continually went 'one step too far', substantially redefining public tolerances and certainly inciting public awareness and discussion of the nature of imagery in the graphic environment, from billboards to magazines. The new century brought Toscani's departure from the company, following the highly volatile campaign showing photographs of convicts on America's Death Row. It marked the end of an important era in advertising.

Under the editorship and creative direction of renowned designer Tibor Kalman, Benetton's promotional magazine *Colors* also broke new ground, handling themes such as racism in a manner that was both controversial and visually stunning. Kalman reigned over the first 13 issues (1991–5), blasting his way through one taboo after another. Few can forget the enormous photographs of condoms in issue No 3 (1992) which flashed around the public domain causing shock and embarrassment.

1

2

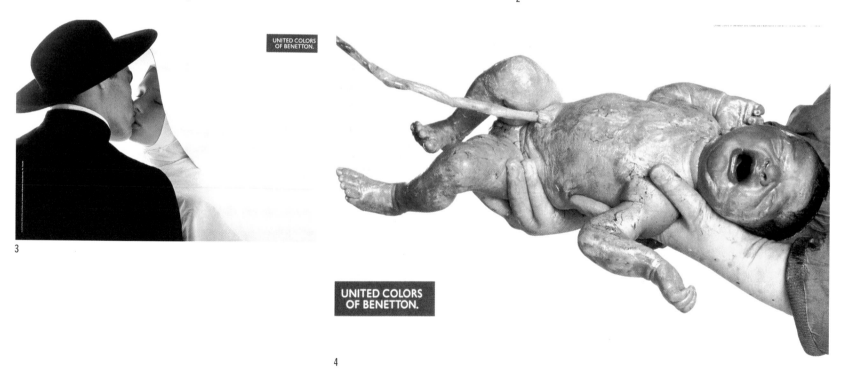

3

4

5,6 Front cover and inside spread from Benetton's promotional magazine, *Colors* No 4, spring/ summer 1993. This issue, edited by Tibor Kalman, explored how race affects our lives and how racism can take many forms. Photographs by Oliviero Toscani and design by Paul Ritter.

7,8 Front cover and inside spread from *Colors* No 3, fall/winter 1992, edited by Tibor Kalman. This issue was known for its large size – approximately 47 x 30 cm (18 ½ x 11 ½ inches) – and its huge photos of condoms, which were shocking at the time. Cover photograph by Steve McCurry, Magnum; spread photograph by Oliviero Toscani.

COLORS

We've told you about skin color, wax ear consistency and nose size. Now, what do you really want to know about On vous a tout dit sur la couleur de la peau, la consistance du cérumen et la nez. Et maintenant, que voulez-vous vraiment savoir sur les autres races? people of other races? On en était sûrs.

5

6

COLORS

7

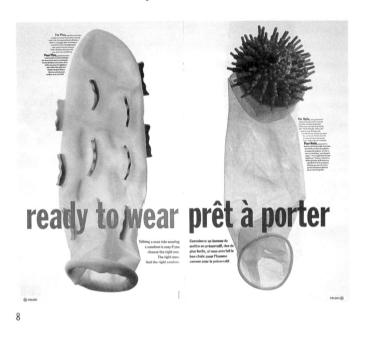

ready to wear prêt à porter

8

1 'Safer Dancing', illustration from a poster by Michael Linnell of the Lifeline Project, Manchester. UK 1992.

2,3,4 Covers of booklets created by Michael Linnell of the Lifeline Project, Manchester, aimed (largely) at young people exposed to or using drugs. UK 1990 (2) and 1992 (3, 4).

Exposing truths, fighting against the odds: drugs education and AIDS campaigning

Smaller projects with equally big ideas are represented here by Lifeline Publications in the UK and the Treatment Action Campaign in South Africa.

The Lifeline Project in Manchester produces highly researched, informative publications for a wide range of groups engaged in or affected by drug use. Operating on the assumption that most of their users are young and distrust authority, their chosen format is that of humorous comics, largely conceived and drawn by Michael Linnell. Their audiences are carefully targeted and researched, and consequently their publications communicate with a realistic knowledge of lifestyles, dress, behaviour and language. Highly popular and widely used throughout the UK, their publications provide a fundamental challenge to ineffectual mass media campaigns (see page 193).

Fighting the even greater challenge of HIV and AIDS in South Africa, the Treatment Action Campaign battles against the stigma of being HIV positive, and the image of powerlessness that goes with it. They campaign openly and brashly, taking on the power of drug corporations in order to bring down the cost and accessibility of anti-retroviral medication. At the same time, their marches and dramatic T-shirts bring the taboo of being HIV positive out into the open, as well as making a healthy, defiant, fighting stand, overcoming an image of hopelessness.

They are shown here in a photograph by Gideon Mendel, a photojournalist who has spent much of the past decade documenting the AIDS crisis in Africa. His work has become renowned for its sensitive and positive portrayal of people living with AIDS, often conveying their personal stories of hope. Mendel is also committed to the use of his work in campaigns and educational projects in the countries where the photographs have been taken.

1

2

3

4

5

1,2 Cover and spread from a booklet promoting the Fashion Targets Breast Cancer UK T-shirt campaign. Cover photograph by Mario Testino and spread photograph by Phil Poynter. UK 2000.

3,4 Spread and front cover from the British fashion and style magazine *Dazed & Confused* No 46, September 1998, guest editor Alexander McQueen, photographer Nick Knight. Cover model Aimee Mullens. The inside spread is from the fashion essay 'Access-Able', exploring the beauty in disability. Conceived by Alexander McQueen, photographed by Nick Knight. UK 1998.

Exposing truths, fighting against the odds: breast cancer and disability

A health promotion battle was to be fought with the help of T-shirts in the 1990s. The Breakthrough Breast Cancer charity was launched in 1991 in the UK to raise money for an urgently needed new centre for breast cancer research. The Fashion Targets Breast Cancer campaign, launched by the American fashion industry in 1994, brought its 'target' logo T-shirts to the UK in 1996 to raise money for Breakthrough. The campaign was endorsed and supported by media celebrities, supermodels, fashion editors, top designers and photographers. It was a huge success — and in 1997 the UK's first Breast Cancer Research Centre opened as part of the Institute of Cancer in London.

Thousands of T-shirts have since then been sold by the Fashion Targets Breast Cancer UK campaign. Moreover, it overcame the taboos of cancer and sex (breasts) and raised awareness of the disease and the necessity for regular self-examination. It continues to run a highly energetic campaign. Why all the rush? As of the year 2000, more than 1,000 women in the UK were dying of breast cancer every month — one of the highest mortality rates from the disease in the world.

The fashion world continued to break down stereotypes and taboos when fashion designer Alexander McQueen and photographer Nick Knight produced a fashion essay for UK style magazine *Dazed & Confused*, aiming to challenge preconceptions about beauty. They explored notions of beauty in relation to disability — in their own words, 'a joyful celebration of difference'. The high visibility of the images — some of which also formed large displays in the Main Hall of London's newest major art museum, Tate Modern — went a long way towards promoting an imaginative coupling of disability with artistry. UK definitions and depictions of beauty and style might now include forever the idea and appreciation of the imperfect body.

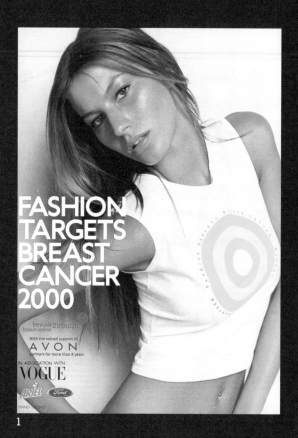

1

THE CLASS OF 2000

2

3

DAZED

¡CONFUSE!

46

ONCE YOU START YOU CAN'T STOP ISSUE

SEPTEMBER 1998 UK£2.50 US$4.50
IT4S IRFL.340 £2.35 1.200 ISSN 0961-9704

FASHION ABLE?

09
9 770961 976093
AIMEE MULLINS BY NICK KNIGHT

ALEXANDER
McQUEEN
GUEST
EDITOR
ISSUE

Children and violence: school shootings and child abuse

The sight of children carrying weapons and guns with their lunchpacks — on Art Spiegelman's cover illustration for *The New Yorker* in September 1993 — was an early indication of one of the strangest new fears of the United States. For decades, children and guns were an unholy combination with children the victims of guns or gun accidents. Reports of children wielding guns — in classroom massacres, for example — are a relatively new development that has prompted visual statements from graphic designers.

The 'Oragun' poster by Visual Mafia shown here comments on an incident in 1998 when a 15-year-old high school student in Springfield, Oregon, went on a shooting rampage, killing his parents, one student and injuring 23 others. James Victore's 'Fair Game' poster appeared coincidentally around the time of the Columbine High School massacre in Littleton, Colorado, in April 1999, when two students walked into the cafeteria and began shooting and throwing bombs. Sixteen people were killed, 20 were wounded. (Barely a month later, a student at a school in Georgia shot six classmates.) The various projects on these pages present

images that are both tragic and thought-provoking.

Graphic campaigns on the issue of children suffering from abuse or neglect are also shown here. The British charity Barnardo's — committed to helping children and young people threatened by disadvantage, abuse and neglect — resorted to shock advertising to put their message across in January 2000. Ad agency Bartle Bogle Hegarty produced a powerful and upsetting image of a baby injecting heroin (see page 213): in actual fact, a composite of a baby in a studio wrestling with a candy bar, superimposed on the horrific environment. The Committee for Advertising Practice (CAP) ruled the advert

likely to cause offence and advised the media not to carry it. But Barnardo's put up a fight, arguing that their motives were pure and that the image was aimed at raising awareness among adults. The Advertising Standards Authority (ASA) later rejected all complaints and deemed the image justified. With a few alterations, the ad campaign carried on for a long time afterwards.

In 2002, Saatchi & Saatchi produced posters and a TV advertisement to launch the second phase of the Full Stop campaign to end child abuse, headed by the National Society for the Prevention of Cruelty to Children in Britain. The NSPCC

1

2

message was that everyone has a responsibility to take action to end child abuse. Saatchi & Saatchi responded by producing a highly memorable TV advertisement, in which a cartoon child is taunted and kicked around by a parent in live action surroundings (accompanied by slap, bang, wallop sounds and cartoon music). At the end of the ad, the cartoon child slowly undergoes a startling transformation into a real child. This shocking realization is not easily forgotten.

Sadly, child cruelty is considered to be widespread in the UK. This was highlighted painfully in the year 2000 by one of the worst cases of child abuse in English criminal history – the case of eight-year-old Victoria Climbié who died of abuse at the hand of her great aunt and the aunt's boyfriend, undetected by social services and others. Campaigns such as the Barnardo's ad continue to attempt – by whatever means necessary – to put their vital message across, even if it means showing us things we don't want to see and shocking us to our senses.

3

4

5

1–5 'Real Children Don't Bounce Back', stills from a TV ad and posters created to launch the second phase of the NSPCC's ongoing Full Stop campaign to end child abuse. Designed by Saatchi & Saatchi for the National Society for the Prevention of Cruelty to Children. UK 2002.

6–9 Controversial ad campaign for Barnardo's, the children's charity, intended to raise funds and promote awareness of threats to childhood. By ad agency Bartle Bogle Hegarty. UK 2000.

1

2

REAL CHILDREN DON'T BOUNCE BACK.
Together we can stop child abuse. FULL STOP. ● NSPCC
Call our Helpline for advice or visit www.nspcc.org.uk 0808 800 5000

3

REAL CHILDREN DON'T BOUNCE BACK.
Together we can stop child abuse. FULL STOP. ● NSPCC
Call our Helpline for advice or visit www.nspcc.org.uk 0808 800 5000

4

REAL CHILDREN DON'T BOUNCE BACK.
Together we can stop child abuse. FULL STOP. ● NSPCC
Call our Helpline for advice or visit www.nspcc.org.uk 0808 800 5000

5

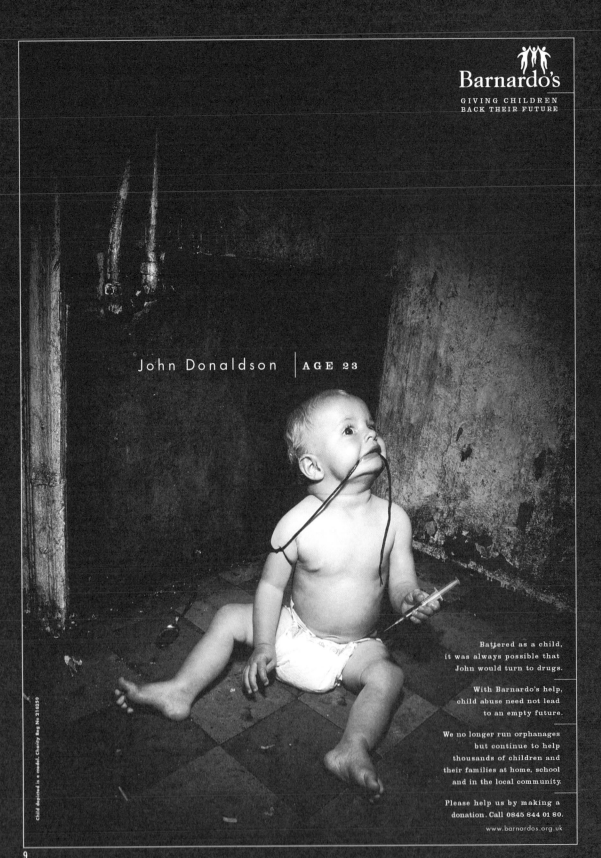

New directions: gay and lesbian rights in the 1990s

After the AIDS crisis defined the 1980s and forced the gay and lesbian communities to consolidate their strength against a common enemy, the 1990s saw new directions in activism accompanied by strong graphics.

The internationally renowned direct action group Lesbian Avengers, founded in 1992, benefited from a manifesto and logo designed by Carrie Moyer, which are now graphic icons of lesbian power. In 1991 Moyer teamed up with photographer Sue Schaffner to form Dyke Action Machine (DAM!), and together they defined a decade of lesbian visibility and assertiveness through their graphic campaigns. Their early examples of culture jamming — in which they inserted lesbian images into well-known advertising campaigns for the likes of Gap or *Family Circle* — subverted prevailing heterosexual roles and conceits and allowed a new, highly visible view of lesbian reality to emerge. Other projects took them into more controversial topics such as gay marriage, again subverting the easy heterosexual assumption that gay marriage is what all gays want. They expertly embraced new technology and their website continues to be one of the most entertaining spots in cyberspace, combining activism, information and imaginative design.

The New York-based collective Gran Fury was responsible for some of the most striking and dominant posters on AIDS awareness throughout the 1980s, many of them created for the energetic AIDS activist coalition ACT UP (see pages 22–3). As the 1990s moved on, so too did Gran Fury and key members such as Marlene McCarty and Donald Moffett set up the design studio Bureau, continuing to produce highly politicized work.

Other visual icons of the 1980s AIDS crisis and the fight for gay rights were produced by artists who tragically died during that era. The artist David Wojnarowicz, for example, produced powerful and iconic images of gay male experience in the United States at that time, such as the 1991 screenprint 'Untitled (One day this kid …)'. He died of AIDS, aged 37, in 1992.

The early 1990s move towards lesbian and gay radical activism also saw the founding in 1990 of Outrage!, the UK queer rights group. Renowned for their outspokenness — even their T-shirts rattled UK sensibilities — they rejected the intransigence of slow-moving, mainstream politics and its channels, and achieved results (such as better treatment from the police) through provocative occupations and demonstrations (see page 217).

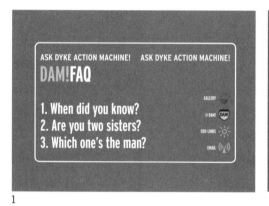

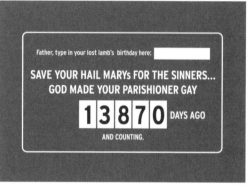

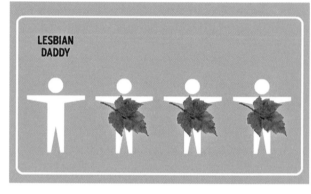

1

2

3

214

1 'The Rules', leaflet designed by Siân Cook for the volunteer-led charity Gay Men Fighting AIDS. UK 2001.

2 'Untitled (One Day This Kid ...)', screenprint for the AIDS activist group ACT UP by David Wojnarowicz and a grim statement about homophobia from the height of the US AIDS crisis. USA 1991.

3 'You and Your Kind Are Not Wanted Here', an oversized street poster for the American Civil Liberties Union that addresses and demands queer rights. Designed by Marlene McCarty and Donald Moffet at Bureau. USA 1994.

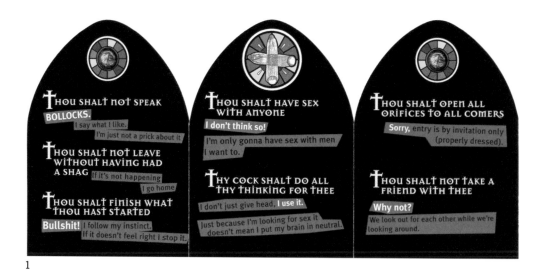

1

One day this kid will get larger. One day this kid will come to know something that causes a sensation equivalent to the separation of the earth from its axis. One day this kid will reach a point where he senses a division that isn't mathematical. One day this kid will feel something stir in his heart and throat and mouth. One day this kid will find something in his mind and body and soul that makes him hungry. One day this kid will do something that causes men who wear the uniforms of priests and rabbis, men who inhabit certain stone buildings, to call for his death. One day politicians will enact legislation against this kid. One day families will give false information to their children and each child will pass that information down generationally to their families and that information will be designed to make existence intolerable for this kid. One day this kid will begin to experience all this activity in his environment and that activity and information will compel him to commit suicide or submit to danger in hopes of being murdered or submit to silence and invisibility. Or one day this kid will talk. When he begins to talk, men who develop a fear of this kid will attempt to silence him with strangling, fists, prison, suffocation, rape, intimidation, drugging, ropes, guns, laws, menace, roving gangs, bottles, knives, religion, decapitation, and immolation by fire. Doctors will pronounce this kid curable as if his brain were a virus. This kid will lose his constitutional rights against the government's invasion of his privacy. This kid will be faced with electro-shock, drugs, and conditioning therapies in laboratories tended by psychologists and research scientists. He will be subject to loss of home, civil rights, jobs, and all conceivable freedoms. All this will begin to happen in one or two years when he discovers he desires to place his naked body on the naked body of another boy.

2

3

QUEER as FUCK

THIS FAGGOT'S NOT FOR BURNING

I CAN SEE QUEERLY NOW

4 Slogan T-shirts from OutRage!, claimed to be the world's longest surviving queer rights direct action group. The T-shirt slogan 'This Faggot's Not for Burning' refers to Prime Minister Margaret Thatcher's statement of firmness in the 1980s, 'This Lady's Not for Turning' (changing her policy). UK 1994.

5 Photograph showing an OutRage! demonstration for lesbian and gay rights taking place at Downing Street (near the Prime Minister's residence at No 10). UK 1994. Photograph by Steve Mayes.

4

5

1 'We Are All Innocent, We Are Armed – Where is Feminism Going? A Proposal That Starts From Our Cities', poster publicizing an exhibition and talks by the group Las Muñequitas Contratacan (The Little Dolls Fight Back) and the creators of the magazine *Lunátika* (Moody Women). They were invited to show their work in Italy by the women of the Ya Basta! organization. Designed by Margarita Sada. Mexico 2001.

2 Front cover of *WAC Stats: The Facts About Women*, a book containing statistics on rape, abortion, AIDS, sexual harassment and other realities for women. Published by the Women's Action Coalition (WAC), cover design by Gail Vachon and WAC logo by Marlene McCarty. USA 1992.

3 Web page from the SpiderWomen website. USA 2002.

Images of women: breaking with traditions and stereotypes

A gallery of snapshot-images is presented here, touching on some of the issues relating to women since the early 1990s.

At the start of the decade Jacky Fleming's book of collected feminist cartoons, *Be A Bloody Train Driver* (1991), became a bestseller in the UK. Blasting away any assumptions that feminist views no longer had an audience, they were sharp, acerbic and very funny. (They needed to be – by the end of the decade, women depressingly would still number less than seven per cent of directors of companies on the FTSE 100 index.)

At the same time, the New York-based Women's Action Coalition (WAC) – active 1992–4 – was campaigning for abortion rights and against violence against women. They made strategic use of press and broadcast coverage as well as the strong, memorable graphics of Marlene McCarty – designer of the 'all-seeing eye' logo – and Bethany Johns.

Mexican designer Margarita Sada's work emerged towards the other end of the decade, giving graphic expression to a generation of young feminists in Mexico who wish to continue the struggle in a

different way, and desire a new identity for changing times. Sada works with the young group Las Muñequitas Contratacan (The Little Dolls Fight Back), designing the feminist magazine *Lunátika* (Moody Women; see page 8) as well as posters concerning violence against women, gender rights, the rights of indigenous women and the freedom of female political prisoners.

Digital-age feminists also made radical use of new technology. The United States-based SpiderWomen website acts as a focal point for contemporary feminist issues and debate, incorporating news, actions, statistics, surveys and a newsletter. Designer Diane Gromala, meanwhile, explores women's relationships with their bodies through new technology and graphics (the interface between woman and machine) by creating a typeface that continually responds to her body impulses. She thus pre-empts a truly interactive digital age when our bodies or impulses will be able to control our computers. In July 2001, Gromala described her work thus:

'Using a "wearable device", sensors measure my body's output like an ECG (electro-cardiograph). The sensors repond to changes to my internal

chemical balance, my bio-waves and my internal state of being and mind. By linking myself to a computer, the output from my senses can augment and change the output from the computer.

'Looking for a means to illustrate my research into computer-augmented output, I have developed a series of typefaces which I term "BioMorphic Typography". This new form, an always morphing typeface, continually responds to the impulses received from my body. It demonstrates that a computer can respond to a user's changing physical states.'

1

2

3

4 Jacky Fleming's feminist cartoons in the form of postcards. From her best-selling book, *Be a Bloody Train Driver*, published in the UK in 1991. Another popular collection, *Never Give Up*, followed in 1992.

5 Booklet fold-out depicting designer Diane Gromala and her experiments with BioMorphic Typography, where her body's physical state directly affects the typographic output of her computer. The experiments use letterforms based upon the classic Roman characters engraved on Trajan's Column in Rome (c. AD 110). USA 2001.

4

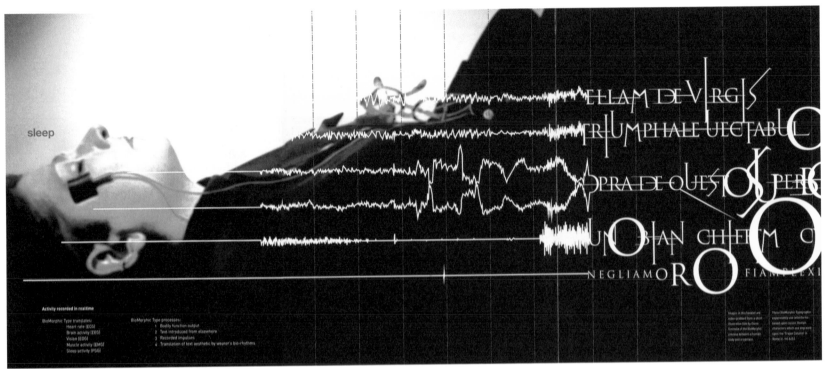

5

1 Street flyer announcing a meeting at a college in London's East End. UK 1995.

2 'Which is the Crime?', electronic poster by Petulia Mattioli created around the time of the war in Afghanistan for RAWA, the Revolutionary Association of the Women of Afghanistan. Italy 2001.

Images of women: the graphic symbolism of the veil

A significant but ambiguous sign of our times has come into play for women in the twenty-first century: the graphic symbolism of the veil of Islam. Its stereotypes and associations are many – it can be read as a sign of restriction or repression; as a political statement (for example, a rejection of Western values); or as a commitment to Islam and an expression of faith.

In recent years other confusing interpretations have been added, such as associations with oppression linked to fundamentalism or fears linked with terrorism. Such associations have magnified the culture clash between East and West, particularly after 9/11.

The image of the burqa came sharply into focus during the war in Afghanistan in 2001.

Arguments ensued over whether toppling the Taliban regime would 'free' women from their burqas – or whether the wearing of the burqa was a matter of individual religious belief and respect, and beyond Western attempts to label it as a sign of oppression. It proved to be a difficult and many-sided debate.

Nevertheless, the burqa became a graphic symbol used in posters and other visual material striking out against the Taliban regime during the war in Afghanistan. In Petulia Mattioli's poster 'Which is the Crime?', it became a focal point for a statement by RAWA, the Revolutionary Association of the Women of Afghanistan. (Founded in 1977, RAWA has declared itself 'the oldest political/social organization of Afghan women struggling for peace, freedom, democracy and women's rights

in fundamentalism-blighted Afghanistan'.) At a time of heavy debate in the West about right or wrong (on the subject of the war), the poster was meant to show that a 'crime' against women was still taking place – as the entire poster represents a prison-like viewpoint from inside a burqa.

An earlier example of use of the burqa (and the powerful readings surrounding it) can be seen in a project which aimed to visualize Western society's fears about Islam, or the spread of Islamic culture. 'New Liberty 2006' was one of a number of computer-generated collage-images set in cities around the world. It was produced by the Moscow-based art group AES (Tatiana Arzamasova, Lev Evzovitch and Evgeny Svyatsky) as part of its futuristic 'Islamic Project', launched in 1996 as an installation and performance that interacted with the public.

The Islamic Project first opened in Moscow, then travelled around the world. It proved to be controversial (for example, in the United States in 1998) as the images, including 'New Liberty 2006', were viewed by some local Muslim communities as reinforcing bad stereotypes of Muslims (for example, that all Muslims are alleged terrorists). But the artists insisted that the exaggeration of fears was the way to promote dialogue and bring such issues into the open for discussion – the true intention of the project. Although some might consider the image an extreme or even misguided attempt, the artists' sentiment was admirable. For the clash of cultures will only give way when an era of communication takes hold.

1

IF YOU LOVE FREEDOM, YOU ARE AGAINST FUNDAMENTALISM. RAWA: REVOLUTIONARY ASSOCIATION OF THE WOMEN OF AFGHANISTAN. WWW.RAWA.ORG
PETULIA MATTIOLI FOR RAWA. www.petuliamattioli.com

2

3 'Forbidden to go out without the chador, forbidden to work, to educate themselves – the Taliban have abolished the rights of women in Afghanistan', poster by Nous Travaillons Ensemble (We Work Together). France 1998.

4 'New Liberty 2006', one of a series of images from the 'Islamic Project'. Produced by group AES. Russia 1996.

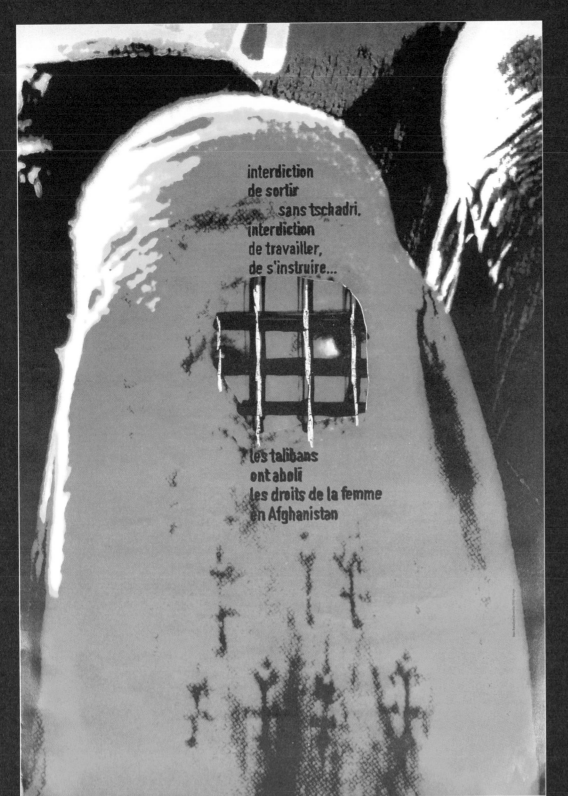

3

4

1 Front cover and inside pages from the book, *Latino USA: A Cartoon History*, by Ilan Stavans and illustrated by Lalo Alcaraz. Published by Basic Books. USA 2000.

2 Huey (speaking) and his little brother Riley (on the right), leading characters from *The Boondocks*, the controversial comic strip and website by Aaron McGruder. USA 1999.

3 An aboriginal flag waves as a plane writes 'Sorry' in the sky on annual National Sorry Day (26 May) in Australia, 2001. Photograph by Glenn Campbell.

4 'The Baby Bottle' (aka 'Teach Your Children Well'), anti-racist poster by James Victore. USA 1992.

5,6 'Racism and the Death Penalty', front and back of a poster/mailer designed by James Victore for the National Association for the Advancement of Colored People (NAACP). USA 1993.

Fighting racism and the Right: stereotypes, history and institutions

The ongoing fight against racist attitudes and stereotypes in ethnically diverse societies, such as the United States and Australia, is graphically described here in images that range from comics to sky-writing.

Sharp-witted Huey Freeman (named after the Black Panther, Huey P Newton) and his little brother Riley, involved in gangsta culture, are leading characters from *The Boondocks,* the controversial, pioneering US comic strip by Aaron McGruder, launched in 1999. It tells the story of two young African-American boys (Huey and Riley), who go to live with their grandfather in a white Chicago suburb. This provides the basis for exploring white racial anxieties, current black stereotypes (as well as past) and other territory most writers or cartoonists will not touch.

Originally an online strip on a website, it was launched in 160 newspapers and became the most successful debut strip in the history of Universal Press Syndicate. Since then it has taken on delicate issues ranging from drugs and violence to education, has drawn complaints as well as praise, and has become renowned for generating debate about the role of the cartoon in newspapers across the United States. Its website (www.boondocks.net) remains a focal point for fans, as well as an outlet for any material that might be censored by the mainstream papers.

James Victore's sharply direct posters against racism and discrimination are well known in the United States. In 1993 he tackled the issue of racism and its relationship with the death penalty in a poster for the National Association for the Advancement of Colored People (NAACP) to promote their documentary film *Double Justice.* It dealt with 'the continuing impact of race, and particularly the race of crime victims, in determining whether a death sentence will be imposed'.

Hitting closer to home, his poster 'The Baby Bottle' showing a bottle with racist words in the place of measure-markings—acts as a reminder that prejudice or racial hatred can be 'fed' to our children at an early age, even by seemingly 'casual' remarks heard inside or outside of the home.

Graphic projects or campaigns have also been used to redress historical injustices—by presenting a different view of history or by demanding rights for those denied them. The book *Latino USA: A Cartoon History*, written by Ilan Stavans and illustrated by Lalo Alcaraz, is a humorous, whirlwind tour through the history of Latinos (Spanish-speaking people) living in the United States. The tour is made accessible and entertaining through its comic format and a narrative delivered by cartoon actors in a 'theatre of history'. At the same time, it is deadly serious in its attempt to define the different Latino subgroups, bring a sense of reality to the statistics, break down imposed stereotypes, retell historical events and celebrate cultural contributions.

In the photograph shown here, a plane writes 'sorry' in the sky, creating a graphic memorial for National Sorry Day (26 May) in Australia. Since 1998, National Sorry Day has allowed non-Aboriginal Australians a day to hold community activities and actions in order to show regret for 'crimes' committed by their ancestors against the indigenous people of the continent. Some are alarmingly recent: until 1970, an official policy involved the removal, by force if necessary, of Aboriginal and Torres Island children from their families in order to 'assimilate' them into white society—a practice that grew out of white society's attempt to 'reclaim' the mixed race children of white men and Aboriginal women. Thus National Sorry Day carries on, not as an attempt to blame—but as an attempt to acknowledge, and to remember.

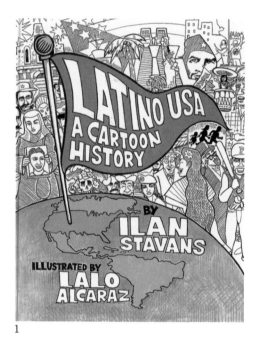

1

8

161

2

3

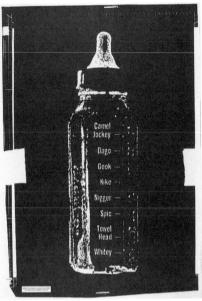

4

Racism and the Death Penalty

"Double Justice" combines historical information about the racially biased use of the death penalty with contemporary research that demonstrates the continuing impact of race, particularly the race of crime victims, in determining whether a death sentence will be imposed. A moving visual commentary highlighted by the magic of computer animation, "Double Justice" takes information that for too long has been confined to scholarly works, law books and legal briefs and makes it accessible to the general public.

5

all men are created equal

Racism and the Death Penalty

Capital Punishment

double justice

"The impact of our heritage of slave laws will continue to make itself felt into the future. For there is a nexus between the brutal centuries of colonial slavery and the racial polarization and anxieties of today. The poisonous legacy of legalized oppression based upon the matter of color can never be adequately purged from our society if we act as if it had never existed."

6

1,2 'French of All Countries' (literal
translation, see text).
Poster and banner protesting
against the immigration laws
of the time. Designed by
La Fabrique d'Images. France 1996.

Fighting racism and the Right: the diversity of Europe

In the culturally and economically diverse countries of Europe, issues such as immigration and asylum-seeking give rise to prejudice, racism or extremist attitudes. Moreover, the cast of characters and the issues involved change from country to country.

Such intolerance will always provoke responses from graphic designers and activists, working individually or for campaigns to combat extremism or right-wing views, or loss of liberties for ethnic minorities.

'French of All Countries' is the literal translation of a poster and banner designed by La Fabrique d'Images (Olivier Darné and Hélène Le Bechec) in France in 1997, but a broader meaning is 'regardless of colour or background, we are all French'. The images were used on demonstrations in Paris against the immigration laws of the time – and, in the view of the artists, as a blow against the racists who claim 'the country belongs to them'. The poster can also be seen as a celebration of the cultural and racial diversity of France, where a significant percentage of the population originates from Algeria or other former French colonial territories in Africa or the Middle East. Therefore race continues to be an ongoing issue, particularly provoked by extreme right-wing politicians such as Jean-Marie Le Pen (see also page 227).

In Germany, the plight of refugees is confronted by Berlin designer Sandy K. His poster and postcard 'Free Movement is Our Right' (shown here in different versions) protests against the 'Residenzpflicht', a law which since 1982 has restricted the movements of refugees in Germany. Apparently they cannot leave their local districts, where they must live in isolated buildings under permanent surveillance. They must apply (and pay) for a travel permit, an application which can always be rejected. They are therefore inclined to cross their district borders illegally, risking prison or deportation. This poster, created in 2001, is part of the campaign against this residential law.

Sandy K has also produced work for the well-known anti-racist campaign 'Kein Mensch Ist Illegal' (No One is Illegal). The poster series (see overleaf) designed in 1999 and distributed throughout Germany, aims to counter the dominant, mass media view of illegal immigrants as a huge 'faceless' mass. The posters tell stories from the lives of four such people, showing the daily difficulties they must confront (due to their lack of legal papers) with regard to four areas: work, health, education and just being in a public place.

Also shown is a photograph (by Marily Stroux) of Sandy K's posters being held by members of a photo workshop – part of a project for refugee children –

"La Fabrique d'Images" – 1996   Photographie de Lionel Joyeux

1

taking place at Hamburg harbour. (In the workshop, the children are given cheap pocket cameras to photograph and reflect on their situation and surroundings.) In the background are container ships which act as refugee accommodation, and which are severely overcrowded. It is alleged that around 1,700 people live on such ships, around 700 of them children. The refugees, however, cannot get a permit to stay in the country because they are defined as 'economic' refugees.

The French Right makes an appearance in the poster 'L'alliance' (The Alliance) by Nous Travaillons Ensemble (We Work Together), which protests against the alliance of the French Right with the National Front in May

1998 – a marriage made in hell, symbolized by a wedding ring that causes a gangrenous finger. Also shown is an anti-racist, anti-fascist poster by Vincent Perrottet (working with Les Graphistes Associés) entitled 'We Don't Need A Führer'. It combined the faces of Adolf Hitler and extreme right politician Jean-Marie Le Pen, and was carried in an anti-racist demonstration in France in 1990. Its timing is significant, for despite Le Pen's recent challenge to Jacques Chirac for the presidency of France in 2002, he has been a long-established presence in French politics, coalescing extreme nationalism and racism.

3,4 'Free Movement is Our Right!', poster and postcard by Sandy K, produced as part of a campaign for the rights of refugees. Germany 2001.

»free movement is our right!«

4

3

1 'No One is Illegal', poster series by Sandy K for the anti-racist campaign 'Kein Mensch Ist Illegal', and distributed throughout the country. Germany 1999.

2 Photograph by Marily Stroux of a photo workshop for refugee children taking place at Hamburg harbour. Germany 1998.

3 'The Alliance', poster by Nous Travaillons Ensemble (We Work Together). France 1999.

2

Kein
Mensch ist illegal

„Meine Freunde wußten,

daß ich kein Visum mehr hatte.

Sie hätten dringend

einen Krankenwagen für mich rufen müssen.

Aber wie sollte ich an die nötigen

Papiere kommen,

unter welchem Namen sollte

ich eingeliefert werden?

Das war total schwierig,

unlösbar."

Menschen ohne gültige Papiere und somit ohne Krankenversicherung wird von den meisten Ärztinnen und Krankenhäusern eine Behandlung verweigert. Stattdessen müssen sie mit Denunziation und Abschiebung rechnen.

Kein Mensch
ist illegal

„Plötzlich standen sie vor mir

und einer wollte

meinen Ausweis sehen.

Aber ich kam nicht mehr dazu

ihn rauszuholen.

Sie warfen mich direkt zu Boden

und drückten mir

die Kehle zu."

Sich ohne gültige Papiere in der Öffentlichkeit zu bewegen bedeutet: sich unsichtbar machen, nicht auffallen – aus Angst, entdeckt und abgeschoben zu werden. Selbst in ihren Wohnungen sind Illegalisierte vor Razzien nicht sicher.

1

4,5 'We Don't Need A Führer', anti-racist/anti-fascist poster showing the combined faces of Adolf Hitler and extreme right politician Jean-Marie Le Pen. By Vincent Perrottet, working with Les Graphistes Associés. France 1990.

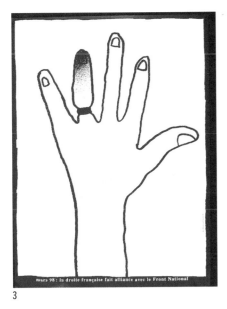

3

mars 98 : la droite française fait alliance avec le Front National

4

ON N'A PAS BESOIN DE FUREUR !

5

Kein Mensch

ist

illegal

„Ich werde noch ganz verrückt,

den ganzen Tag

allein im Zimmer herumsitzen.

Ich will einfach zur Schule gehen

und von den anderen lernen.

Einfach lernen.

Aber keine Schule

hat mich genommen."

Kindern, Jugendlichen und Erwachsenen ohne gültige Papiere wird das Recht auf Bildung abgesprochen. Die meisten LehrerInnen und RektorInnen weigern sich aus Furcht vor den Konsequenzen, Illegalisierte zu unterrichten.

Kein Mensch ist

illegal

„Ich mußte versuchen Arbeit zu finden,

um die nächste Monatsmiete zu bezahlen.

Arbeiten ist ein großes Problem,

denn jede Firma, bei der du anfragst,

will erstmal deine Papiere sehen,

immer geht's um Papiere,

Papiere ..."

Um überleben zu können, sind illegalisierte Frauen oftmals zur Prostitution gezwungen. Menschen ohne gültige Papiere müssen zu schlechtesten Bedingungen arbeiten – ohne eine Garantie auf Lohnauszahlung. Sie sind schutzlos der Ausbeutung und Willkür der Vorgesetzten und KollegInnen ausgesetzt.

1 Poster by US artist John Baldessari, one of a series of anti-fascist statements created for a project that was organized and displayed by the Secession (independent artists' association) in Vienna. Austria 2000.

2,3,4 Poster by Sandy K for a series of anti-fascist concerts organized by the PDS (socialist party). Germany 1997.

Fighting racism and the Right: art and design against facism

A smiley face turns into a fascist icon in a poster artwork by American artist John Baldessari, one of a number of artistic statements produced by both Austrian and international artists commenting on the political situation in Austria in early 2000. (Jörg Haider's far-right Freedom Party had become part of the new Austrian coalition government that took power in February 2000, leading to intense anti-government demonstrations, street performances and other initiatives.) The posters were part of a project entitled 'Project Facade' which took place from February to October 2000. It was organized by the Secession, an independent artists' association in Vienna and one of Austria's leading institutions for contemporary art. Their building is a famous landmark, and each poster in this project was displayed on the right-hand wing of the front facade for two weeks. Other artists involved included Louise Bourgeois, Joseph Kosuth and Paul McCarthy.

In Germany, a poster depicting a large red (left) ear was created by Berlin designer Sandy K for a series of four anti-fascist concerts organized by a local branch of the PDS (socialist party) in 1997, with information photocopied and pasted on later for economy. Apparently people sometimes scribbled 'Stasi' on the posters sited in the street (the Stasi was the hated secret service of the former GDR/East Germany). The PDS grew out of the former ruling party of East Germany, and it is understandable that some people might have associated the big ears with bad memories of being subjected to spying or 'listening in'. The Stasi was much feared, and its network of informers was formidable, including many ordinary members of the population.

1

2

3

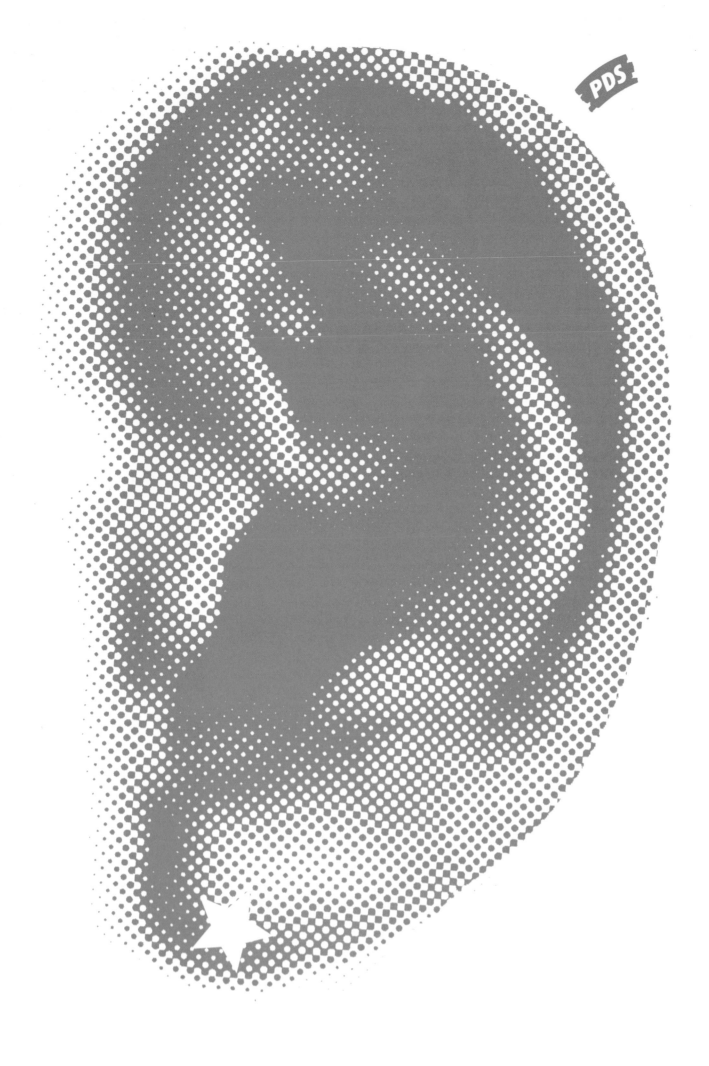

4

Human rights and optimism: the pride and hope of Southern Africa

With all the difficulties and devastation that Africa has had to bear over the last decade – the end of apartheid, AIDS, despots, natural disasters, civil war – it is still a continent of great hope and inspiration. Two projects emanating from Southern Africa – one from Zimbabwe, the other from South Africa – encapsulate its hopeful energy and enthusiasm. Both projects were born in optimistic times and contexts and although their countries have since suffered set-backs, disillusionment or crisis, their quality of hope remains undiminished.

In 1996 in Zimbabwe, graphic designer Chaz Maviyane-Davies created designs for a series of posters based on 13 articles from the UN Declaration of Human Rights, intended to be sent to human rights groups, schools, social institutions, galleries or any other source able to further the cause of human rights throughout Africa and elsewhere. But instead of depicting the horror or wretchedness of human rights abuses (one of Africa's main stereotypes), he decided to take a positive stance on the subject. This became the 'Rights' calendar for 1997. In his own text on the calendar itself, he describes his approach as 'the celebration of the human spirit – to emphasize the cultural diversity that abounds and above all, demand that the viewer looks outside him or herself. After all "Rights" are our strength and if these can be related to pride and dignity, instead of uselessness and apathy, then we can begin to

define a world that we can believe in again.'

Making a short visit to England from Harare, he completed the complex images on the latest Quantel Graphic Paintbox and then produced the posters as a calendar for 1997. It stands as a lasting tribute to Africa as a place of strength, beauty and imagination, as well as being a weapon in the fight for human rights.

The first democratic elections of April 1994 which made Nelson Mandela state president gave birth to 'the new South Africa'. In 1995, Orange Juice Design – headed by creative director Garth Walker and based in Durban – started publishing *i-jusi* (Zulu for 'juice'), an experimental non-commercial magazine committed to developing a design language rooted in the new South Africa experience, and promoting South African graphic design to creatives worldwide.

However, turning their backs on the apartheid years did not mean that the new era was going to be one of glowing idealism and pretty pictures. *I-jusi* was colourful, subversive, wild, cynical and full of irreverence and bite. Featuring everything from Durban street signage to traditional Zulu culture, *i-jusi* produced some of the freshest, most intriguing images around – with an energy that was explosive. It achieved great international success – so much so that a digital version of the magazine has been created for the web at www.i-jusi.com. Like the new South Africa itself, *i-jusi* continues to be a mass of contradictions, beauty, strangeness and wonder.

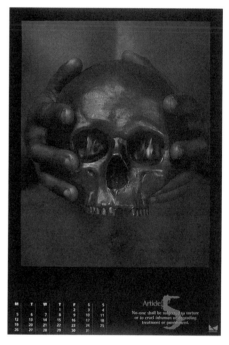

1 'Black & White: For the Sins of Our Fathers', front cover of *i-jusi* No 8, designed by Garth Walker of Orange Juice Design and showing different aspects of racial segregation (apartheid) as manufactured products of previous generations. South Africa 1999.

2 Front cover of *i-jusi* No 9, the magazine created by Orange Juice Design. Cover design by Jean Hofmeyr. South Africa 1999.

3 Spread from *i-jusi* No 9, designed by Damian Stephens. South Africa 1999.

4 Spread from *i-jusi* No 9, designed by Wilhelm Krüger. South Africa 1999.

5 Promotional poster for 'Bruno Signs', inserted into *i-jusi* magazine. Bruno, a refugee from the Congo (to escape the war in 1997), paints unique advertising signs and banners that decorate the streetside haircutting salons of Durban and beyond. Not only is he famous for the signs but he also invents the hairstyles on the signs, developing his own popular form of 'Bruno Style'. South Africa 1999.

6 Spread from *i-jusi* No 11 (the type issue), designed by Wilhelm Krüger. South Africa 2000.

7 Spread from *i-jusi* No 11 (the type issue), designed by Shani Ahmed. South Africa 2000.

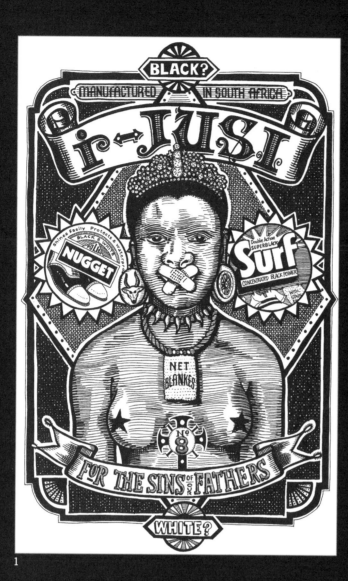

5

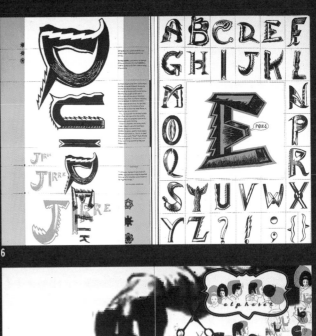

6

7

Notes

Legacy of the Graphic Revolution

1 See Liz McQuiston, *Graphic Agitation*, Phaidon Press, London 1993, for examples of all these.

2 Roger Sabin, *Comics, Comix & Graphic Novels: A History of Comic Art*, Phaidon Press, London 1996, pp. 182–8.

3 Douglas Crimp with Adam Rolston, *AIDS Demo Graphics*, Bay Press, Seattle 1990, pp. 12–16.

4 Liz McQuiston, *Suffragettes to She-Devils: Women's Liberation and Beyond*, Phaidon Press, London 1997, pp. 166–7.

5 The ACT UP website is at www.actupny.org.

6 Dana Bartelt and Marta Sylvestrová, *Art as Activist: Revolutionary Posters from Central and Eastern Europe*, Thames & Hudson, London 1992, pp. 13–24.

Chapter 1

1 Chiapaslink, *The Zapatistas: A Rough Guide*, Chiapaslink/ Earthright Publications, Ryton, Tyne & Wear 2000, pp. 13–24.

2 After the passing of the Criminal Justice Act, the next (Labour) government went even further with the Terrorism Act, which took effect in February 2001, broadening the definition of terrorism and criminalizing support for organizations viewed as terrorist, which would include the Zapatistas and other organizations abroad. See the article 'Warning: Terrorist Material' by Zac Goldsmith, in Anita Roddick, *Take It Personally*, Thorsons/HarperCollins, London 2001, pp. 46–7.

3 George McKay, *Senseless Acts of Beauty: Cultures of Resistance Since the Sixties*, Verso, London 1996, pp. 135–58.

4 Paul O'Connor, 'Undercurrents, or "the news you don't see on the news"', *Filmwaves*, issue 13, April 2000, Edgware UK, pp. 22–7.

5 'The Revolution Will Not Be Emailed', article source attributed to *Worldwide Resistance Round-Up, People's Global Action*, reproduced in *SchQUALL, SchNews* issues 201–250 and *SQUALL* magazine, published by Justice?, Brighton 2000.

6 Homepage for GASCD: Governments Accountable to Society and Citizens=Democracy, a website and CD aiming to raise awareness of the anti-globalization movement and inspired by the 2001 Quebec City protests. www.gascd. com, 8 February 2002.

7 The Greenpeace website is at www.greenpeace.org.uk and GenetiX Snowball is at www.fraw.org.uk/gs/.

Chapter 2

1 Naomi Klein, *No Logo*, Flamingo/HarperCollins, London 2000, pp. 7–26.

2 Publications, promotional materials and correspondence from California DOC (Doctors Ought to Care) is located at the California Medical Association, San Francisco 1993; and more recently at www.bcm.tmc.edu/ doc, September 2001.

3 Laurel Harper, *Provocative Graphics: The Power of the Unexpected in Graphic Design*, Rockport, Gloucester 2001, p. 55.

4 'The Point of Purchase' by Gareth Williams, in Jane Pavitt (ed.), *Brand.new*, V&A Publications, London 2000, pp. 184–213.

5 Naomi Klein, ibid., pp. 387–91. See also: Maggie O'Kane, 'McDonald's Clash Sets Record', *Guardian*, 9 December 1995, p. 3 and McSpotlight website at www.mcspotlight.org.

6 See 'The McLibel Trial' at www.mcspotlight.org.

7 Michael Moore, *Stupid White Men*, HarperCollins, London 2002.

8 Letter to the author, 21 November 2001.

9 The name 'El Cartel de Medellín' is a joke. The group met in a studio on Medellín Street – but the name is also that of a famous Colombian drug mob.

10 Andy Beckett, 'Blueprint for Britain', *Guardian Weekend*, 4 May 2002, pp. 17–27.

Chapter 3

1 Mark Laity, 'Reporting the War', *Britain's Gulf War*, Harrington Kilbride, London 1991, pp. 62–5.

2 Philip M Taylor, *War and the Media: Propaganda and Persuasion in the Gulf War*, Manchester University Press, Manchester 1998 (2nd edn), pp. 11–26 and 51–7.

3 Stealth aviation technology involves a radical new way of designing aircraft by modifying shape and texture (materials) which results in changing the radar 'signature' on a display screen, i.e. the aircraft does not show on a radar screen or appears to be much smaller than it is, hence it becomes electronically 'invisible'.

4 J C Herz, *Joystick Nation*, Abacus/Little Brown, London 1997, p. 207.

5 This refers particularly to the model map used on BBC2 *Newsnight*, operated by an enthusiastic presenter. It now resides in the Imperial War Museum in London, along with a model map from the Falklands War – acquired by curators who, even at that earlier point in time, saw the attraction of such a display for the general public.

6 For insight into the concerns expressed by people involved in making the Gulf War's broadcast graphics (in US television news), see Philip B Meggs, 'Post War, Post Mortem: Made for Television', *Print* magazine (USA), September/October 1991, pp. 54–63 and 132.

7 Peter Kuper, 'Protest Graphics Live!', *Print* magazine (USA), March/April 1992, p. 111.

8 'Bosnia' is the shortened name for Bosnia-Herzegovina, one of the six republics of the former Yugoslavia.

9 Vikram Dodd, 'Now for the Moment of Truth', *Guardian* Media Section, 21 February 2000, p. 9.

10 Post-World War II Yugoslavia, led by Tito (Josip Broz), was comprised of six republics: Bosnia-Herzegovina, Croatia, Macedonia, Montenegro, Serbia and Slovenia, and the two provinces of Kosovo and Vojvodina (both linked to Serbia). After the breakaway in the early 1990s of Bosnia, Croatia, Macedonia and Slovenia, in 1992 a new Yugoslav federation was formed by Serbia and Montenegro. By the end of the 1990s, after a decade of wars, Yugoslavia still remained a federation of Serbia (including Kosovo and Vojvodina) and Montenegro.

11 Daoud Sarhandi and Alina Boboc, *Evil Doesn't Live Here: Posters from the Bosnian War*, Princeton Architectural Press, New York and Laurence King, London 2001, pp. 13–17.

12 'Suffering into Art: Howson and Bosnia' by Richard Cork, in *Peter Howson: Bosnia*, Imperial War Museum, London 1994, pp. 35–42. Exhibition catalogue.

13 Matthew Collin, *This is Serbia Calling: Rock'n'roll Radio and Belgrade's Underground Resistance*, Serpent's Tail, London 2001, pp. 99–131 and 175–80. Also, author's interview with Manja Stojic (formerly a resident of Belgrade), 7 October 2002.

14 Ivo Skoric, 'A Clenched Fist Becomes Milosevic's Vexation', 3 March 2000. (Subject: <nettime> Poster War in Belgrade), www.nettime.org/ nettime.w3archive/200003/ msg00032.html.

15 Michael Ignatieff, *Virtual War: Kosovo and Beyond*, Chatto & Windus, London 2000, p. 196.

Chapter 4

1 'What does Cathy Davies, creator of NeedCom, have to say about her project?', www.pbs.org/weblab/ needcom/press/artists.html.

2 ''Tis the season for giving? See how America really feels about panhandlers on groundbreaking market research site', press release, 15 November 1999, www.pbs.org/weblab/needcom/ press/releases.html.

3 Author's interview with Michael Linnell, Director of Communications, the Lifeline Project, Manchester, UK, 22 August 2001.

4 Wayne Ellwood, 'We all have AIDS', *New Internationalist*, issue 346, June 2002, pp. 9–12. The statistics given in the article originate from *AIDS Epidemic Update*, UNAIDS/ WHO, December 2001.

5 Chris McGreal, 'Shamed and Humiliated – the Drug Firms Back Down', *Guardian*, 19 April 2001, front page.

6 Liza Ramrayka, 'Full Stop Starts Now', p. 3, and Kendra Inman, 'Change Begins at Home', p. 7, articles in *Putting a Stop to Child Cruelty*, a special supplement produced by the *Guardian* newspaper in association with the NSPCC, London and Manchester 2002.

7 Liza Ramrayka, 'Full Stop Starts Now', p. 3, article in *Putting a Stop to Child Cruelty*, a special supplement produced by the *Guardian* newspaper in association with the NSPCC, London and Manchester 2002.

8 'About Outrage!', www.outrage. nabumedia.com/ aboutus.asp, August 2002.

9 'Boondocks' is an American slang word for the suburbs or somewhere out-of-the-way, as in 'out in the boondocks'.

10 Ilan Stavans, *Latino USA: A Cartoon History*, illustrated by Lalo Alcaraz, Basic Books, New York 2000.

11 The Noborder Network website is at www.noborder.org.

12 Kevin Toolis, 'Race to the right', *Guardian Weekend*, 20 May 2000, pp. 24–31.

13 Sandy K, *Just Posters*, endnotes 19, 31 and 42, Edition Solitude, Berlin 2002.

14 David E Kaplan and Lucian Kim, 'Nazism's New Global Threat', *US News and World Report*, 25 September 2000, pp. 34–5.

15 Patrick Bartlett, 'Germany struggles with neo-Nazi websites', BBC News, 22 December 2000, www.bbc.co.uk.

Select Bibliography and Further Reading

9-11: Artists Respond, vol. 1, Dark Horse Comics, Milwaukie 2002.

9-11: Emergency Relief (A Comic Book to Benefit the American Red Cross), Jeff Mason (ed.), Alternative Comics, Gainesville 2002.

Aulich, James and Sylvestrová, Marta, *Political Posters in Central and Eastern Europe 1945–95*, Manchester University Press, Manchester 1999.

Aulich, James and Wilcox, Tim (eds.), *Europe Without Walls: Art, Posters and Revolution 1989–93*, Manchester City Art Galleries, Manchester 1993.

Bartelt, Dana; Lemel, Yossi et al, *Both Sides of Peace: Israeli and Palestinian Political Poster Art*, Contemporary Art Museum, Raleigh, North Carolina, in association with University of Washington Press, Seattle 1996.

Bartelt, Dana and Sylvestrová, Marta, *Art as Activist: Revolutionary Posters from Central and Eastern Europe*, Thames & Hudson, London 1992.

Bell, Steve and Homer, Brian, *Chairman Blair's Little Red Book*, Methuen, London 2001.

Bircham, Emma and Charlton, John (eds.), *Anti-capitalism: A Guide to the Movement*, Bookmarks Publications, London 2001 (revised edition).

Blechman, Nicholas, Niemann, Christoph and Sahre, Paul, *Fresh Dialogue One: New Voices in Graphic Design*, Princeton Architectural Press, New York 2000.

Brown, Michael and May, John, *The Greenpeace Story*, Dorling Kindersley, London 1991 (second edition).

Chiapaslink, *The Zapatistas: A Rough Guide*, Chiapaslink/ Earthright Publications, Ryton, Tyne & Wear 2000.

Clark, Toby, *Art and Propaganda in the Twentieth Century: The Political Image in the Age of Mass Culture*, Everyman Art Library, Weidenfeld & Nicolson, London 1997.

Collin, Matthew, *This is Serbia Calling: Rock'n'roll Radio and Belgrade's Underground Resistance*, Serpent's Tail, London 2001.

Crimp, Douglas with Rolston, Adam, *AIDS Demo Graphics*, Bay Press, Seattle 1990.

Evans, Kate, *Copse: The Cartoon Book of Tree Protesting*, Orange Dog Productions, Biddestone 1998. Introduction by George Monbiot.

Fleming, Jacky, *Be a Bloody Train Driver*, Penguin Books, Harmondsworth 1991.

Fleming, Jacky, *Never Give Up*, Penguin Books, Harmondsworth 1992.

Glenny, Misha, *The Fall of Yugoslavia*, Penguin Books, Harmondsworth 1996 (3rd edn).

Harper, Laurel, *Provocative Graphics: The Power of the Unexpected in Graphic Design*, Rockport, Gloucester 2001.

Harris, Nathaniel, *The War in Former Yugoslavia*, New Perspectives series, Wayland Publishers, Hove 1997.

Hellwig-Schmid, Regina, *Ars Danubiana* (a book accompanying the exhibition 'Ars Danubiana' held during the First International Danube Conference for Art and Culture in Regensburg, Germany, which focused on Serbian artists and their work), KunstKnoten, Regensburg 2001.

Herz, J C, *Joystick Nation*, Abacus/Little, Brown, London 1997.

Ignatieff, Michael, *Virtual War: Kosovo and Beyond*, Chatto & Windus, London 2000.

Isaacs, Jeremy and Downing, Taylor, *Cold War*, Bantam Press/Transworld Publishers, London 1998.

Jacobs, Karrie and Heller, Steven, *Angry Graphics: Protest Posters of the Reagan/Bush Era*, Peregrine Smith Books/Gibbs Smith, Salt Lake City 1992.

Klein, Naomi, *No Logo: Taking Aim at the Brand Bullies*, Flamingo/ HarperCollins, London 2000.

Kubert, Joe, *Fax from Sarajevo: A Story of Survival*, Dark Horse Comics, Milwaukie 1998 (paperback edition).

MacArthur, Brian (ed.), *Despatches from the Gulf War*, Bloomsbury, London 1991.

Mantle, Jonathan, *Benetton: The Family, the Business and the Brand*, Warner Books/Little, Brown, London 2000 (2nd edn).

McGruder, Aaron, *The Boondocks: Because I Know You Don't Read the Newspaper*, Andrews McMeel, Kansas City 2000.

McGruder, Aaron, *Fresh for '01… You Suckas!*, Andrews McMeel, Kansas City 2001.

McKay, George, *Senseless Acts of Beauty: Cultures of Resistance Since the Sixties*, Verso, London 1996.

McQuiston, Liz, *Graphic Agitation*, Phaidon Press, London 1993.

McQuiston, Liz, *Suffragettes to She-Devils: Women's Liberation and Beyond*, Phaidon Press, London 1997.

Moore, Michael, *Stupid White Men… and Other Sorry Excuses for the State of the Nation!*, Regan Books/HarperCollins, New York 2001.

Pavitt, Jane (ed.), *Brand.new*, V&A Publications, London 2000.

Peter Howson: Bosnia, Imperial War Museum, London 1994. (Essays: 'Facing Fear: Peter Howson in Bosnia' by Robert Crampton and 'Suffering into Art: Howson and Bosnia' by Richard Cork.) Exhibition catalogue.

Road Alert!, Road Raging: Top Tips for Wrecking Roadbuilding, self-published, Newbury, October 1997 (revised edition). Out of print but an electronic version can be accessed on the web at www.eco-action.org/rr/index.html.

Roddick, Anita, *Take It Personally*, Thorsons/HarperCollins, London 2001.

Ross, Stewart, *The War in Kosovo*, New Perspectives series, Wayland Publishers, Hove 2000.

Sabin, Roger, *Comics, Comix & Graphic Novels: A History of Comic Art*, Phaidon Press, London 1996.

Sacco, Joe, *Safe Area Gorazde: The War in Eastern Bosnia 1992–95*, Fantagraphics Books, Seattle 2000.

Salisbury, Mike, *Art Director Confesses: 'I Sold Sex!, Drugs & Rock'n'roll'*, RotoVision, Crans-Près-Céligny 2000.

Sarhandi, Daoud and Boboc, Alina, *Evil Doesn't Live Here: Posters from the Bosnian War*, Laurence King, London 2001.

Saunders, Dave, *20th Century Advertising*, Carlton Books, London 1999.

SchNews Annual, a compilation of issues 101–150, Justice?, Brighton 1997.

SchNews Round, a compilation of issues 51–100, Justice?, Brighton 1996.

SchNews and SQUALL Yearbook 2001, SchNews issues 251–300 and SQUALL magazine, Justice?, Brighton 2001.

SchQUALL, SchNews issues 201–250 and SQUALL magazine, Justice?, Brighton 2000.

Spiegelman, Art, *Maus: A Survivor's Tale (vol. I: My Father Bleeds History)*, Penguin Books, Harmondsworth 1987.

Spiegelman, Art, *Maus: A Survivor's Tale (vol. II: And Here My Troubles Began)*, Penguin Books, Harmondsworth 1992.

Stavans, Ilan, *Latino USA: A Cartoon History*, illustrated by Lalo Alcaraz, Basic Books, New York 2000.

Symons, Mitchell, *The Bill Clinton Joke Book*, illustrated by John Jensen, Chameleon Books/André Deutsch, London 1998.

Taylor, Philip M, *War and the Media: Propaganda and Persuasion in the Gulf War*, Manchester University Press, Manchester 1998 (2nd edn).

Walls, David, *The Activist's Almanac: The Concerned Citizen's Guide to the Leading Advocacy Organizations in America*, Fireside/Simon & Schuster, New York 1993.

Warford, Mark, *Greenpeace – Witness: Twenty-five Years on the Environmental Front Line*, André Deutsch, London 1996. Introduction by the Dalai Lama.

Websites

ACT UP – www.actupny.org
Adbusters – www.adbusters.org
AES group – www.aes-group.org
Animal Liberation Front – www.animalliberationfront.com
Billionaires for Bush or Gore – www.billionairesforbushorgore.com
The Boondocks – www.boondocks.net
Radio B92 Website – www.b92.net
Car Busters – www.carbusters.ecn.cz
Dyke Action Machine (DAM) – www.dykeactionmachine.com
Water for Human Kind – www.eauhumanite.com
Eco-action – www.eco-action.org
Free Range Graphics – www.freerangegraphics.com
GenetiX Snowball – www.gene.ch
Civic Initiatives – www.gradjanske.org
Graffiti – www.graffiti.org
Hello Mr President – www.hellomrpresident.com
I-jusi – www.i-jusi.co.za
Indymedia – www.indymedia.org
McLibel Support Campaign – www.mcspotlight.org
Vegetarian and Vegan Information – www.meatstinks.com
Noborder Network – www.noborder.org
Otpor! – www.otpor.com
Outrage – www.outrage.nabumedia.com
Needcom – www.pbs.org
People for the Ethical Treatment of Animals (PETA) – www.peta.org
Think Again – www.protestgraphics.org
Revolutionary Association of the Women of Afghanistan – www.rawa.org
Reclaim the Streets – www.reclaimthestreets.net
Respect for Animals – www.respectforanimals.org
Schnews – www.schnews.org.uk
Spiderwebart Gallery – www.spiderwebart.com
Stop the War Coalition – www.stopwar.org.uk
Treatment Action Campaign – www.tac.org.za
Undercurrents – www.undercurrents.com
Vogue Sucks – www.voguesucks.com
Stop Huntingdon Animal Cruelty Campaign (SHAC) – www.welcome.to/shac
Witness – www.witness.org

Page numbers in italic type
refer to captions/images

A

ABC News *135*
Abeido, Issa *174*
Aboriginals *222*, *223*
Absolut Vodka 124, 145
Abuelas de la Plaza de Mayor
    116–17
ACT UP (AIDS Coalition to Unleash
    Power) 10, 22–3, 23, 34, 195,
    214, *216*
Adbusters 8, 35, *35*, 62, *62*, 77,
    79–80, 92, *92–5*, 96, *97*
advertising
    Benetton ads 81, *92*, 176, *177*,
        192, 204, *204–5*
    multinational corporations 77,
        78–9
    social causes 195
    subvertising 7, *8*, 10, 77, *77*, 78,
        79, 79, 84, *84–9*, 92, 191
    see also billboards
Advertising Standards Authority
    (ASA) 57, 210
AES Group 111, 220, *221*
AES+F Group *113*
Afghanistan 37, 182, *183*, 196, 220,
    220–1
Africa
    AIDS epidemic 193–4
    human rights 198, *199*, 230,
        230–3
    independence movements 14
Ahmed, Shani *233*
AIDS activism 6, 19–23, 122,
    191–2, 195
    ACT UP 22–3, *23*, 34, 193, 214,
        216
    Africa 192, 193–4, 206, *207*
    Benetton ads 192, 204, *204*
    in Russia 81
air pollution 62, *64*
Albanians, Kosovo War 154
Alcaraz, Lalo 196, 222, *222*
alcohol 78
Alternative Comics *181*
American Civil Liberties Union 35
American Institute of Graphic Arts
    96, *96*
American Red Cross *181*
Amir, Yigal *128*, 176, *177*
Amnesty International *70*
ANC (African National Congress)
    198
Anderson, Todd *210*
Andropov, Yuri *107*
Animal Liberation Front (ALF) *56*
animal rights 6, 18, 36, *56–8*, 56–9,
    90
anti-globalization movement 6–7,
    28–30, 35–7, *36–7*, 68, *68–75*
    internet and 7
    J18 (International Carnival
        Against Capitalism) 35, 36, 44,
        45
    Latin America 72, *72–5*
    mass protests 36, 44–54, *44–55*
    Zapatistas influence 32
Aoba, Masutera *66*
apartheid 17
Arafat, Yasser 172, *172*, *173*
Argentina *35*, 37, 62, 72, *74–5*, 82,
    116–17, *117*
Art Workers' Coalition *17*
Arzamasova, Tatiana 111, 220
Ashdown, Paddy *102*
Asher and Partners *86–7*
asylum-seekers 6, 196, 224
Atelier de Création Graphique *71*
Attyah, D *128*, 182, *183*
Australia, Aboriginals 196, 222, *223*
Austria 198, 228
Avzner, Igor 126, 159, 168, *170–1*
Avzner, Ivana *159*

B

Bachman, S A *128*, 182, *183*
Bachollet, Jean-Paul 19
badges 98, *164*, 190
Baghdad 120
Bailey, David *57*

Baldessari, John 228, *228*
Bali nightclub bomb *5*
Balkan wars 5, 119, *121*, *122*,
    123–6, 140–71
Balmazovic, Djordje *126*, 154
Baltic States 126, 130, *130–1*
Band Aid 18
bandana masks 36, 50, *51*
banners 198, 224, *224*
Barfboro campaign 78, 84, *84–5*
Barnardo's 195, 210–11, *213*
Barnbrook, Jonathan *33*, 36, 68, *69*,
    79, 92, *93–5*, *104*
Barr, Jeremy *105*
Barrera, Eduardo *115*
Bartelt, Dana 174, *174*
Basrawi, Claudia *137*
Batjic, Olivera *158*
BBC 198
begging 192, 202, *202–3*
Beijing 24
Belgrade 110–11, 124–6, 154
    mass protests 160, *160–1*
    NATO bombs 123, *124–6*, 125,
        158, 166, *166–7*
    Otpor! 10, 125–6, *127*, 160, 162,
        162–5, 164, 168
    Radio B92 125, 158, *158–9*, 166,
        168
Bell, Steve 102, *102*
Beltrán, Erick 114, *114*, *115*
Benetton 81, *92*, 176, *177*, 192, 204,
    204–5
Berger, Carin *23*
Berger, Joshua *68*
Berlin Wall 6, 25, *26–7*
Berlusconi, Silvio 198
Bernard, Pierre 19, 68, *71*
Bextor, Sophie Ellis *59*
billboards 191
    AIDS activism 23
    anti-fascism *197*
    anti-globalization movement *70*
    anti-war *120*
    branding 78
    British politics *105*
    environmental campaigns *62*
    post-Soviet Europe *108*
    subvertising *77*, 79, 84, *86–9*
Bilton, Nick *210*
black power 15, *15*
Blair, Tony 81, 102, *103–4*, 184,
    185, *187*
Blechman, Nicholas *98*, 154,
    156–7, 192, 200, *200*
Bleck, Nancy *77*
Blum, Dr Alan 78, 84, *85*
Bokser, Yuri 81, 106, *106–7*
Bookmarks *186*
Bosnian War (1992–5) 110, *121*,
    123–4, 140, 154, 160
    Benetton ads *204*
    Channel Four season *122*, 123
    comics 19
    ethnic cleansing 123
    graphic novels 152, *152–3*
    siege of Sarajevo 19, 124, 144–5,
        144–7, 150, *150–3*, 152
    Trio design group 144–5, *144–8*
    UN's role *119*, 123
Both Sides of Peace 127
Botswana 194
Bourgeois, Louise 228
Boyd, Andrew *97*
branding 5, *6*, 10, 77, 78–9, 80, 81,
    84
Breakthrough Breast Cancer 194,
    208
breast cancer 194, 208
Brent Spar incident (1995) 34
Brezhnev, Leonid *107*
Britain
    AIDS activism *216*
    anti-capitalism protests 36, 44,
        45–7, 46, 50–1, *53*
    asylum-seekers 196
    breast cancer awareness 208,
        208
    child abuse 194–5, 210–11,
        212–13
    gay and lesbian rights 214, *217*
    genetically modified (GM) food
        60–1, 61
    Gulf War 132
    political satire 81, 102, *102–5*

road protests 32–3, *34*, 38–9,
    38–9, 40
British National Party 196
Broughton, Zoe 33
Brown, Gordon *103*
Browns design studio 188, *188*
Bucan, Boris 141, *142*
Buenos Aires 37, 72, *74*
bumper stickers 96, *133*, 211
Bureau 214, *216*
burqa, symbolism of 220, *220–1*
Bush, George, Sr 17, *82*, 96, 136,
    136, *139*, 192
Bush, George W 36, 54, *54*, 62, *62*,
    63, 80–1, *80*, 96, *97*, *100–1*, 102,
    104, *128*, 182, 184, *187*
Bush, Jeb 96
Buy Nothing Day 92, *95*

C

calendars
    human rights 198, *199*, 230,
        230–1
    Serbian *107*, 110–11, *112–13*
California Department of Health
    Services 77, *86–7*
Calvin Klein *77*, 79
Camel cigarettes 78, 79, 84, *88–9*
Campbell, Glenn *222*
Campbell, Naomi *58*
cancer 194, 208
capitalism *see* anti-globalization
    movement
Caplin, Steve 82, 116, 117
Car Busters 35, 62, 62
caricatures, political 81, 102
Carnival Against Capitalism 44, 50,
    52
cars 62, *62–3*
El Cartel de Medellín 82, *116*
cartoons
    anti-war *134*
    political satire 96, *100*, 102, *102*
Castro, Fidel 82, 116
Cath Tate Postcards 17
Catholic Church 23, *204*
CBS *134*, *135*
Ceausescu, Nicolae 24
Central America 17, 68
Central Europe 24–5, 81–2, 106,
    110
Channel Four *121*, 123
Chantry, Art *191*
Chechnya 106, *107*
Cheney, Dick *62*
Chernobyl 18, *20–1*
Chiat Day 188
children
    child-soldiers 10
    violence against 10, 194–5, 210,
        210–13
Chile 82, 116, *117*
China
    Cultural Revolution 14
    Tiananmen Square protest 24, 25
Chirac, Jacques 198, 225
Cho, Frank *181*
CIA 162, 182
Ciganovic, Borka *155*
Citizens Committee for the Right to
    Keep and Bear Arms *211*
Civic Initiatives 168, *168–70*
civil disobedience 32
civil rights 15
Clarke, Rob Carlos *57*
Clement, Edgard *73*
Clinton, Bill 80, 82, *82*, 96, *98*, *101*,
    123, 172, *172*
Clinton, Hillary *99*, *101*
Cobbing, Nick *39*, *90*
Coca-Cola 145
Cold War 4, 6, 23, 24, 80, 118
Collin, Matthew 158, *159*
Collins, David *120*
Collins, Mike *96*
Colors magazine 192, 204, *205*
Colosio, Luis Donaldo 117
Columbine High School massacre,
    Littleton 194, 210
comics
    anti-racism 196
    drugs awareness 193
    graphic novels 18–19, 124, 152
    Gulf War *121*
    and 9/11 127–8, 180, *181*

Nozone 65, 122, *191*, 192, 200,
    200–1
Zimbabwean election 178, *179*
Committee for Advertising Practice
    (CAP) 210
Committee to Help Unsell the War
    17
communism 4, 23–5, *24–7*
computer games 121
computer viruses 7
Concordia University 50, *51*
condoms 204, *205*
Conrad, Michael G *132*
Conservative Party (UK) 32, 102,
    102–5
Consumer Project on Technology
    35
Cook, Siân *32*, *216*
Corporate Watch *44*
corporatism *see* anti-globalization
    movement
La Corriente Eléctrica 10–11, *30–1*,
    32, 37, 72, *73*, 82
Courtelis, Niko 68
Criminal Justice Act (UK, 1994) 32,
    33, 39, *39*
Crimp, Douglas 23, *23*
Croatia 110, 123, 124, 140–1,
    140–3, 154
Crumb, Robert 16
Cuba 82, 116, *116*
Cuerden Valley road protest *38*,
    38–9
culture jamming 79–80, 92, 214
Cunningham, Scott *136*
cyberactivism 34–5, 62
Czech Republic 81
Czechoslovakia 24, 25, *25*

D

Dagon, Gadi *176*
Dancuo, Nenad *142*
DANI *122*, 144
Dark Horse Comics *181*
Darné, Olivier 224
Davies, Cathy 8, *8*, 192, *192*, 202,
    202–3
Davos, anti-capitalism protests 36,
    48, *48–9*
Dazed & Confused 194, 208, *208–9*
deforestation 62
democracy 10
    post-Soviet Europe 106
    US presidential elections 80–1,
        96, *96–101*
Democratic Party (USA) 96, *96*
Dennis, Adrian *46*
Depczyk, Jacek *121*
Dereta, Miljenko *160*, 168, *168–70*
Dewar, Donald *103*
digital technology 34–6
    see also electronic posters;
        internet; websites
direct action 7
disability 194, 208, *208–9*
Djelilovic, Asim 145, *149*
Doctors Ought to Care (DOC) 78,
    78, 84, *84*
Documenta X exhibition, Kassel
    (1997) 197
Dongas Tribe 32
Donoghue, Michael *42–3*, *46–7*
Doran, Brett *96*
Dosen, Predrag 141, *141*
Douglas, Noel *186*
Dragosavac, Slavica *112*
Drewinski, Lex *195*, *196*
Drooker, Eric *181*
drugs
    AIDS treatment 194
    drugs awareness campaigns
        191–3, 206, *206*
Dubrovnik 140, 141, *142*
Dumb Animals campaign 57
Durban 192, 194
Dyke Action Machine (DAM!) *193*,
    195, 214, *214–15*

E

Earth First! 32, *33*, 61
Earthworks Poster Collective 16
East Ender 39
Eastern Europe 24–5, 81–2, 106,
    110
ecology movement 15, 17, 18, *18*
Eekhoff, Paul *92*

El Emrany, Fawzy 174
elections
    Britain 102, *102–5*
    Mexico 114, *114–15*
    United States 80–1, 96, *96–101*
    Zimbabwe 178, *178–9*
electronic posters
    9/11 *181*
    women's rights *220*
    Zimbabwean election 178, *178–9*
Elizabeth II, Queen 17, *18*
emails 7
embroideries, Kosovo War 154,
    154–5
Emerald City Communications *62*
English, Ron 84, *89*
environmentalism 5–6, 17, 18
    anti-globalization protests 62,
        62–5
    road protests 8, *29*, 32–3, *34*,
        38–9, *38–9*, 40
    water 66, *66–7*
Esso/Exxon *35*, 62, *62–3*
Estonia 130
Ethiopian famine 18
Europe, immigration 224–5, *224–7*
European Community 130, *130*
European Union 198
Evans, Kate 35, 39, *39*
Evzovitch, Lev 111, 220
extremism 196

F

Fabijanic, Damir *142*
La Fabrique d'Images 224, *224*
Faldin, Alexander *24*, 106, *107*
Faldina, Svyetlana *24*
FAMA International 124, 150,
    150–1
El Fantasma de Heredia 10–11, *35*,
    37, 62, *64*, 66, 68, *70*, 72, *73–5*,
    82, 116, *117*
fascism 196, *196–7*, *227–9*, 228
Fashion Targets Breast Cancer 194,
    208, *208*
fast food 68, *68*, 90, *90–1*
faxes 6
feminism 15, 17, 196, 218, *218–19*
FIA Art Group 110, *110–13*
FIFA (Fédération Internationale de
    Football Association) 188, *188*
Fifth Estate 41, *41*
film, Vietnam War 120
Finck, Jockel *54*
flash-movies 182, *182*
Flaunt 194
Fleming, Jacky 196, 218, *219*
Fluck, Peter 102
flyers *53*, *220*
Focus Communications *126*, *159*,
    168, *170–1*
food
    fast food 68, *68*, 90, *90–1*
    genetically modified (GM) food
        36, *60–1*, 61
Forbes, Dan *68*
fox hunting 56
France
    immigrants 224, *224*
    neo-Nazis 198
    racism 225, *226*
    student protests 14
Frare, Therese *204*
Free Range Graphics 35, *62*, 182,
    182
Free Trade Area of the Americas
    (FTAA) 36, 50, *50–2*
Freedom Party (Austria) 198, 228
French Communist Party 19
Fridkes, Vladimir 111
Friends of the Earth 92, *95*
Frogopolis *96*
FRON't *126*
Fuera de Registro *31*, 37, 72, *73*,
    82, 114, *114–15*
fur, anti-fur campaigns 36, *57–8*,
    57–8

G

G7 summits 32
G8 summits 32, 36, 54, *55*
G17 Plus 168, *170–1*
Gabriel, Peter 188
Gap 78
Garvey, Christopher *210*
GASCD *50*

gay and lesbian rights 17, 195, 214, *214–17*
Gay Men Fighting AIDS *216*
Gees, Johannes 48, *48–9*
Geldof, Bob 18
genetically modified (GM) food 36, *60–1*, 61
GenetiX Snowball 36, 61, *61*
Genoa, anti-capitalism protests 54, *55*
Gentleman, David *63*
Germany
  anti-fascism 228, *228–9*
  anti-racism 196–8, *196–7*
  immigrants 224, *225–7*
  neo-Nazis 198
Gisele *58*
Giuliani, Carlo 54, *55*
global corporations 5, 30, 76–80
  see also anti-globalization movement
global warming 62, *63*
Goines, David Lance *138*
Gonzalez, Elian 116, *116*
Gonzalez, Humberto *116*
Gorazde 152, *153*
Gorbachev, Mikhail 23–4, *24*, 81, 106, *107*, 130
Gordon, Jesse *63*
Gore, Al *97*
Gorry, Drew 192
Gothenburg, anti-capitalism protests 54, *54*
governments
  image-building and manipulation 77
  satire and lampooning 80–2, *80–2*
graffiti 127, *173*, *176*, 191
Gran Fury 22–3, *23*, 214
Graphic Commentaries, Zimbabwean election 178, *178*
graphic novels 18–19, 124, 152
Les Graphistes Associés 225, 227
Grapus 19, 22
Greenham Common 17–18, 32
Greenpeace 18, 34, 36, *38*, 39, 61, *61*, 62, 80, *90*
Greens 18, *19*
Griffin, Rick 16
Gromala, Diane 196, 218, *219*
Grozny 106, *107*
Guardian 123, 196
Guest, Julia *60*
Gulf War (1991) 6, 119, 120–3, *120–1*, 132, *132–9*, 136, 200, *201*
Gush Shalom 172

H
hacking, internet 7
Hadzihalilovic, Bojan 144, *145*
Hadzihalilovic, Dalida 144, *145*
Hadzihalilovic, Fuad 144, *145*
Hague, William 7, *105*
Haider, Jörg 198, 228
Hamilton, Paul 35, *62*, *63*
Hamnett, Katharine 57
Hanson, Tod *38*
Haring, Keith 195
Hart, Steven *134*
Hatt-Mulabegovic, Leila 144
Havel, Václav 81
health activism 194
Heath, Michael *134*
Hendel, Eytan *138*
Henigsman, S *143*
Herz, J C 121
Hildebrandt, Greg *181*
Hildebrandt, Tim *181*
Hilgemann, Georg *124*
Hitler, Adolf *197*, 225, *227*
HIV 193–4, 206
Hofman, Fabián *117*
Hofmeyr, Jean *232*
Holmes, Brian 37, *51*
Holmes, Nigel *135*
Holocaust 19, *22*
homosexuality 195, 214, *214–17*
Hoon, Geoffrey *187*
Howard, Michael *39*
Howson, Peter 123
human rights 8–9, 188, *188–9*, 230, *230–3*
Hungary 106, *108–9*
hunt saboteurs 32

Huntingdon Life Sciences 36, 56, *56*
Huntington, Caleb 50

I
i-jusi 198, *198*, 230, *232–3*
Ignatieff, Michael *120*, 128
Ilic, Mirko *113*
immigrants 17, *195*, 196–7, 198, 224–5, *224–7*
Independent Media Centers (IMCs) 33, 40–1, *40*, *41*, 54
Indymedia 33, 40–1, 44, 182
Institutional Revolutionary Party (PRI) 82, 117
International Monetary Fund (IMF) 5, 29, 30, 36, 37, 44, 48, 72, 82
International Organization for Migration (IOM) *108*
internet
  online newsletters 8, 41
  protest movements on 6–7, 8
  see also websites
Iraq
  Gulf War (1991) 119, 120–3, *120–1*, 132, *132–9*, 136, 200, *201*
  Iraq War (2003) 8, *129*, 184, *184–7*
Iron Curtain 23–5, *24–7*, 106
Islam, symbolism of the veil 220, *220–1*
Islamic Project 220, *221*
Israel 5, *80*, 126–7, *128*, 136, *138*, 172, *172–5*, 174, 176, *176–7*
Italy 198
ITN 123, *123–4*

J
J18 (International Carnival Against Capitalism) 35, 36, 44, *45*
Jacobs, Sandra *176*
Jadallah, Ahmed *173*
Jarecke, Kenneth *136*
Johns, Bethany 218
Johnson, Steve *34*
Jordan, Alex 19
Justice? 33, *33*

K
Kallaur, Andrei *210*
Kalman, Tibor 192, 204, *205*
Kapic, Suada 150, *150–1*
Karmarama *185*
Karp, David *176*
Kasumagic, Emir *150*
Katevatis, Evie 35
Keenan *159*
'Kein Mensch ist Illegal' 197, 224, *226–7*
Kelly, Dr David *187*
Kennedy, Liz *134*
Kinnock, Neil *102*
Kirby, David *98*, 192, *204*
Klein, Naomi 30, *31*, 78
Klein, Oded *128*
Knickerbocker *63*, *200–1*
Knight, Nick 194, 208, *208–9*
Kojadinovic, Nenad *159*
Kosovo War (1998–9) *120*, 123–4, *126*, 140, 154, *154–7*, 166
Kostovic, Cedomir 145, *148*, *149*
Kostunica, Vojislav 126, *171*
Kosuth, Joseph 228
Kroninger, Stephen *139*
Krüger, Wilhelm *232*, *233*
Kubert, Joe 19, 152, *152*
Kuper, Peter *121*, 122–3, 192
Kuwait 132
Kuznjecov, Marica *159*
Kyoto Treaty 36, 54, 62

L
Labour Party (UK) 81, 102, *103–5*
Lacic, Svetlana *155*
Lasn, Kalle 79
Latin America 72, *72–5*, 82, 114, *114–17*, 116–17
Latvia 130
Lauren, Ralph 194
Law, Roger 102
Lawrence and Beavan *91*
Lawyers Committee for Human Rights 188
Le Bechec, Hélène 224
Le Masurier, Marion 67
Le Pen, Jean-Marie 198, 224, 225, *227*

Le Quernec, Alain *73*
leaflets, Otpor! *163*, *165*
Leeds Postcards 17
Lehn, Ernesto *30–1*
Leko, Andreja *154*, *155*
Lemel, Yossi 36–7, 68, *70*, *80*, *119*, 126, *128*, *138*, 172, *173–5*, 174, *177*
Lenin 24, 106
Lertola, Joe *134*
Lesbian Avengers 195, 214, *214*
lesbians *193*, 195, 214, *214–15*
Lewinsky, Monica 80, 96, *98*
Libération 55
Lifeline Project 192, *193*, 206, *206*
Linnell, Michael *193*, 206, *206*
Lithuania 126, 130, *130–1*
Liu Xingrui *66*
Live Aid 18
Ljubicic, Boris *140*, 141, *142*, *143*
LM magazine 123
Loesch, Uwe *197*
London
  anti-capitalism protests 36, 44, *45–7*, 46, 50–1, *53*
  anti-Iraq War protests 184, *184*
London Mayday Collective *37*, *53*
Lopez, Heraclito *73*
Lopez Castro, Ricardo *73*
Lukova, Luba 11, *13*, 62, *65*, 68, *68*, 195
Lunátika 8, 218, *218*
Lynx anti-fur campaign 18, 36, 57, *57*
Lyons, Steven *138*

M
M11 Link Road protest 32–3, 38, *38*, *39*
MacArthur, Brian *120*
McAlpin, Loring *23*
McCarthy, Paul 228
McCartney, Mary 57, *57*, *59*
McCartney, Stella 36, 57, 58
McCarty, Marlene 214, *216*, 218, *218*
McCracken, Pete *68*
McCurry, Steve *205*
Macdiarmid, Peter *184*
McDonald's 10, 24, 30, 36, 46, *47*, *78*, 80, *80*, 90, *90–1*
Macedonia 154, 166
McGruder, Aaron 196, 222, *222*
McGuinness, Matthew *210*
McInformation Network 90, *91*
McLibel Trial 10, 80, 90, *90–1*
McQueen, Alexander 194, 208, *208–9*
McSpotlight website 80, 90, *91*
Madrid, Ana Bertha *115*
Magallanes, Alejandro 37, 62, *64*, *73*, 114, *114*, *115*, 116, *117*, *117*
Major, John *39*, 81, 102, *102*
Manchester 192, *193*, 206
Mandela, Nelson *198*, 230
Mani, Anand R *92*
Mansour, Sliman 174
Mao Tse-tung 14
maps, and warfare 122, 124, *135*, 150, *150–1*
Marcos, Subcomandante 32
Marek, Mark *200*
Marinovic, Saki 168, *168–170*
Markovic, Mira *170*
Marlboro *77*, 78, 79, 84, *84–8*
Martinez, Dylan 55
masks 36, 50, *51*
Mason, Jeff *181*
mass demonstrations
  anti-globalization 36, 44–54, *44–55*
  anti-Iraq War protests 184, *184*
  Belgrade 160, *160–1*
Mateu, Gabriel 35, 37, 72, 82, 116
Matic, Veran 158
Mattioli, Petulia 220, *220*
Maviyane-Davies, Chaz 8, *12*, 127, *178*, *178–9*, 198, *199*, 230, *230–1*
Mayes, Steve *217*
media activism 10, 33–4, 40–1, *40–3*
Meessen, Vincent *126*
Melchett, Lord 36, 61
Mendel, Gideon 206, *207*
Messinis, Dimitri *166*

Mexico 117
  elections 114, *114–15*
  feminists 218, *218*
  social comment 82
  Zapatistas 8, 30–2, *30–1*, 36, 72, *72–3*, 82
Mexico City 32, 37, 72, 82
Microsoft *125*
Middle East 126–7, 172, *172–5*, 174
Mika, Chen *176*
Miller, Erik *119*
Milosevic, Slobodan 25, 110, 123, 124–6, *124*, *127*, 140, 154, 158, 160, *162*, *165*, 166, 168, *170*
miners' strike (1984–5) 17
Minkler, Doug 78, *78*, 84, *85*
mobile phones 6
Moffett, Donald 214, *216*
Moldova 106, *108*
Monroe, Marilyn 124
Montenegro 154, 166
Montes de Oca, Héctor *115*
Moore, Michael *80*, 81
Morris, David 80, 90, *90*
Moscoso, Victor 16
Mosqueda, Enrique 68
Moyer, Carrie *193*, 195, 214
Mugabe, Robert 127, 178
multinational corporations 5, 30, 76–80
Las Muñequitas Contratacan *193*, 218, *218*
murals *116*, 127
Muslims 220

N
Nader, Ralph 10, *15*, 35, 96, *97*
National Association for the Advancement of Colored People (NAACP) 222, *223*
National Front (France) 198, 225
National Society for the Prevention of Cruelty to Children (NSPCC) 194–5, 210–11, *212*
nationalism 196
NATO (North Atlantic Treaty Organization) 5
  bombs Belgrade 123, *124–6*, 125, 158, 166, *166–7*
  Bosnian War *122*, 123
  Kosovo War 154
  and peace movement 17, *22*
Nazis 19, 22, *22*, *196–7*, 198
Ne Pas Plier *37*, 50, *51*
NeedCom 192, *192*, 202, *202–3*
neo-Nazis 198
Netanyahu, Binyamin 176, *176–7*
Nevin, Charles *100*
New Activism 28–9
New World Order 5, 80, 82
New York City 127, 180, *180–1*, 193, 195
New York Times Magazine 162
Newbury by-pass 33, 39
newsletters
  online 41
  SchNews 33, *33*
newspapers
  Israeli *172*
  spoof 36
Nice, anti-capitalism protests 36, 48
Nicolaou, Mykel *187*
Niemann, Christoph 154, *156–7*
Nike 30, 36, 44, *44*, 78, 79, *79*, 123, *124*
No Shop 92, *95*
Noborder Network 196
Northern League 198
Nous Travaillons Ensemble *138*, 221, 225, *226*
Novak, Ranko *140*
Nozone 65, 122, *191*, 192, 200, *200–1*
nuclear weapons *see* peace movements
NYC Comic Book Museum 180

O
Observer 122, 136, *136*
O'Connor, Paul 33
Olympic Games 124, 144, 145
One Another 35, 62
Orange Juice Design 198, *198*, 230, *232*

Orlic, Milka *155*
Orosz, István *108*
Otpor! 10, 125–6, *127*, 160, 162, *162–5*, 164, 168
OutRage! 195, 214, *217*

P
Paisley, Rev Ian *102*
Palestine Liberation Organization *172*
Palestinians 5, 126–7, 172, *173–5*, 174, 176
Palisano, Louis *134*
Palmer Hargreaves *57*
Pan Am *5*
panhandlers 192, 202, *202–3*
Paris-Clavel, Gerard 19
Pavlovic, Ozren 150, *150–1*
PBS Online 192
PDS 228, *228–9*
peace movements
  anti-nuclear protests 6, 15, *15*, 17–18, *22–3*
  Middle East 126, 172
Peace Now 172, *172*
Pearce, Lippa *119*
Peláez, Ricardo *72*
Pemberton, Jeremy 57
People & Planet 34, 62
People for the Ethical Treatment of Animals (PETA) 34, 36, 58, *58–9*, 90, *91*
People's Global Action 8, 34, 36
Peres, Shimon 172
Perrottet, Vincent 225, *227*
personal politics 6, 18–19
Philip Morris 78
Physicians for Human Rights *189*
Pinochet, General Augusto 82, 116, *117*
pins, 9/11 *180*
Pitzer, Chris *181*
playing cards, Iraq War 184, *186*
Plazm 68, *68–9*
Pócs, Péter *108*
Poland
  posters 19, 106, *108*
  satire *80*
  Solidarity 24, *25*
politics
  branding of political parties 77, 80, 81
  post-Soviet Europe 106, *106–13*
  satire and lampooning 80–2, 102, *102–5*
  US presidential elections 80–1, 96, *96–101*
pollution 62, *64*
postcards *7*, 8
  anti-globalization movement *70*
  anti-racism 224, *225*
  Balkan wars 124, *125*, 144, 145, *146–8*
  feminism *219*
  Gulf War *132*
  9/11 *180*
  social causes *193*
Poster Collective 16
posters *7*
  AIDS activism 23, *191*
  anti-fascist *196–7*, *228–9*
  anti-fur campaign 57, *57*
  anti-globalization movement 52, *68–71*, *74–5*
  anti-racism 194, 222, *223–5*, 224
  Belgrade's mass protests *160*
  Bosnian War 124, 144, 145, *148–9*
  Croatian War *140–3*, 141
  decline of Communism 24–5
  drug advice *206*
  environmental campaigns 62, *62–5*
  gay and lesbian rights *214*
  Gulf War 136, *136*, *138–9*
  illegal immigrants 195, 197
  Iraq War *129*, 185, *187*
  Israeli peace movement 172, *172–5*, 174
  Kosovo War 154, *156–7*
  Lithuanian independence 130, *130*
  NATO bombing of Belgrade *166*
  9/11 *181*, *183*
  Otpor! *164–5*
  Palestinian 127

perestroika 23–4, *24*
political discontent 81
post-Soviet Europe *106–10*
post-war 188, *188*
protest graphics 15–18, *15–17*
Serbian elections *168–9*
subvertising 84, *85*
US presidential elections 96–7
women's rights *193*, 218, *218*, 220
Potter, Keith R *138*
Poynter, Phil 208
Prado, Claudia *115*
Prague, anti-capitalism protests 36, 48
Private Eye 102, *104*
Protic, Dragan *126*, 154
Pugliese, Paul *134*
Punk 17, *18*, 192, 200
Putin, Vladimir 106, *107*

Q
al-Qaida 11
Quebec City, anti-capitalism protests 36, 50, *50–2*
Queer Nation 195

R
Rabin, Yitzhak *128*, 172, *172*, 176, *176–7*
racism *194*, *195*, 196–7, *205*, 222, *222–9*, 224–5
Radio B92 125, 158, *158–9*, 166, 168
Rajicic, Nada 110, *110*
Rambow, Gunter *19*
Ramirez, Andres *73*
Ramírez, Ruth 116, *116*
Rather, Dan *134*
Ratinsky, Ben-Ami *174*
Raye, Robynne *96*
Reagan, Ronald 17, 22, *22*
Reclaim the Streets 8, 34, *36*, *44*
Red Cross *148*
Reebok Foundation 188
refugees 6, 196, 224–5, *225–7*
Reid, Jamie 17, *18*
Reisinger, Dan *126*, *172*
Republican Party (USA) 96, *96*
Resner, Drago *150*
Respect for Animals 36, 57, *57*
Revolutionary Association of the Women of Afghanistan (RAWA) 220, *220*
Reynolds, R J 78–9
riots, anti-capitalism 44
Ritson, Mark *79*
Ritter, Paul *205*
Road Alert! *38*
road protests 8, *29*, 32–3, *34*, 38–9, *38–9*, 40
Road Raging 39
Robins, Jim *100*
Robinson, Geoff *56*
Rocky *52*
Rodríguez Romo, Sebastián *115*
Rogic, Sinisa *158*
Rolston, Adam 23
Romania *24*
Rowson, Martin *83*, 102
Russia 81, 106, *107*, 111
Rwanda *189*

S
Saalfield, Catherine *23*
Saatchi, M+C *103*
Saatchi & Saatchi 195, 210–11, *212*
Saatchi & Someone *120*
Sacco, Joe *19*, *137*, 152, *153*
Sada, Margarita 37, *73*, *193*, 196, 218, *218*
Saddam Hussein 6, 81, *82*, *132–3*, 136, 184
Sagahón, Leonel 37, *73*, 82, *115*
Sahre, Paul *98*, 154, *156–7*
Saito, Makoto *29*
Salem, Anabella *35*, 37, 72, 82, 116
Salisbury, Mike *88*
San Francisco *183*
Sandy K 197, *197*, 224–5, 225–9, *228*
Sarajevo, siege of (1992–96) 19, 124, 144–5, *144–7*, 150, *150–3*, 152
Sarfis, Thierry 66, *66*
satire 8–10

political 80–2, *80–2*, 96, *96–105*, 102
subvertising 10, 77, *77*, 78, 79, *79*
Schaffner, Sue *193*, 195, 214
Schmidt, Harold *128*
SchNews 33, *33*, 34, *40*, 41
Schwartzkopf, General Norman *137*
Seattle, anti-capitalism protests 36, 44, *44*
Secession 228, *228*
See Red Women's Poster Collective 16, *16*, 17
Segar, Mike *58*
Serbia 25, 81, 110–11, 119, 123, 124–6
    Belgrade's mass protests 160, *160–1*
    Bosnian War 123, 124
    calendars *107*, 110–11, *112–13*
    Croatian War 123, 124, 140
    elections 168, *168–71*
    Kosovo War 123, 154
    NATO bombs Belgrade 123, *124–6*, 125, 158, 166, *166–7*
    Otpor! 10, 125–6, *127*, 160, 162, *162–5*, 164, 168
    Radio B92 125, 158, *158–9*, 166, 168
Shango 178, *179*
Shapiro, Eric *134*
Sharon, Ariel 172
Sharp, Stanislav 110, *110*, 112
Shatman, Lydia 50
Sheasby, Morgan *210*
Shell 34
Sibík, Jan *26–7*
Skart *126*, 154, *154–5*
sky-writing 222, *223*
Slovenia 123, 140
smart technology 121, 122
smoking, anti-tobacco protests *77*, 78–9, *78*, 84, *84–9*
social causes 6, 190–233
    AIDS 206, *207*
    Benetton ads 204, *204–5*
    breast cancer awareness 208, *208*
    disability 208, *208–9*
    drug use 206, *206*
    gay and lesbian rights 214, *214–17*
    human rights 230, *230–3*
    immigration 224–5, *224–7*
    NeedCom 202, *202–3*
    Nozone 200, *200–1*
    racism 222, *222–9*, 224–5
    symbolism of the veil 220, *220–1*
    violence against children 210–11, *210–13*
    women's rights 195–6, 218, *218–19*
Solidarity 24, *25*
solidarity movements 17
South Africa
    AIDS activism 192, 194, 206, *207*
    elections *198*
    human rights 230, *232–3*
    i-jusi magazine 198
South Atlantic Souvenirs 17
Soviet Union *see* USSR
Spain *22*
SpiderWomen 196, 218, *218*
Spiegelman, Art 18–19, *22*, 124, 210, *211*
Spira, Maurice *41*
Spitting Image 80, *82*, 102, *102*
Spy 99
Srebrenica 123
Staeck, Klaus 16
Stalin, Joseph 106, *106*
Starbucks 78
Stasi 228
Stavans, Ilan 196, 222, *222*
stealth aircraft 121
Steel, Helen 80, 90, *90*
Steinberg, Ned *134*
Steinberg, Wolfram *54*
Stengel, Konstantin *92*
Stephens, Damian *232*
Stewart, Martha *215*
stickers
    anti-globalization movement 72, *73*
    anti-tobacco protests *84*
United States of America
    AIDS activism 22–3, *193*, 195, 214
    breast cancer awareness 208

McLibel campaign *91*
9/11 *180*
Otpor! *163*, *165*
    Serbian elections *170*
    US presidential elections *96*
    violence against children *211*
Stojanovic, Slavimir *158*
Stojic, Manja *160*
StopEsso campaign *35*, 62, *62–3*
Stop Huntingdon Animal Cruelty (SHAC) 36, 56
Stop the War Coalition *187*
Straw, Jack *187*
Stroux, Marily 224–5, *226*
Student Strike Workshop 16
subvertising *7*, 8, 10, 77, *77*, 78, 79, *79*, 84, *84–9*, 92, 191
Sun 133
Sunday Times Magazine 103
Svyatsky, Evgeny 111, 220
Swampy 33, *38*, 39
Swarte, Joost *201*
symbolism of the veil 220, *220–1*
Symons, Mitchell *101*

T
T-shirts *6*, 190–1, 198
    AIDS activism 194, 206, *207*
    anti-fast food activism *90*
    breast cancer awareness 208, *208*
    gay and lesbian rights *217*
    Otpor! *164*
Taliban 196, 220, *221*
Tartakover, David *126*, *128*, 172, *172–3*, 176, *176–7*
Tate Modern, London 208
TBWA *105*
Tel Aviv *176*, 176
television
    Balkan wars 123
    censorship 124
    Gulf War (1991) 120–2, *121*
terrorism 5
    memorials 5
    9/11 *10–11*, 11, 37, 54, 127–8, 180, *180–3*, 182
    symbols 196
Testa, Andrew *29*
Testino, Mario 208
Texas, Bill 62, *97*
text messaging *7*
Thatcher, Margaret *7*, 17, 81, 82, 102, *105*, 116, *117*, *217*
THINK AGAIN *128*, 182, *183*
Time magazine *107*, *135*
Time Out 58
Tito 111, 140, *148*
tobacco, anti-tobacco protests *77*, 78–9, *78*, 84, *84–9*
Tobocman, Seth *121*
Tomic, Dusica *154*
Tomorrow, Tom *84*
Toolis, Kevin 196
Toscani, Oliviero 192, 204, *204–5*
Treatment Action Campaign 192, 194, 206, *207*
Trio design group 8, 124, 144–5, *144–8*
Tudjman, Franjo 123, 140
Tudor, M *143*
Twyford Down road protest 32, 38, *39*
typefaces *33*, *69*, *104*, 218, *219*

U
UNAIDS/WHO 194
Undercurrents 33, 40, *40*
underground press 16
Ungerer, Tomi *17*
UNICEF 188, *188*
United Nations (UN) 5
    Balkan wars *119*, 123, *148*, 152, 154, 172
    and Cuba 82
    Declaration of Human Rights *199*, 230
    Earth Summit (2002) 37
    Gulf War 132
    Iraq War 184
    Security Council 110
    Zimbabwean election 178

and Cuba 82, 116, *116*
    cultural imperialism 68, *68–9*
    gay and lesbian rights 214, *214–16*
    Gulf War (1991) 6, 119, 120–3, *120–1*, 132, *132–9*, 136, 200, *201*
    Iraq War (2003) 184, *184–7*
    and Latin America 116
    neo-Nazis 198
    9/11 *10–11*, 11, 37, 54, 127–8, 180, *180–3*, 182
    political satire 80–1
    presidential elections 80–1, 96, *96–101*
    racism 222
    Vietnam War 15, 16–17, *17*, 120, 122, 132
    violence against children 194, 210, *210–11*
Universal Press Syndicate 222
US Department of State *108*
US Federal Trade Commission 79
US Supreme Court 81, 96
USA Playing Card Company *186*
USSR
    Cold War 4
    disintegration of 80
    and Lithuanian independence 130
    perestroika 23–4, *24*, 81
    see also Russia

V
Vachon, Gail *218*
Valencak, Ivan 168, *168–9*
Vallen, Mark *136*
Vardi, Stephen *134*
veil, symbolism of 220, *220–1*
Victore, James 68, *68*, *80*, *191*, 192, *194*, 196, 210, *211*, 222, *223*
video activism 8, 33, 34, 40, *40*, 132
Vidstrand, Erik *84*
Vietnam War 15, 16–17, *17*, 120, 122, 132
Vilnius 130, *130–1*
violence
    against children 194, 210–11, *210–13*
    against women 195
    animal rights movement 6
Virus Foundry *33*, *69*, *104*
viruses, computer *7*
Visual Mafia 210, *210*
Vojvodina 140
Volpi, Mauricio *115*
Vukovar 140, 141, *143*

W
Walesa, Lech 24
Walker, Garth *198*, 230, *232*
'walking glasses', Belgrade mass protests 160, *160–1*
war 118–28
    Croatia 110, 123, 124, 140–1, *140–3*, 154
    'distancing' 10
    Gulf War (1991) 119, 120–3, *120–1*, 132, *132–9*, 136, 200, *201*
    Iraq War (2003) 8, *129*, 184, *184–7*
    Kosovo War *120*, 123–4, *126*, 140, 154, *154–7*, 166
    Vietnam War 15, 16–17, *17*, 120, 122, 132
    War on Terrorism 37, 54, *104*, *128*, 182, *182–3*, 184, 196
    see also Bosnian War
Washington, DC 44
water 66, *66–7*
'Water for Human Kind' 66, *66–7*
weapons, 'smart' 121, 122
Web Lab 192
websites *7*, *33*, 34, 191
    Adbusters 92
    anti-fur campaign 58, *58*
    anti-multinational campaigns 80
    anti-racism 222, *222*
    gay and lesbian rights 214, *214*
    Independent Media Centers 40–1, *40*
    McLibel campaign *91*
    NeedCom 192, *192*, 202, *202–3*
    neo-Nazi 198
    spoof websites 34–5, *58*, 96, *97*
    women's rights 218, *218*
    Zimbabwean election 178

see also internet
Wells, Deborah *134*
whaling *18*
Williamson, Jan *96*
Wilson, Wes 16
Wilson-Max, Ken 127, 178, *179*
Winter Olympic Games, Sarajevo (1984) 124, 144, 145
Witness *119*, 188, *188–9*
Wladyka, Marcin *80*, *108*
Wojnarowicz, David 195, 214, *216*
women
    symbolism of the veil 220, *220–1*
    women's rights 195–6, 218, *218–19*
Women in Black 172
Women's Action Coalition (WAC) 195–6, *218*, 218
Woodcock, James 78
World Bank 29, 36, 48
World Conservation Union (IUCN) *29*
World Summit on Sustainable Development (2002) 66
World Trade Organization (WTO) 29, 36, 44, *44*, 54
World War 3 Illustrated 121, 122–3
World Wide Web 6
    see also internet; websites
Wright, Micah Ian *129*, *187*

Y
Yahoo 137
YearZero 41, *41*
Yellowhammer 57, *57*
Yeltsin, Boris 24, 81, 106, *107*
Yesh Gvul 172
Yevtushenko, Yevgeny 106
youth movements 14–15
Yugoslavia 106, 110–11, *110–13*, 123, 140, *148*, 154, 168

Z
Zagreb Arts Fund 140
Zajedno 160, *160–1*
Zanu PF 11, *12*, 178
Zapatistas 8, 30–2, *30–1*, 36, 72, *72–3*, 82
Zelenovic, Lenka 154
Zimbabwe 8, 127, 178, *178–9*, 230

Acknowledgements

The author wishes to give special thanks to the following for consultation and generous assistance in the making of this book:

Francesca Amat-Tito, London
Jeremy Barr, London
Stephen Buckle, London
Victoria Clarke, London
Vivian Constantinopoulos, London
Christine Davis, Bristol
Nickie Hirst, London
Sharon Hocking, Catherine Kennedy and Paul Rogers, Ravensbourne College of Design and Communication, Chislehurst, UK
Tom Hor, London
Sandy K, Berlin
Jed Leventhall, London
Michael Linnell, Director of Communications, Lifeline Project, Manchester
Chaz Maviyane-Davies, Boston
George and Luz McQuiston, Bradenton, USA
Michael Moody, Imperial War Museum, London
Richard Oliver, London
Emmanuelle Peri, London
Colin and Elinor Renfrew, London
Sinisa Rogic, Belgrade
John Sauven, Campaigns Director, Greenpeace UK
Lydia Sharman, Department of Design Art, Concordia University, Montreal
Manja Stojic, London
Mari West, London
Ken Wilson-Max, London
Verdi Yahooda, London

Phaidon Press
Regent's Wharf
All Saints Street
London N1 9PA

Phaidon Press Inc.
180 Varick Street
New York, NY 10014

www.phaidon.com

First Published 2004
© 2004 Phaidon Press Limited

ISBN 0 7148 4177 3

A CIP catalogue record for
this book is available from
the British Library.

Designed by Harry Pearce &
Nicole Förster, Lippa Pearce
Printed in Singapore

Publisher's Note

This work is intended as a survey
of contemporary political and
social agitation via graphics since
the early 1990s. The publishers
wish to make it clear that the views
expressed in the images contained
in this publication are not their own
but those of the individuals and
organizations that created them.
The publishers do not consider
that these views are necessarily
justified, truthful or accurate.

The materials included
demonstrate the utilization of
graphic art by individuals and
bodies with differing aims.
Those employing graphic means
to spread their views are of
varying repute, and range from
governments through to terrorist
organizations and include, amongst
others, various pressure groups
and commercial institutions.
This book depicts the many
graphic methods used and portrays
the lengths to which people will
go in order to communicate their
views to the public. The inclusion
of such work is for the purpose of
criticism and review of the use of
the graphic medium and in no way
indicates that the publishers agree
with the sentiments expressed
therein, nor that the targets of any
of the illustrations are deserving
of such treatment.